Dancing on Live Embers

Addressing discomfort and resistance are very important. You do that without flinching and I like that. I also like the excerpts from interviews and quotes by those working in leadership positions and at the grassroots level.

—Gayle Nye, community and labour educator

The conversations between Tina and Barb are powerful. The lessons from their experience will be a valuable eye-opener for those who have the courage to read these conversations with an unbiased eye.

—Carol Anderson, Associate Director of Education, American Federation of State, County and Municipal Employees Union

Dancing on Live Embers:
Challenging Racism in Organizations

Tina Lopes and Barb Thomas

design and illustration
Margie Adam

Between the Lines
Toronto

Dancing on Live Embers

First published in Canada in 2006 by
Between the Lines
720 Bathurst Street, Suite #404
Toronto, Ontario M5S 2R4
1-800-718-7201
www.btlbooks.com

Distributed in the U.S.A. by
SCB Distributors
Gardena, California

Fifth Printing September 2014

National Library of Canada Cataloguing in Publication

Lopes, Tina, 1961-
    Dancing on live embers : challenging racism in organizations / Tina Lopes, Barb Thomas.

Includes bibliographical references.
ISBN 1-897071-04-3

    1. Discrimination in employment—Canada. 2. Racism—Canada. 3. Canada—Race relations. 4. Work environment—Canada. I. Thomas, Barb, 1946- II. Title.

HT1521.L66 2006   331.6'2'0971   C2005-907298-9

Front cover art: Stephanie Martin
Author photographs: Tina Lopes by Kendall Townend; Barb Thomas by Rainer Soegtrop
Photographs on pages xi, 9, 150, 153, 154, and 157, courtesy of Pat Case
Photographs in Section 4: Rainer Soegtrop and Kendall Townend
Cover and text design: Margie Adam, ArtWork
Printed in Canada by union labour

Between the Lines gratefully acknowledges assistance for its publishing activities from the Canada Council for the Arts, the Ontario Arts Council, and the Government of Canada through the Book Publishing Industry Development Program.

Table of Contents

Acknowledgements

We are grateful to many people and organizations which have strengthened our work and shaped this book. There are some whom we do not know personally, but whose writing and Web sites are listed in our bibliography. And there are those we want to acknowledge by naming them here.

Organizations where we have done racial equity work, separately or together: AIDS Committee of Toronto (ACT); American Federation of State, County and Municipal Employees; Arise Women's Shelter; Canadian Labour Congress; Canadian Union of Public Employees; Children's Aid Society of Toronto; Children's Services Division, City of Toronto; Catholic Children's Aid Society of Toronto; Central Toronto Community Health Centre Communication; Energy and Paperworkers' Union; Community Resource Connections of Toronto; Education Wife Assault; Family Service Association of Hamilton; Family Service Association of Toronto; Federal Department of Canadian Heritage; Huron County Women's Shelter; Labour Council of Toronto and York Region; Law Society of Upper Canada; Marin Institute, Marin County, California; Mennonite Central Committee Canada; Metro Network for Social Justice; Municipality of Edmonton; Municipality of Metropolitan Toronto (now the City of Toronto); Ontario Coalition of Agencies Serving Immigrants; Ontario Public Service Employees Union; Parkdale Community Health Centre; Planned Parenthood of Toronto; Public Service Alliance of Canada; Saskatchewan Government Employees Union; Saskatchewan Federation of Labour; Service Employees International Union, Canadian Region and Local 1199 in New York; Social Services Division, Municipality of Metropolitan Toronto; Toronto Community Housing Corporation; United Way of Calgary, and Woodgreen Community Centre.

People we interviewed: We interviewed many people to find out about their work, their strategies, and their frustrations. In some cases we went back to people to see if our work together had shifted things in their organizations. Our thanks to Jennifer Adkins, Julie Ball, Julie Black, Cesar Cala, Alicia Caro, Zemeta Chefeke, Romita Coudhury, Peter Crosby, Vilma Dawson, Lisa Hari, Brian Hoffart, Linda Kongnetiman, Kelley Myers, Valerie Pruegger, Ruth Ramsden-Wood, Marie Rebalbos, Teresa Woo-Paw, and Paul Zarnke. We want to especially acknowledge the courage and leadership of Jean Morgan and Suzanne Clemanis who taught us so much.

People whose stories are featured in this book: Racial equity work happens in community, in connection with so many others who yearn and work for justice. We interviewed the following people because we wanted to feature their work that had inspired us. Then we sent them draft manuscripts to ensure that our presentation of their work and our learning from it would be useful to other people. For their work and contributions to this book, we thank Jenny Ahn, John Cartwright, Pat Case, Evelyn Murialdo, Winnie Ng, David Onyalo, Hazelle Palmer, Rainer Soegtrop, Amal Umar, Hieu Van Ngo, and Hassan Yusseff.

Our readers: We circulated various parts of this book to colleagues and friends to review as we went, and we sent our daunting, unedited manuscript to eighteen people who not only reviewed it but also sent us e-mails, marked up manuscripts, and comments by telephone. They are people working in a variety of organizations and positions across this country and the United States. Our love and gratitude to Nora Allingham, Carol Anderson, Bev Burke, Pat Case, Lois Coleman Neufeld, Diane Dietrich, Bev Johnson, Tarik Khan, Hari Lalla, Susan Lillico, Don MacKay, D'Arcy Martin, Stephanie Martin, Denise Nadeau, Gail Nye, Adrian Paavo, Nan Peacock, Dawn Philips, and Janet Wilson. We are particularly thankful to Eveline Shen for her careful eye and insights that were so important for the chapter "Between Us." We're profoundly grateful to Charles Smith for his wisdom, generosity, and attention to detail with the entire book. His excitement about this project kept us going.

Technical Help: We taped not only interviews with others but also the conversations between ourselves to stimulate our writing of this book. It was Karen Ellis, Tamara Glenn, and Christian Morey who transcribed our often-inaudible meanderings. Sylvia Fernandes helped keep our finances on the straight and narrow. Many thanks to them. We are grateful for the skill and generosity of Rainer Soegtrop who made sure we had photographs of ourselves and of those who are featured in the book. We also appreciated the care and support for our work by the staff of the Elmhirst Inn where we did some of our most focused writing over the past three years. We were lucky to have the rigorous, curious, and compassionate editorial eye of Beth McAuley on our manuscript. Paul Eprile of Between the Lines believed in this book from the beginning and was unstinting in the time he devoted to it. And we are enormously grateful for the politics and art of Margie Adam for bringing our work into visual form.

People who provided perspective and support: As writers, we recognize our limits. We don't have words to convey our appreciation for the ongoing love, attention, and perspective from a few people who weathered with us the most discouraging moments of trying to produce this book. We are deeply grateful that Margie Adam, Jenny Brooks, Karen Ellis, Kristi Magraw, Christian Morey, Julian Morey, Janny Thomas, Ariela Weisfeld, and Penny Winestock are in our lives and that we still draw on the teachings and inspiration of the late Marlene Green and Fran Endicott. In the most critical moments, Ariana Lopes Morey and D'Arcy Martin nurtured us, shored up our faith in ourselves, and celebrated the work of this project.

Tina is particularly grateful to her parents, Francisco de Assiz Lopes and Lita Lopes, for the dignity and fierce determination with which they respond to the racism they experience in Canada.

Barb wants to thank her parents, Eleanor Jean and Arthur Johnson, for their early teaching that all communities are connected.

Funding: Funding support for this project was provided by the Multiculturalism Program, Department of Canadian Heritage. The views expressed are those of the authors and do not necessarily reflect those of the Multiculturalism Program, Department of Canadian Heritage or the Government of Canada. In particular, we acknowledge Kass Sunderji, a friend and colleague whose encouragement got us started over five years ago.

Foreword

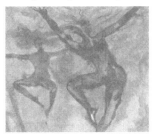

The modern human rights movement is less than sixty years old. A mere seventy years ago, racism was either ignored or indeed supported by those with power in society. It is easy with our habitually worm's-eye view of history and because of our continued resistance to equality rights goals to forget that, in some respects, we have come a long way and yet, in other respects, it is as if time has stood still.

If the road travelled seems wearisome, it is because—even though those direct forms of racism are often identified and addressed—equality and human rights advocates are still faced with denial that the phenomenon exists in the current discourse about "institutional," "adverse effects," or "systemic" racism. So blank are the stares from many of those with whom they attempt to reason that at times it seems as though advocates are probing for the discrimination that is buried within our institutions with a divining rod.

The fact is that even if White people do not see, feel, and hear racism, people of colour know it is still there within our institutions. People of colour and Aboriginal peoples have always known that we are put on this earth with no worse or no better a set of mental or physical faculties than those of White folk, so if you do not see us at the decision-making levels of society's institutions, do not blame us; the fault lies with the written and unwritten rules operating just outside the employers' and service providers' consciousness.

Direct racism has certainly played a part in making sure that for centuries the scales have been truly tipped against people of colour. Such discrimination has created rules that have become embedded within the major systems of our society. Although many of the obviously nasty rules have been eradicated, the balance remains tilted. We do not need any further studies to establish that, for racialized and Aboriginal peoples, unequal representation and outcomes continue within most of these systems.

Dancing on Live Embers: Challenging Racism represents a very serious contribution to understanding how organizational racism in all of its chimerical characteristics works and provides concrete approaches for handling its elusive nature. Through their own voices and those of other agents of change, Tina Lopes and Barb Thomas have described some of the major challenges facing those who—using tools that they have had to fashion for themselves—attempt to bring about organizational anti-racist change in society's institutions. But this book is more than a description of problems and solutions from the trenches. It is at one and the same time a complete resource for all of those who seek strategies for anti-racist organizational change.

In 1985, in Ontario (Human Rights Commission) v. Simpsons Sears Ltd., the Supreme Court of Canada rejected the commonly held thesis that intent is a necessary ingredient in discrimination. The principles of *Simpsons Sears* are easy to understand and just as easy to apply. When a seemingly neutral provision adversely affects an individual or group, and does so on the grounds described in human rights legislation, the provision must give way and those applying it must accommodate the individual or the members of the group to the point of undue hardship.

In *C.N.R. v. Canada (Human Rights Commission)*, better known as the *Action Travail des Femmes* case, the Supreme Court of Canada reaffirmed and strengthened its reasoning in relation to the concept of adverse effects. After relying on and applying Madam Justice Rosalie Abella's definition of discrimination, the Court concluded:

> In other words, systemic discrimination in an employment context is discrimination that results from the simple operation of established procedures of recruitment, hiring and promotion, none of which is necessarily designed to promote discrimination. The discrimination is then reinforced by the very exclusion of the disadvantaged group because the exclusion fosters the belief, both within and outside the group, that the exclusion is the result of "natural" forces, for example, that women "just can't do the job". To combat systemic discrimination, it is essential to create a climate in which both negative practices and negative attitudes can be challenged and discouraged.

A majority of the opportunities that our courts have been given (or have taken) to elaborate on the concept of systemic discrimination have been in relation to religion in the context of employment or public schooling. The paucity of judicial and human rights decision-making in relation to the adverse effects of discrimination on the ground of race means agents of anti-racist change must draw their guidance partly from lived experience.

Among those employers and service providers who concede that systemic discrimination exists, the predisposition has been to accommodate the individuals rather than to attack the root causes. *Dancing on Live Embers* fills a gap created by a lack of judicially mandated change and by the repeated tendency to do the minimum when addressing racism within organizations.

Tina Lopes and Barb Thomas are two of the most experienced anti-racism thinkers and practitioners in Canada. Together they have an accumulated forty years of experience observing, working in and bringing about change in organizations—they *know* how organizations think and act. Readers of *Dancing on Live Embers* will benefit from this rich experience and find the strategies they need in order to bring about change in their organizations between its covers.

I was honoured to have been asked to work with Tina and Barb on this project. As a book, *Dancing on Live Embers* will never be far from my desk.

Patrick Case,
LL.B., LL.M (Osgoode), Former Chair Canadian Race Relations Foundation;
Co-Chair, Equality Rights Panel, Court Challenges Program of Canada

Introduction

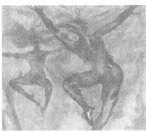

Over the past twenty-five or more years, many organizations have made some attempt to advance racial equity in their operations. Yet many of these same organizations are not more anti-racist or equitable than they were before they tried to change. Indeed, some of our work may have given organizations the language they need to better mask the same old inertia and resistance to really tackle racism. In the late 1990s we became seriously discouraged about the losses we experienced in the anti-racism movement. Employment Equity legislation in Ontario was repealed, the Ontario Anti-Racism Secretariat was closed down, and the British Columbia Human Rights Commission was closed. There was a new permission to dismiss equity initiatives. This widening gap between talk about equity and daily realities of racism led to widespread discouragement and, in some cases, cynicism on the part of anti-racism activists. Was systemic change in organizations really possible?

We also began to examine the effectiveness of our own work. Organizations were requesting the same kinds of "training" they had done fifteen years earlier. This pushed us to analyze our work in a more systematic way. We started to look critically at who was benefiting from anti-racism work and whether our work was contributing to real racial equity. This book captures what we continue to value about our past work and brings to light the newly emerging thinking and strategies in our approach.

What's This Book About?

Dancing on Live Embers investigates how racism, White power and privilege work in the ordinary, daily moments of organizational life. It holds up familiar workplace interactions for scrutiny and analysis, and looks for openings to advance racial equity and justice. This is our primary focus, because unexamined White power and privilege continue to be central obstacles to racial equity in organizations. They are also powerful factors shaping current global politics, economics, and relations between peoples and nations.

As activist educators with an international perspective, we see our anti-racism work in organizations as ever more urgent, given how profoundly it is shaped by the global context. We live in a world made unequal by centuries of empire and colonialism. The wealth of the North is based on the deprivation of the South. The lands and resources of Aboriginal peoples in the Americas have been seized and exploited for the benefit of European settlers and their descendants. These inequities continue to cause people to migrate for work and to struggle for access to basic resources.

Currently, of the one hundred largest economies in the world, fifty-three are multinational corporations.[1] International trade policies are increasing corporate economic and political control, which is felt in communities and workplaces across the country. But people blame each other for the loss of jobs or for oppressive working conditions where harassment thrives. We live in a post–9/11 context where fear of "terrorism" by "the other" has been promoted on a global scale. We firmly situate our racial equity organizational work in this shifting context.

This book is a structured exploration of our racial equity work together, in a variety of organizations, predominantly in southern Ontario, over the past fourteen years. It also offers lessons from activists and their struggles from whom we have learned and been inspired. This book is *not* a comprehensive survey of equity work across Canada. It also does not explore the distinct political, economic, and cultural goals of Aboriginal Peoples. Their rights of self-government, and First Nations' land claims confirmed through treaties, are beyond the scope of this book; and it does not provide examples of racial justice work from every region of the country.

Our choice to look at the *internal workings of organizations* (which include institutions, workplaces, community groups, and so on), rather than what they do in the world, is intentional. First, organizations are where we have done most of our work together. Requests from a variety of organizations have come to us in many forms. We're asked to respond to racial discrimination complaints, provide "equity training," develop policy, evaluate community programs, or to help equity committees achieve more effective outcomes.

Second, organizations are *workplaces where White and racialized*[2] people are likely to have the most contact with each other. It's where people spend a great deal of time. The ways in which workplaces are structured and the "normal" ways they operate, either challenge or reinforce White privilege and racialized hierarchies in the larger society.

Third, *organizations are neglected sites of struggle for social movement activists* whose focus is "out there" but whose own workplaces often reflect the very inequities they fight in the world. We have spent many years of paid and volunteer labour in coalitions, unions, women's organizations, and community agencies. We want to support more courageous work to create equity here, too.

Anti-racism is our entry point to our equity work, and racial equity is the goal of our work. We are a racialized and a White woman doing anti-racism work together in ways that challenge all forms of oppression within an organization. We can't isolate, for example, the racism a clerical worker may experience from the sexism and class that shapes the organization of her work. We find the words of George Dei, Leeno Luke Karumanchery, and Nisha Karumanchery-Luik helpful in explaining our focus:

> We still work within an understanding of oppressions as connected. The saliency of race is
> an "and/with" rather than an "either/or" analysis that stresses the centrality of race and the
> connection of race with class, gender, ethnicity and sexuality. We feel this to be a strategic
> way of maintaining the gaze on race, which has so often been ignored and/or silenced in
> both public discourse and in the imagination of our oppressor. ... It is both a strategic and
> pragmatic approach that maintains a deserved focus on a particular oppression in order to
> deal with it comprehensively, all the while recognizing that it does not stand alone in a hierarchy of oppressions.[3]

We analyze the persistent and specific ways in which White privilege manifests itself between us—Tina and Barb—even in the course of doing racial equity work. We do this for a couple of reasons: first, we want to highlight the fact that "racial equity doesn't just happen,"[4] even between committed anti-racism activists. It requires ongoing, sometimes unpleasant, work. Second, racial equity requires White people to learn, and acknowledge their learning about racism, from racialized colleagues and friends. We think we show clearly that White people cannot do real anti-racism work without an ongoing apprenticeship to racialized people willing and able to make that enormous effort. Third, we hope that by offering an examination of how White power and privilege works between us, we can encourage such frank explorations between racialized and White activists.[5]

Who's This Book For?

This book is for people, who, for a variety of reasons, are trying to create more equitable organizations. Perhaps you are front-line staff who are frustrated by the gap between the practices of your organization and the needs of people you serve. Some of you are managers who feel morally as well as legally responsible for an equitable workplace. You may be administrative support people who are tired of being treated with disrespect. You could be political leaders in unions, on boards of directors, or in political parties who want to use your power for social justice. Maybe you are union stewards dealing with racism in the workplace and union. Or, you may be the designated organizational conscience—"the diversity co-ordinator" or "the equity director"—the person responsible for making the organization do what it knows it should, and who is often punished for doing your job well.

This book is also for people who are hesitant—people who feel something needs to be done about racism but are nervous about doing anything for fear of making things worse. We encourage your instinct to act. We want this book to reassure you that you will make mistakes in the course of trying something, and that it's important to do it anyway. These pages attest to the fact that *not acting* is an action.

As our readers, you work (paid or volunteer) in the full gamut of workplaces—community health centres, unions, universities and colleges, community organizations and coalitions, social housing, all levels of government, media, retail outlets, chambers of commerce, women's shelters, and religious organizations—and you may have completely different analyses of racism and a diverse vocabulary for talking about it. We hope you find something familiar here, that can guide you more comfortably to what is unfamiliar.

Many of the people we work with often feel isolated and don't have an immediate community with whom to share and analyze stories and with whom to strategize further action. We hope our writing will make you feel less crazy, encourage you to find the support and courage you need to keep going, and inspire you to share your own stories and knowledge with the rest of us.

This book is also for the many creative in-it-for-the-long-term activists who have found the strength and stamina to keep working towards racial equity with heart, mind, and spirit. We have been inspired by you; we try to honour your work through a few stories in this book.

There are many sections in this book that might make you feel uncomfortable.

If you're a White person looking for tactical solutions to racism and hoping to remain unscathed, this book may alarm you.

If you're a person of colour beleaguered by racism, tired of playing by the rules, and just want someone to come into your organization and read White people the riot act, this book may infuriate you.

If you think all racialized people doing racial equity work are angry, vengeful, and taking advantage of White people's guilt, this will not be an easy read.

If you want to help racialized people but you don't want to take direction from them, you may want your money back.

If you think White people who do anti-racism should never admit their mistakes, this book will be a real downer.

What's in This Book?

In SECTION ONE, "What Is Racial Equity Work?," we outline the goals of this work and who can benefit from it. We examine some of the pressures on organizations we've been involved with at this particular political and economic moment. We review the shifting frameworks and practices that have shaped racial equity work over the past thirty years, and we conclude with an outline of the key elements of our work now.

SECTION TWO, "Phases in Organizational Change: Measuring Shifts in Power," provides a series of situations and stories in which people are grappling with racism. For each situation, we analyze how power is working and suggest some tools and strategies we've tried to use, with varying results, in each case. After some of the situations, we try to make it explicit just how easily unequal power dynamics are reproduced between White and racialized equity activists. In this section, we also include the stories based on interviews with people in five different organizations and sectors. These stories offer proof that organizational power can be used in the service of racial equity.

The situations and true stories in section two are organized into three phases of organizational change that we have identified in our work: (1) getting beyond training; (2) getting to how things work; and (3) keeping racial equity on the agenda. Each of these phases reflects our experience of initial enthusiasm, alarm, and backsliding in organizations. We summarize each phase with a version of "Building Blocks for Equity," which highlights some common openings and blocks of that phase.

SECTION THREE, "Making the Links: Racial Equity in Organizations and Social Movements," provides examples of two organizations where people have chosen to put different kinds of power—organizational authority, social identity privilege, personal courage, and charisma—at the service of racial equity and movement-building work.

In SECTION FOUR, "Between Us," we examine how racism has distorted our friendship and our capacity to work together. White privilege and racism have played out between the two of us over and over again. It would be dishonest to simply provide tools and strategies without examining the emotional demands that racial equity work requires of people. We draw on our experience with each other to bring to the surface what it takes to honestly confront White privilege when it arises and attempt to transform it.

SECTION FIVE, "More Tools and Strategies," highlights the craft of anti-racism organizational change work. We include some sample policy and analytical tools we have developed and which we think might be helpful to readers. We offer these with gratitude to the many organizations and people who, in the service of their own equity work, were willing to test these out.

We close with a glossary of words we use and a selected bibliography that includes print and Internet resources we have found useful in our work. These resources keep in mind the busy and practical lives of those readers who cram their learning into a bus ride or a plane trip on their way to the next meeting.

A Word about Credit

It is our everyday experience that White people, in particular, are more likely to credit Barb with anti-racism knowledge than they are to credit Tina. One of the ways that racism gets expressed is that White people are viewed as the experts on racism, even though they are not its targets. In fact, they are its beneficiaries. But, even faced with Tina's evident knowledge and skill, many people still assume that Barb is the "expert" on racism.

To counter this tendency, we highlight Tina's expertise in this book as an accurate reflection of her work. Too often such recognition is viewed with suspicion. It's seen as a "token" gesture that confers unearned credit to a racialized person. We want to be clear: this is about merit. A racially divided society (and workplace) requires this kind of clarity to ensure the expertise of a racialized woman is appropriately recognized. Similar interventions are unnecessary for White people.

Finally, we take every opportunity to stress that White people learning from people of colour and Aboriginal people is essential to the integrity of racial equity work. We try to make Barb's learning from Tina as transparent as we can in our dialogues in section four, "Between Us," and in a couple of the case studies in section two. We invite you to monitor your own assumptions about the authors' author-ity as you read this book.

Who We Are

TINA LOPES is a facilitator, educator, and mediator who works with people in organizations to create alternative ways of having and using power in their particular context. Working with community agencies, social service organizations, federal and municipal government departments, women's organizations, law firms and unions, she facilitates sessions in human rights, anti-oppression organizational change, conflict mediation, and strategic planning. Her work has taught her that the most creative options often come from people who have the least power within an organization. A racialized woman who emigrated to Canada as a teenager, she is the target of discrimination. As a straight, able-bodied woman now in her forties, she is also a person with privilege. She continues to research the connections between social transformation, organizational change, and spirituality.

BARB THOMAS worked initially as an activist/educator in community settings in Canada and the Caribbean. Her work has always focused on issues of racism, class, and solidarity and learning from the South. While continuing her community activism, she began working with the labour movement in 1980, and currently she is employed as a temporary, part-time education officer with the Ontario Public Service Employees Union. Her strengths are in equitable program design, facilitator training, and in processes that help people work together to analyze and address systemic problems strategically. She is a White, straight, able-bodied woman in her late fifties, committed to challenging White supremacy in herself. Her passion is work that builds inclusive, effective organizations and social movements, where people can use their hearts and spirits as well as their minds to create something collective.

Together, we have been doing racial equity work, in one way or another, as colleagues and friends since 1990.

What Is Racial Equity Work?

What Is Racial Equity Work?

Shifting Power through Organizational Change

We have found that any effort to effect real organizational change requires an analysis of power. Yet many mainstream theories of organizational development and change make no reference to the ways in which power is embedded in the social identities of managers, workers, and service recipients, or to the impact organizational power has on the lives of people.

Rapid and continuous changes in technology, materials, product development, and markets have made constant change a given in most organizations. Yet this change is generally regarded as taking place without drastically altering how people are assessed, controlled, and compensated; in other words, disparities in power are not questioned. Shifts may be made in how areas of work are defined, the number of employees working in the organization, and the systems of production, but the people who make the decisions remain the same. There are countless organizational change models aimed at increasing efficiency, productivity, and innovation in an organization; few include an explicit discussion about how power dictates the ways in which people in organizations see, value, and interact with one another.

In their book, *Reading Organization Theory*, Albert J. Mills and Tony Simmons challenge the existing texts on organizational theory, which are largely silent about race, gender, class, and other forms of discrimination.[1] They maintain that we live in a time dominated by organizations, and that these organizations and capitalism have "evolved hand in hand."[2] Most organizations are hierarchical, with control and decision-making powers lying in the hands of the few people in senior management positions. Even in the not-for-profit sector, employees are rewarded for generating the greatest number of products, programs, and services at the lowest cost. As a result, "interpersonal relationships within organizations are largely impersonal, manipulative, mistrustful, and mediated by money."[3] Organizations, they argue, have an immense influence on our social and psychic lives, often resulting in a lack of self-esteem, a sense of powerlessness, unhealthy levels of stress, sexual harassment, pay inequities, racism, physical injury, and a segregated work life.

In our attempts to facilitate anti-racism/racial equity organizational change, we aim to make these types of relationships, and their impacts, explicit. Our discussions move back and forth between analyses of how systems work and how people are affected by decisions made within those systems. Racism, sexism, class, and other forms of discrimination shape both the systems and the people who implement them. Embedded in the organizational systems, and in the social identities of people, are disparities in power that affect the life opportunities of individuals, regardless of what they merit based on their skills, competencies, and hard work.

Fran Endicott speaking at the 10th Anniversary of the Toronto District Board of Education Race Relations Policy, 1989

We measure the success of our efforts to bring about organizational change through the positive results experienced by those with the least power within an organization. If we have been successful in the process, people with the least power will have a healthier work environment, their contributions will be properly assessed and valued, and they will be able to actively transform their organization rather than be assimilated into it. If this type of transformation is allowed to occur, the organization benefits immensely from increased productivity, reduced absenteeism and conflict, improved staff morale, and having greater relevance to diverse communities.

Who Are the Players?

People with Organizational Power

One of the biggest challenges of racial equity work is that we are often hired by the people with the most power in an organization to engage in a process that ought to shift how power is used and by whom. As a result, it can become easy to believe that the purpose is primarily to convince the people with power that it is in their interests to change the systems and culture of the organization. Many studies and research projects have been undertaken in order to demonstrate the costs of discrimination and inequity to the organization and to society as a whole. Strong cases exist which appeal to the reason and the principles of people with power, so that they will agree to review and change the systems they develop and oversee.[4] If we want to create greater racial equity, we cannot ignore the decision-makers in organizations and still be effective. However, while people with power are an essential focus, they are neither the only, nor the most important, aspect of the work.

Internal Change Agents

Racial equity work often depends on the internal pressure from people with less power in the organization who risk acting as catalysts for change. Often these are racialized workers and some White allies who might sit on a "diversity committee," lodge a complaint of racism, put racism on the staff meeting agendas, or advocate for the least powerful people the organization serves. No matter how valid the issues, and how careful the presentation, these workers are often described as "trouble-making," "aggressive," or "seeing racism everywhere." They are often isolated from one another and must worry constantly that their efforts to challenge racism will put their jobs at risk.

It is essential, therefore, to build the capacities of the change agents inside the organization and to create the conditions for them to carry out their role. Anti-racism organizational change confirms the racism they have identified in the organization, provides tools to frame their analysis, connects change agents with one another, and widens the space in the organization for their voice(s) to be heard.

Potential Change Agents

There might also be people in the organization who are receptive to racial equity ideas but have not had the tools to grapple with it. Given the appropriate supports, they may develop additional knowledge and skills to recognize the importance of increasing racial equity for themselves, their organization, and their communities. Effective organizational change work builds community and broadens the connections between pockets of people inside and outside the organization. It will take the unified efforts of people acting in solidarity with one another to bring into existence the equitable organizations we seek.

External Communities

In its initial stages, and throughout its process, facilitators of anti-racism organizational change, as well as internal change agents, rely on external pressure from equity-seeking communities to persuade decision-makers to examine the roots of inequities within the organization.[5] Therefore, organizational change must contribute to the mobilizing and strengthening of equity-seeking communities as an important aspect of the change process.

Shifting Approaches to Dealing with Racism

In developing an organizational change process for racial equity, it is important to review earlier efforts to deal with racism in Canadian workplaces. This is necessary in order to identify which approaches have actually challenged racism and which efforts tended to allow inequitable power relations to remain unaltered.

Multiculturalism became Canadian federal policy in 1972 with the *Multiculturalism Act*. The language of multiculturalism suggests that power inequities exist because people of the dominant Canadian culture do not adequately understand the cultures of immigrants from countries other than Britain and France. Emphasis is placed on recognizing the importance of providing services in languages other than English and French, and challenging organizational norms regarding dress codes, accents, food, and other overt forms of bias. The more covert forms of control and ways of maintaining power within work-place organizations tend to be left intact, though some models of organizational change do attempt to pose questions regarding hiring processes, pro-gram development, and service delivery.

Delegation from Central America visiting Toronto City Hall, 1980

As a result of multicultural-ism, organizations began to hire racialized people in entry-level positions, often because they spoke a language that was needed if the organization was to serve a new community of service users. The programs developed for these communities often remained peripheral to the "real work" of the organization, and the staff who worked in these positions were rarely given opportunities to apply their skills and knowledge in other parts of the organization.

A critique of multiculturalism in the 1970s and 1980s, both in Britain and in Canada, reflected a shift in an understanding about the roots of racism. The emerging anti-racism movement insisted on posing questions about power squarely in the midst of any discus-sions of racism and other forms of inequity in an organization. Anti-racism educators began to question the emphasis placed on people's ethno-cultural differences and pointed to the ways in which organizations are structured to reinforce inequities. The term "systemic racism" was coined as a way of capturing the notion that racism is a product of the normal ways in which work is structured, monitored, and rewarded. The difficult and often painful discussions about an individual's racist behaviour were secondary to this emphasis on racism as a by-product of seemingly neutral mechanisms for doing business.

Many organizations have avoided this approach, stating that the language of anti-racism is too confrontational and negative for people in their organization. Even when organizations have hosted anti-racism workshops, many White staff arrived reluctantly, afraid that they would be attacked or labelled as racist. Some found these discussions diffi-cult, feeling implicated by systems they did not create, angry at what they saw as general-izations about White people, and hurt that they were set apart from racialized people.

In these workplaces, despite the relief that many racialized people felt at finally having an explicit discussion of the differential impacts of racism, many were cautious. Some were cynical about yet another organizational initiative that, as with so many others, would probably end before any real change took place. Others were placed in the awkward position of having to reassure their White colleagues that they were not racist, and to publicly oppose the need for anti-racism work. There were also some that preferred a multicultural approach that was less conflict ridden and more acceptable to the majority of people in the workplace. As a result, anti-racism organizational change would often stall due to the high levels of discomfort and resistance in the organization. An anti-racism approach was generally seen as divisive, emotionally wrenching, and, ultimately, ineffective.

Yet organizations that are serious about transforming power, and that are committed to grappling with racism, often return to an anti-racism model. Anti-racism/anti-oppression movements recognize that inequitable power exists in our society. Unless this inequity in all its forms is actively challenged, it reproduces itself whether we intend it to or not, in our organizations. If there is to be real equity, there is no way to bring it about without taking an honest and critical look at the ways in which the normal, seemingly neutral systems of most organizations benefit White people and disadvantage racialized people. While it is impossible to challenge existing power relations without moments of tension and discomfort between members of the dominant group and racialized peoples, it is possible to make those moments a productive part of a process that builds alliances and common cause among these groups.

Avoiding Real Change through "Diversity"

Perhaps in reaction to the anti-racism approach, many organizations have hired consultants to facilitate processes for "celebrating" or addressing diversity. The argument is that "diversity" is more inclusive as it embraces all forms of inequity and discrimination. The danger is, of course, that in trying to be inclusive of all forms of inequity, that none will be addressed effectively. This is particularly true of racism, a topic which produces real discomfort in the workplace.

The underlying assumption of the diversity change processes seems to be that people with organizational and/or socially conferred power need to be persuaded that people who look or act in ways that are different from them are benign, perhaps even useful to the organization. Educational sessions often take the form of providing socially dominant groups in the organization with selected pieces of information about "others" so that "they" can be brought into an organization, which remains essentially unchanged.

The term "diversity" can mean anything. For example, if we wanted to, we could talk about people's diversity in terms of where they went to school, whether they are the oldest, youngest, or middle children in their families, their food preferences and tastes in fashion. Human diversity simply exists and is not in and of itself a problem. Indeed, environmentalists and scientists are telling us that diversity is essential for our survival. The actual problem is discrimination and the resulting inequities.

It's not clear how the concept of diversity would be any more effective than the earlier approach of multiculturalism as it appears to be equally reluctant to name systemic and social inequities. Real disparities of power among people and within organizational systems are usually left unaddressed in a diversity framework.

Margie Adam

Connecting Workplace Inequities to Global Inequities

Few of us learn about the connections between capitalism, the demand for cheap sources of labour and materials, and societal inequities such as racism, sexism, and classism. Most organizations and the people who manage them believe that their organization has been structured for the greatest efficiency and productivity. They see these structures as neutral at best, perhaps a little impersonal, but never brutally inequitable. It is important to place racial equity work in the context of privatization and the "enclosure of commons," the newest forms of restructuring under globalization.

Richard Bocking provides useful definitions of the terms "enclosure" and "commons":

The term "commons," derived from ancient usage in rural England, is now applied to those things to which we have rights simply by being members of the human family: the air we breathe, the fresh water we drink, the seas, forests and mountains, the genetic heritage through which all life is transmitted, the diversity of life itself. There is also the commons that humankind has created: language, a wealth of scientific, cultural, and technical knowledge accumulated over the ages, our public universities, our public utilities, our health and education systems, the broadcast spectrum. And there is the commons that we have specifically declared to be public assets, like our parks and community squares. A commons, then, is synonymous with community, cooperation, and respect for the rights and preferences of others. Enclosure, on the other hand, refers to exclusion, possession, monopoly, and personal or corporate gain.[6]

Enclosure, or the privatization of public resources and services, happened on a grand scale through imperialism and colonialism. As Edward Said puts it, "At some very basic level, imperialism means thinking about, settling on, controlling land that you do not possess, that is distant, that is lived on and owned by others."[7] Here in Canada this process began with the dispossession of Aboriginal peoples by British and French governments. Then, as now, this process was about the accumulation of wealth, as James Blaut describes: "Colonialism in its various forms, direct and indirect, was an immensely profitable business and considerable sums of money were invested in efforts to learn as much as possible

Tina Lopes

UN World Conference
Against Racism,
Durban, 2001

about ... the regions to be conquered, dominated, and perhaps settled, in order to facilitate the administration and economic exploitation of these regions."[8]

Today, privatization and the enclosure of our modern-day commons are being carried out by transnational corporations whose owners have much the same worldview as their European ancestors. The ownership of the essentials of life is now being transferred to these transnational corporations at a rapid rate. Transnational corporations have enormous influence on national governments all over the world, and they exercise this influence through a number of mechanisms, the most well known of which are the World Trade Organization, the International Monetary Fund, and the World Bank.

Even as social programs are reduced and human rights are diminished, the rights and freedoms of these transnational corporations are strengthened and protected in trade agreements such as the General Agreement on Trades and Services (GATS) and the North American Free Trade Agreement (NAFTA). Under Chapter 11 of NAFTA, corporations can sue nation states for compensation if any national policies have the impact of reducing their profits.

In Canada, cuts to social programs are made in order to justify large tax breaks for wealthy individuals and profitable corporations. This process is happening in many other countries as part of the globalization of economies. It is what is known as "structural adjustment." In a study released by the Canadian Centre for Policy Alternatives, Andrew Jackson explains that cuts to corporate taxes between 2000 and 2010, plus the elimination of the surtax and capital tax, will reduce federal government revenues by $12.6 billion.[9] Governments are pressured to reduce spending by cutting social programs and lowering labour and environmental standards. Current government responsibilities to maintain adequate shelter, health care, healthy food, care for children and the elderly, access to clean water and adequate heat, are then shifted to individuals, communities, and charities.

The connections between this evolving corporatization and the cuts in federal and provincial spending in Canada are made clear in Elmear O'Neill's article "From Global Economies to Local Cuts: Globalization and Structural Change in Our Own Backyard."[10] O'Neill argues that the reduced transfer of funds from federal to provincial levels and from provincial to municipal levels has meant that essential social services such as health care, education, and income support are increasingly being paid for by individual Canadians rather than by taxes gathered from corporations. She adds that the growing amalgamation of services in numerous cities and provinces has resulted in "a shift from a universal basic minimum standard of community care to a 'charity' model" in which a non-representative few decide who is deserving of public funds and who is not.[11] Increasingly, the privatization of health care, care of the elderly, public utilities and prison systems has resulted in poorer quality of services for Canadians and greater profits for corporations.

The cutbacks disproportionately affect women who are both the majority of public-sector workers and users of public services. For example, in British Columbia, spending cuts implemented since 2002 have resulted in a loss of more than twenty thousand public-sector jobs, nearly three-quarters of which were held by women. In a news release in December 2004, the Canadian Centre for Policy Alternatives argued that cuts to public services, changes in education policy and weakened legal protections for workers have also combined to undermine key employment conditions for women.[12]

Aboriginal women, women of colour, and low-income women, in particular, bear the brunt of these cuts, which makes the struggle for racial equity more essential and yet more difficult to undertake. Faced with constant threats of downsizing, fewer people are willing to complain about discrimination and harassment in the workplace; fearing the growing lack of services, few service users challenge workers who treat them poorly; confronted with rising unemployment, there is greater resistance to employment equity initiatives; due to the lack of affordable housing and overcrowded shelters, fewer women are leaving abusive relationships; and the growing costs of child care, elder care, education and health care, mean fewer people can afford to stay healthy.

Protecting human rights and fighting for racial equity at the organizational level is as essential as the resistance to trade agreements that benefit only multinational corporations at the international level. Both processes create inequities and hardships in many communities.

Keeping the Focus on Racial Equity at Home

There continues to be debate about whether racism is currently a problem in Canada. A growing number of academics, politicians, and journalists argue that it is a concern of the past and that it is time to consider other "more pressing social issues." This should not be surprising. Studies indicate that most White people persist in believing that racism is much less of a problem than racialized people think it is, even though there are countless well-researched and documented studies indicating its prevalence in many spheres of society, including employment, education, housing, policing, media, politics, and the arts.

In his exploration of the huge difference in perception about racism between White and African Americans in the United States, Tim Wise suggests that one reason for it is that White people "find the notion of widespread mistreatment hard to digest."[13] He argues that this happens "especially when one has been socialized to give more credence to what members of one's own group say, than what the racial 'other' tells us is true." White and racialized people who have been engaged in anti-racism work in Canada can confirm that this is not just an American phenomenon; a similar gap exists between White and racialized Canadians. An Ipsos-Reid survey, conducted in March 2005 to mark International Day for the Elimination of Racial Discrimination, indicates that about four million Canadians, or one in six adults, has been the target of racism.[14] According to the survey, approximately one in ten, or 13 per cent, believe that racism has decreased in their community during the past five years, while about 17 per cent indicate they believe that racism has been rising. While the poll does not indicate the racial identity of those who believe racism has decreased versus those who indicate that it has increased, it's quite possible that the differences may be attributed, at least in part, to differences in race.

There is ample evidence of the existence of racism in the everyday lives of racialized and Aboriginal peoples. Being on the receiving end of overt or subtle racism creates intense and constant stress, which boosts the risk of depression, anxiety, and anger—factors that can lead to or aggravate heart disease. Some research suggests it can also manifest itself in respiratory and other physiological problems. Camara P. Jones, research director of Social Determinants of Health for the Centers for Disease Control and Prevention and a leading specialist on the health impact of racism, comments:

> We know that black folks are at higher risk of hypertension, but in childhood, there are no differences between Black and White blood pressure rates. By the time you get into the 25 to 44 year old group, you start to see changes. We have evidence that in White folks, blood pressure is dropping at night, but not in Black people.[15]

She further explains her theory for this:

> There's a kind of stress, like you're gunning your cardiovascular engine constantly if you're Black, that results from dealing with people who

Protest against homelessness and clear-cut forestry

are underestimating you, limiting your options. It results from little things like going to a store and if there are two people at the counter, one Black and one White, the White person will be first approached ... the stresses associated with racism are chronic and unrelenting.[16]

While this particular study focused on people of African descent, there is no doubt that the conclusions of the study apply to other racialized peoples.

A recent article quotes a British study of 4,800 people which found that those who felt victimized by discrimination and forms of racism were twice as likely to develop psychotic episodes over the next three days.[17] It also states that a group of Harvard University researchers have documented that a 1 per cent increase in incidents of racism translates to an increase of 350 deaths per 100,000 African Americans.

Therefore, it is no exaggeration to say that racism must be survived on a daily basis. Not only is it a hazard to one's health, it threatens access to the basic necessities of life, while continuously doing damage to one's emotional, psychological, spiritual, and social well-being. Poverty among racialized groups is rising, unemployment is increasing for racialized workers, the curriculum taught to our children continues to reinforce White privilege, and significant numbers of racialized children and youth are suffering as a result. Racial profiling in policing, the differential treatment of Aboriginal and racialized people in the criminal justice system, and the over-representation of Aboriginal and racialized people in prisons is well documented. Immigration policies continue to bring highly educated racialized professionals to Canada knowing they will not be permitted to practise their professions, and racialized women continue to earn less than White men, White women, and racialized men.[18]

It is no surprise, then, that racism distorts what might otherwise be decent and amicable exchanges between White and racialized people in the workplace. Some of the distortion is not just about racism—it's about the inequitable distribution of resources and the human desire to be "successful" and well rewarded. When racism is mixed into this already conflict-laden environment, it becomes harder to disentangle, but its presence is undeniable, particularly to racialized people who are its targets.

The knowledge, skills, and analysis required to proactively address racism in the workplace will become increasingly important in Canada in the coming years. According to a Statistics Canada study, *Canada's Visible Minority Population in 2017,* released in March 2005, about one in five Canadians will be a "visible minority" by 2017. Researchers concluded that over 75 per cent of all "visible minorities" will live in Toronto, Vancouver, and Montreal, and over half the population of Toronto and Vancouver will be racialized peoples. This same study predicts that in 2017, "for every 100 visible minority persons old enough to leave the labour force ... there would be 142 old enough to join the labour force."[19] Clearly, challenging racism is going to become increasingly important as Canadian society and its workplaces become more racially diverse.

Workers of Colour Conference, Toronto and York Region Labour Council

Our Approach to Racial Equity Work

Our approach to organizational change for racial equity requires a creative tension between an examination of systems and a challenge to individuals who implement those systems. Both aspects require an understanding of different forms of power: power in systems, the power of individuals, the power of symbols, and the collective power of equity-seeking communities.

Power in Systems

We need to give people the tools for analyzing the inequitable impact of the apparently neutral systems that drive an organization. These systems contain power and can function as a force for keeping things the same. Few of us have been encouraged to analyze how the policies, processes, and practices, both formal and informal, impact people. The development of policies and procedures is often left to boards of directors, senior managers or policy analysts, people who embody power (and who often have trouble acknowledging the power they represent). What they do is rarely discussed openly, and is often shrouded in mystery. The implication is that the majority of us are neither qualified nor entitled to critique organizational systems.

Analyzing an organization's systems for racism is an invitation to take an honest look at systems for developing programs and providing services, as well as at hiring and promotional practices. It challenges the organization to examine whether current programs and services serve all communities or tend to favour traditional clients over new ones. It recognizes that employment systems might not always reward competence and hard work, and might be vulnerable to favouritism and bias. Racial equity initiatives ensure that a workplace's policies, practices, and procedures function fairly and effectively for everyone.

Power of Individuals

It is important in racial equity work that we explore how the life experiences of individuals mould what individuals learn about their own and other people's social identities and how these identities are valued differently by our society. It also shapes how individuals think about acting for social justice. This, along with the types of power afforded or denied by the organization in which they work, affects how individuals act to challenge or perpetuate inequities in the organization. Power is not in and of itself a bad thing. Individuals with power can use it to bring about results that benefit all people and communities. A denial of power only results in its abuse.

In our work we pay attention to how people with power can be effective allies with those who are the targets of oppression. Work in this area has largely tended to explore how people with power can provide support to those with less power. This approach has kept the focus almost exclusively on the people experiencing oppression. If it is to be effective, racial equity work must ensure that people with power have opportunities to examine their own experiences of unearned privilege. Self-directed questions could be, "How does privilege shape my life as a man or as a White person?" rather than "How do racialized people experience racism, or women experience sexism?" People with privilege must also grapple with the difficult question of why they would want to share the power they have. This would shift the ways in which people think about solutions. Instead of sending women for self-defence courses, we might hear about men gathering to talk about maleness, power, and violence. White people might challenge employers on the number of White people hired as a result of networks and friendships, instead of debating the merits of employment equity. It's about people getting clear about the power they have and the strategic ways they could use it for equity, rather than getting paralyzed by guilt.

World Social Forum, Brazil, January 2005

Rainer Soegtrop

Power of Symbols: Using Symbols and Stories to Create Meaning

How do we bring about the radical change in power relations necessary for creating an equitable organization? We need to draw on the intellectual, emotional, psychological, and spiritual aspects of everyone in the organization to bring about real transformation. Otherwise the organization tends to shift in ways that are largely superficial. The change process for an individual person and for an organization is similar in that new symbols and stories must be created that imbue the process with meaning and value.

In *Organization Theory: Modern, Symbolic and Postmodern Perspectives*, Mary Jo Hatch describes how organizational theorists are looking at the ways in which stories and symbols are essential tools for transforming the values and assumptions of an organization.[20] In fact, these theorists are finding that symbols and stories are just as significant as structures, policies, and procedures in producing and reproducing an organization.

This is clearly evident when organizations create or revise their mission, vision, and values statements. Stories about how the organization came into being, why it still exists, inspiring tales about the first organizers, service users and volunteers, memories of deeply satisfying moments can be a source of great energy and passion for the people involved in that organization. We have had people weep with each other, laugh long and hard, and speak passionately about why they chose to join the organization. This is often a place from which to build discussions about creating a more equitable workplace. There is often a great deal in common between a vision of racial equity and the values of most organizations.

Yet all too often, the most powerful stories and symbols are at odds with the way an organization's mission and vision are lived. People's energy and job satisfaction are depleted when this is the case. For instance, an organization might say that its employees are its

Marie-Andrée L'Herureux

CEP Women's Conference, October 2005

most valuable resource, that it welcomes initiative and innovation from staff, and that it values collaboration. Yet, as Hatch points out, the same organization uses daily productivity reports and time sheets and has offices that are easy to monitor visually and that deter people from conversing. This conveys something quite different: employees must be closely monitored and coerced into being productive.[21] Employees respond with resentment and mistrust.

For real organizational change to take place, the existing symbols of the organization may need to be replaced with new words, objects, and ways of doing things. When the assumptions of people within the organization are symbolically challenged, new and different values can be incorporated into the culture, and will function along with established organizational principles.

This is not a linear or a uniform process, and it has looked different in the various organizations with which we have worked. In one organization, the symbolic challenge occurred when the CEO and the union president stood before the assembled staff and spoke as the two leaders of the organization about the importance of racial equity. The challenge was, of course, twofold: it was a novel experience for staff to see the union president acknowledged by the CEO for her organizational leadership; it was also significant to have both leaders commit the time and resources to address the entire staff about racial equity. At an individual level, the CEO had to change his perception of the union president as an adversary and examine his own assumptions about leadership and who demonstrated leadership qualities.

In another organization, the executive director publicly thanked an African-descent employee who had filed a complaint of racial discrimination for his contribution to changing the organization. This was a radical challenge to the prevailing assumption that workers who complain about racism and other forms of discrimination are troublemakers who damage the organization's public image and cause tensions in the workplace. The executive director had to take responsibility for the ways in which she communicated and reinforced this assumption in her previous reactions towards human rights complaints. She also had to confront her own beliefs about how racialized people in administrative support positions demonstrated commitment to the organization and took risks on behalf of service users.

Some Symbols of "Power Over"

 clocks placed prominently in areas where front-line staff enter and leave

 no doors and little privacy for front-line staff suggest high levels of monitoring

 large boardroom tables seat only one or two people at the head

 leaders/senior people are introduced with first and last names, administrative assistants and receptionists (often women) are often introduced only by their first names

 art work on the walls and in the materials of the organization tend to portray White people in a variety of roles, and the few racialized people in stereotypical roles or as service recipients

 critical documents are only available in English

 all paid statutory holidays are based on Christian days of significance

 meetings are always chaired by the same individual, often a manager

 all staff wear Western clothing

Some Symbols of Racial and Gender Equity

 conducting meetings with people seated in circles

 creating space for silence in meetings and ensuring all participants have an opportunity to speak

 setting aside a room for staff who want a place for quiet reflection

 men ordering/preparing and serving food as often as women

 racialized people are depicted in a variety of roles, including leadership positions, in organizational materials and art work

 interpretation services and translation of documents in the languages of service users

 all employees have the same number of paid holidays which they can use for the observance of their religious days of significance

 staff take turns chairing meetings

 staff choose to wear clothing that reflects their identities

Power of Equity-Seeking Communities

In *The Feminist Case against Bureaucracy*, Kathy Ferguson makes a startling claim: "Compassion, generosity, solidarity, and sensitivity to others are crucial values; that they are more often found in the oppressed than among the oppressors indicates that it is the dominant social order that devalues these traits and distorts them to serve the interests of the powerful."[22] This may appear to be a radical claim that is far from self-evident. Yet as we review where we have seen the greatest evidence of these values, we would agree with Ferguson that it has more often been among those who have experienced oppression. It has been among survivors of torture, African-descent participants in the South African Truth and Reconciliation process, and Aboriginal survivors of residential schools that we have

Barb Thomas

Popular Education Conference, Alberta, 1994

learned the most about the awe-inspiring capacity of human beings to forgive, rebuild, and imagine real alternatives.

It is also from First Nations and Aboriginal peoples, from racialized people born in Canada and those who have emigrated, and from people who have fought for real democracy in their countries of origin and are now here as refugees that we have learned about the power of resistance. They know at a visceral level the depth of commitment required to transform inequitable structures and systems here in Canada. This is not to argue that equity-seeking communities function as a communion of saints. They, as with any other communities, have their disagreements and divisions and can reproduce the normative power relations that exist all around them. Much has been written on how internalized oppression affects the ways in which members of racialized communities treat each other.[23] It is also important to acknowledge the differences in the history of oppression for Aboriginal peoples and people of colour in Canada, and how these differences shape the ways in which these communities are currently racialized in Canada. However, as these communities come together in solidarity over common experiences of racism, they have the power to place necessary pressure on organizations to undertake the change process.

The Power of Not Knowing

A key element of our approach is a willingness to accept that we will not always know the answers to questions that arise as we engage with organizations. This is challenging for both of us and for the people with whom we work. So many of the systems for rewarding and punishing people, from senior managers to front-line workers, have been established to reward people who always know what to do and who take quick action. In our most successful efforts to bring about a real shift in power and equity relations within an organization, we (and the people we worked with) had to spend painful periods of time in which we did not know what to ask, much less what to do. In those moments, we had to have faith that the response most needed would emerge from our admissions to each other as managers, front-line workers, union leaders, and educators that we did not know. Sitting in those interminable silences felt at first like huge failures, but then something would emerge. Our leap of faith required a willingness to be open to a yet unknown possibility, and we were rarely disappointed.

Organizational Change for Racial Equity: An Act of Faith

Perhaps what has changed the most in our work is the recognition that our efforts to encourage organizational change requires an act of faith—in each other, in people's desire for justice, and in whatever impetus there is in the universe for making things better for all beings on the planet. Meaningful, equitable, and sustainable organizational change is not something any of us control, and it is often a mixture of strategy and faith. We do our best with strategies to think as clearly as possible and to act decisively. We appeal to what people value: their wish to be fair, their capacity to care for others, their courage to take risks, and their desire for a different way of relating in the workplace and in society.

Unemployment and Housing protest, Winnipeg

Through their stories we find that people act from the heart: some act out of a desire to atone for the actions of their ancestors; some because they are the daughters and sons of people who resisted before them; others out of a determination to carve out an easier life for their children; some because they could not bear the injustices they witnessed in a dramatic event in their lives; still others out of a need to create and belong to a community.

Without these reasons of the heart, mind, and body, there would be little motivation to embark on a process that exposes how little we know about transforming power relations and challenging racism, and that makes us so vulnerable. All too often, it is only the threat of a human rights complaint that would have legal, financial, and public relations consequences that motivates an organization and its leaders to act. This threat is not enough to sustain a process of transformation.

What does this mean concretely? For those with the power to change organizational policies and practices to advance racial equity, the challenge lies in:

☐ taking full responsibility for the organizationally conferred power that they do have

☐ using this power in ways that have not been rewarded in the past, and may run the risk of being punished in the future

☐ accepting that their efforts to collaborate with people with less organizational power may be viewed with mistrust for some time

☐ a willingness to be vulnerable to criticism, to asking for help and to making mistakes

☐ courage to discuss and challenge their own prejudices

For those with less or little power, the task may be to create alternative bases of power, by creating alliances with others within the organization as well as with those outside it. It is always important to think strategically about ways of working with people who have organizational power and who may want to create change. It's particularly important to ensure that mechanisms for protecting themselves (such as grievances, personnel policies, complaint mechanisms and properly conducted performance reviews) are well maintained during these times.

Throughout this process, we need to shift from one to another competing and complex response, discerning which is the most appropriate in any given moment: a willingness to hold others accountable while not punishing or seeking revenge; a capacity to engage despite a lack of trust; and a clear sense of self-worth that draws the line where it needs to be drawn.

Organizational Change for Racial Equity

❏ resists the assumption that racial equity is a technical product of change that has nothing to do with how we think, the bodies we live in, or the ways we live

❏ begins with the understanding that the process is not linear or simple, and that it will often stall, lurch ahead, lose ground, and occasionally inch forward

❏ recognizes the impact of organizational power on people's social, physical, and mental health

❏ makes explicit the ways in which social identities confer or deny power to people within organizations

❏ poses questions about how seemingly neutral systems perpetuate disparities in power among people in the organization

❏ connects inequities in the organization to broader economic, social, and political inequities locally, provincially, nationally, and internationally

❏ names the fact that people with organizational power either challenge or reinforce inequity through their actions—there isn't a third option

❏ is measured by the ways in which people with less or little power in the organization benefit from the change

❏ allocates resources and attention to building the capacity of internal change agents in various parts of the organization

❏ relies upon and must contribute to strengthening racial equity-seeking communities outside the organization

❏ holds both organizational systems and the individuals who implement them accountable for how power is used in the organization

❏ appreciates that organizational power is not always negative, and that it can be used to create racial equity

❏ values and depends upon people's willingness to admit they do not know how inequities operate in their organization or how to fix the inequities

❏ requires an openness to unknown possibilities emerging out of spaces for reflection among people at all levels of the organization

❏ symbolically challenges the assumptions of an organization

❏ demands radical change of each individual and of all levels of the organization

❏ creates new meaning and values through the development of new symbols, stories, and artifacts

❏ is an act of faith in each person, in the organization's stated values and in the impetus for good that is always available

Phases in Organizational Change

SECTION 2

Phases in Organizational Change: Measuring Shifts in Power

We have both worked in a variety of organizations as employees and as contract workers doing equity work. When decision-makers ask us to help with "diversity" or "equity" in their organizations and they tell us what they want, it's usually with the hope that a simple solution will make a big problem go away. Often these decision-makers have a sense of an immediate tension, but little idea of the scope of the problem. And usually they have not thought about the ways in which power may be working and contributing to the problem. This means we have a responsibility to negotiate with them about what the work is and what the starting points might be. Otherwise, we can further endanger people already vulnerable in the organization and help the organization look good while doing nothing. In these initial negotiations, we may differ from the decision-makers in our purposes, ways of working, and ways of evaluating progress in advancing equity.

For example, we want an intervention to clearly benefit the people who are the targets of discrimination. This is a major indicator of success for us. But from the perspective of a pressured person contracting us to work, measures of success might be that conflict is reduced quickly and that a minimum of money and organizational time is spent in the process. So measuring progress depends on who we think should benefit from equity work, who we see as shouldering the most risk and cost, and how we frame equity as part of the organization's work.

These indicators of progress are not static. Challenging organizations to reassess what results they are looking for is part of the work itself. Indeed, when an organization begins to look critically at how the normal, everyday ways of doing things can reproduce racism, sexism, classism, and other forms of inequality, we know we're getting somewhere. But how do we measure shifts in power in an organization?

This section provides a series of short, fictionalized situations where racism is at work in organizational life and where people are trying to do something about it. For each of these situations, we analyze how power is working and suggest some tools and strategies. After some of the situations, we try to "keep ourselves in the picture," to show how easily unequal power dynamics are reproduced between White and racialized equity change agents. We also include true stories about real people actively challenging racism in five different organizations and sectors. These stories offer proof that each of us can use the power we have in the service of racial equity. We selected these people because they have influenced and helped move our work forward; they are currently engaged in something we thought needed highlighting in this book; and they made themselves available to us for this writing.

The situations and true stories in this section are organized according to three phases of organizational change that we have identified in our work. We call these (1) getting beyond training; (2) getting to how things work; and (3) keeping racial equity on the agenda. Each of these phases reflects our experience of initial enthusiasm, resistance, and backsliding in organizations. At the end of each phase, we summarize important characteristics of that phase with the Building Blocks for Equity tool. Our colleagues Jojo Geronimo and the late Marlene Green developed a way of thinking about how power is exercised in organizations which they called *Building Blocks to Equity*. Power, they said, is either *hoarded or shared* through five activities: decision-making, communicating, allocating resources, use of networks and contacts, and the use of expertise. These are either "blocks"/ obstacles to equity or "building blocks *for* equity." This tool appears again in section five as an interactive checklist for what to look for in an equitable organization.

Marlene Green (above), and Jojo Geronimo (below), North American Alliance of Popular Adult Educators, Alberta, 1994

Barb Thomas

PHASE 1

Getting beyond Training

We have all spent time in organizations (unions, government departments, women's shelters, schools and colleges, businesses, community agencies, and so on) where inequities are blatant and remain unaddressed. For example, in an organization near an Aboriginal community, there are no Aboriginal people in the workplace or in positions of responsibility; tensions and conflicts that are racial, sexual, and classist simmer below the surface unheeded; an employee survey indicates that staff experience racism but are afraid of reprisals if they report it. All the decision-makers are White and able-bodied.

Yet something is pushing the organization to pay attention to racism. Perhaps a new manager with experience in a more equitable workplace is asking questions; or the organization is losing business, clients, or members to other similar organizations; or it's being challenged by its members or clients to move and change. Funding is available for, or contingent on, doing something about equity, and the organization sees an opportunity for more resources. Perhaps a new outreach project is churning up all kinds of questions and possibilities.

But more often than not, it's a crisis that forces an organization in phase one to act: an employee has filed a complaint or grievance alleging racial harassment; tensions are high on the shop or office floor; new people are complaining about the poisonous work environment to which seasoned employees have become inured. In phase one, the organization starts by wanting to put out the fires. This desire to settle trouble spots provides opportunities (as well as limitations) for equity advocates and activists to work.

We provide three situations to illustrate some of the challenges in this phase. "Training Will Fix It" examines the familiar hope of White people that racism will go away with a little education. It also explores the costs to racialized workers when organizations want this kind of quick fix. "'Proving' It's Racism" probes common responses by organizations to racialized workers who point out racism. It uncovers the hidden ways that power works to make racism look so normal that it's impossible to "prove." "Being the 'Diversity Co-ordinator'" explores the challenges of that job and how the structure of this position can be just another way to keep things the same while appearing to address racism. Our true story is "Building Community Coalition and Capacity." For twelve years, community activists have pressured the Calgary Board of Education to integrate English as a Second Language learning into the regular curriculum. This story highlights the necessity of organized community pressure to move organizations to change, particularly phase-one organizations, and it distils some effective strategies to do so.

Training Will Fix It

An organization cannot teach anti-racism. It has to be learned. Teaching and training puts the responsibility on the teachers and trainers to impart the change.

— Rainer Soegtrop, "Leadership in Times of Resistance"

An initial telephone conversation to an equity facilitator goes something like this:

"We are a large social service agency. Your name was suggested by the union. We just want a few, half-day training sessions on diversity for all staff. We need it done by the end of the fiscal year."

"Why do you want training?"

"Oh, we've had a few tensions recently based on cultural differences. We think training could help."

"How did you arrive at a half-day?"

"That's what we thought we could afford. We realize it's just a start."

"What's the rest of the plan?"

"Uh, well, maybe you could make some suggestions. Perhaps we could meet. We're interviewing other possible trainers."

"I only do this work in a team. I'm White; I miss things; I can't make it safer for the people of colour in anti-racism training, if training is what you end up needing."

"Okay, bring someone with you."

On the day of the meeting, the two facilitators are met at the interview by an anxious White manager, Hilda, and an African-Canadian woman, Lorene, who is quiet at the outset. Hilda directs all her greetings and instructions to the White facilitator and fails to introduce Lorene.

As the meeting progresses, it becomes clear that Lorene is on the Access and Equity Committee and is at the meeting as a quasi-representative, although she is clearly not an equal participant in the encounter. The facilitators ask what else is going on in the organization that could have a bearing on the training. Hilda mentions two factors: that the training is, in fact, the result of a grievance settlement on harassment, and that a "Diversity Survey" filled out by the employees has revealed that a high proportion of people fear reprisals from management if they report experiences of racism. The facilitators begin talking about how common reprisals are in organizations—how easy it is to punish people who speak up about discrimination. They mention some of the covert ways in which reprisals happen—distasteful job assignments, increased monitoring of performance, exclusion from information. Hilda protests that, if this is what's going on in her organization, it certainly isn't the intention of the managers to be racist.

When Hilda leaves the room for a moment, Lorene leans forward and reveals that she is the griever to whom Hilda alluded. For three years she had pursued a case of racial harassment and had finally succeeded in getting a settlement, which did not acknowledge harassment but promised a half-day of diversity training to all staff. She said that she has experienced all the forms of reprisals the facilitators just described, and then some, and that reprisals against her continue to go on and are making her sick.

When Hilda returns, the discussion continues about other strategies the organization can take to strengthen equity. Hilda says she will talk to Lorene then let them know. The facilitators ask what criteria they are using to decide on hiring the facilitators. Hilda is vague. She has taken no notes, has no materials ready to hand out, takes no résumés, and cannot elaborate any further on the selection process.

1. What inequities in power do you see in this situation? How is power being used to challenge or reinforce racism?

2. Where are the specific openings for action, to shift how power is working? At what point could you do something different as Hilda? Lorene? the facilitator of colour? the White facilitator?

How Power Is Working

1. **White people see other White people as the "experts" on equity.**

   The White manager calls a White facilitator. When the White facilitator explains why she must work in a team, the manager agrees but doesn't even ask who it will be. Her focus on the White facilitator and her lack of interest in her colleague of colour convey an assumption: serious anti-racist educators are White; people of colour are their side-kicks.

   In a number of subtle and coded ways, Hilda invites understanding and collusion by the White facilitator. She addresses her, even when it's the facilitator of colour who poses a question. She directs all her inquiries to the White facilitator, and her look solicits another White person's grasp of what she's up against in dealing with all "this stuff." When the facilitator of colour poses a challenging question, or explains something effectively, Hilda looks to the White facilitator for support or validation. Hilda credits the White facilitator with points and explanations provided by the facilitator of colour.

2. **White people control the language, "the story," and the action on equity.**

   "A half-day training on diversity" is the initial request, emerging from Lorene's three-year battle to fight racial harassment. "A few tensions based on cultural differences" is Hilda's initial description of the situation. Only through directed questioning does she reveal the story of the grievance and fear of reprisals in the organization. Lorene speaks frankly only when Hilda is out of the room—a clear indication that reprisals are real.

   White people's stated intentions are seen by Hilda as important signals that "they aren't racist." White people are in charge of decisions about what will happen and what will get communicated, and of how resources will be allocated.

3. **Equity is so marginal that training is seen as a fix.**

   Hilda communicates that whatever is wrong isn't very serious, and if it is serious, the trainer doesn't need to know about it. This approach to "trainers" signals the hope that training will fix whatever is wrong in the organization. Training is a way of honouring a commitment and of being seen to take action, but not as part of a long-term strategy. Equity training is definitely separate from the everyday operations of the organization. Equity is seen as an irritant, interfering with the real work of the organization, an unfortunate side effect of a grievance process or of being in a unionized workplace.

   Resources are tightly controlled for "equity work." Indeed, it has taken a problem (and a person of colour) that will not go away, to move this organization to do something. But the need to fix something is an opening for equity work.

4. **Racialized workers are present as proof of good faith, but are not active participants.**

The dynamics between these two women mirror the larger organizational dynamics. The managers are White; racialized workers are concentrated in support staff and front-line positions. Hilda does not think to introduce Lorene to the facilitators. She does not invite her to speak or share her knowledge of the situation that the facilitators are being invited to address. Yet this meeting is happening because of Lorene's leadership, not because of Hilda's.

It's not safe for Lorene to volunteer, uninvited, her observations. Lorene listens and gauges the facilitators and then takes a risk during the break. Lorene's role is unclear. She is present, but not as a griever who would therefore be entitled to union representation. She is there, sort of, as a member of the Access and Equity Committee whose role is unclear and whose authority is minimal. However, she has won a settlement that requires training, and Hilda has to carry this out. Further, Hilda does not want additional problems added to those already on her plate. She's prepared to listen to avoid more of them. These are openings for equity work.

5. **The organization is silent about the impact on racialized workers.**

Lorene confides that this has been a three-year struggle, that she has suffered continual reprisals, and that she is becoming sick. Hilda's explanation has omitted this critical piece. Indeed, the organization took no responsibility for harassment even in the grievance settlement. Even after the survey showed widespread experience of reprisals, Hilda defends the managers' presumed intentions.

TOOLS & STRATEGIES

1. **Training sessions do not provide a quick fix.**

To challenge this assumption:

- signal from the outset, the limits of training as an intervention
- ask what else is going on in the organization that is connected to advancing equity
- probe how training fits into the larger plan
- clarify the dangers of training with no plan

At one point in the meeting, the facilitators talk about how dangerous training could be if it was not part of an overall organizational plan to promote equity. Training could bring to the surface experiences of racism in the organization, the expressions of which would be punished (as the "Diversity Survey" suggested). More likely, with the levels of fear revealed by the survey, the half day would only "go through a few motions," produce more cynicism, and reassure decision-makers that they had "done anti-racism." The task now was to create conditions in the organization where training might have some chance of advancing equity.

2. **Interrupt the inequalities in the meeting.**

    This can be done almost immediately by the facilitators:

    - They can take control of the meeting and introduce themselves to Lorene, and the White facilitator can refuse to collude with Hilda, by denying eye-contact, insisting that Hilda answer her colleague when she has asked a question, and deferring to her colleague's knowledge.
    - They can more deeply probe the limits of Hilda's grasp of the situation and offer alternative frameworks with which to interpret what's going on (see point one above and point three below); this makes it safer for Lorene to participate more if she chooses.
    - They can make sure that Lorene doesn't take any further risks than she already has by not asking her questions that may cause her problems later.

3. **Distinguish between somebody's *intent*, which one can never be sure of, and somebody's *impact*, which can be seen.**

    The situation in the organization is that workers are getting sick, the management is all White, and people of colour and Aboriginal workers occupy the administrative and temporary jobs. At one point, Hilda asserts that if reprisals were going on, it isn't the managers' intent. The facilitators nod and draw a little picture (see figure 1) of two circles, side by side—one contains the word "intent," the other contains the word "impact."[1]

Figure 1: **Parallel Conversations about Racism**

Margie Adam

Source: Alok Mukherjee

They draw a line descending from each circle. They say that, in their experience, parallel conversations often go on between White people and racialized people. White people want to explain what they mean (the intent), and racialized people want to talk about the effect White people's actions have on them (the impact). The result is a damaging, parallel conversation where White people do not take any responsibility for the impact of their actions. The facilitators have found it helpful to acknowledge that well-meaning people often take actions that have the impact of racism. They say that it is not enough to recognize someone's good intentions if the impact of their actions continues to produce racism and no one takes responsibility for that. At that point, Lorene leans forward and says, "That's really interesting!"

4. Shift the "gaze" and focus to the behaviours and actions of White people.

Pose questions about what authority White people have, what and how they communicate, what they are responsible for. One of the ways racism works is to keep invisible the power White people have and the choices they're making. A continued focus on the "inadequacies" of individual people of colour keeps the "gaze" off White people.

5. Broaden the number of players involved.

The union has been active in fighting management's harassment. Since the union has been absent so far from the discussions, the facilitators propose a joint union–management planning process to look at ways to advance equity in the organization. For management, the advantages are that the union, which has pushed them to go this far, would see that they are making good on their commitment; they could benefit from the expertise of the union, whether they wanted to acknowledge that expertise or not; and they would get support from the membership for any training.

For the facilitators, bringing in the union would help build power for real equity work by reducing Lorene's isolation, broadening the information, skills and leadership available, and helping to create conditions for management to be less defensive and more oriented towards problem-solving.

6. Recognize and widen the openings.

The organization is being forced to do something and wants to avoid increased difficulties; an activist of colour is willing to provide necessary information, still behind the scenes; the union has been active in fighting for equity; the organization needs the expertise everyone collectively brings, which includes advice from facilitators about creating conditions for training in order to achieve the desired outcomes. The facilitators have some leverage with which to bargain for better conditions and for interventions that go beyond training.

KEEPING OURSELVES IN THE PICTURE

For the facilitator of colour, this whole meeting is loaded with the same disregard and racism she fights in the world. She realizes that her expertise is unseen and that Hilda only sees her as someone who can provide heartfelt stories that maintain the emotional balance to the intellectual expertise of the White facilitator. In fact, her own experience provides essential information about what Lorene and other racialized people are experiencing in the organization.

The scenario is rife with possible difficulties for the two facilitators. At certain moments the White facilitator's effectiveness is weakened by her own desire to be an "expert." She repeats perfectly clear sentences expressed by the facilitator of colour, and doesn't adequately channel Hilda's respect to her colleague. Here are some strategies both facilitators can use to offset this imbalance:

The racialized facilitator could

- interrupt Hilda's focus on the White facilitator deliberately with comments and questions
- find ways to contribute her own analysis and strategic thinking that is vital to this process
- hold her White colleague accountable for the ways in which she participates in Hilda's racism and for doing her job as an anti-racism educator that requires her to challenge Hilda's assumptions and behaviour
- use her knowledge about, skills in dealing with and analysis of racism to probe the hidden ways in which it might be operating in the policies, practices, culture, and behaviour of the organization

The White facilitator could

- recognize and probe the appeals (often unconscious) of other White people to understand and appreciate their situation
- recognize how she, as a White person, is being constructed as the expert on racism and challenge this (for example, she can deliberately decline eye contact, forcing the White person to speak directly to her colleague; she can ask her colleague questions posed to herself by the White person)
- insist on and hold space for her colleague of colour to use her expertise
- communicate the leadership of her colleague
- communicate the ways she has learned and continues to learn from friends and colleagues of colour about how racism works
- use her assumed connection with the White person to inquire into the behaviour of Whites in the organization. She could ask, for example, "When was the last hiring of a manager of colour?" "Are the managers you're speaking about all White?" "How skilled are managers in recognizing and challenging racism?"

SITUATION 2 "Proving" It's Racism

What condition or circumstance would be sufficient to "prove" the existence and scope of racism to the eyes and ears of those with skin colour privilege?

—George Dei, Leeno Luke Karumanchery, and Nisha Karumanchery-Luik, *Playing the Race Card*

In a union with a diverse membership, an all White management, a new "Equality Committee," and a new Anti-Harassment and Respect Policy, a complaint about racism has shaken things up.

René, a staff rep for two years, has complained that his regional manager has assigned him work on "all activities, including organizing, that concern Aboriginal members." René had tried talking with this manager, explaining that this was not in his job description. He argued that just because he was the only Aboriginal staff rep, he should not be made responsible for all Aboriginal members and potential members in the union. He asked why White staff reps weren't expected to deal with these issues. The regional manager became incensed, told him that he was offended by René's insubordination, and began monitoring his performance. He began asking for written reports of his activities, including calling some of the locals he was servicing. Soon he was sending René memos about his time of arrival at work; in one memo, the regional manager made a distinction between "union time" and "Indian time." Finally, he stopped saying good morning and com-municated assignments by e-mail memos only. René's is the first complaint under the new policy.

An independent investigator's report upholds the complaint. It cites job assignments and performance monitoring as examples of systemic racism directed against René, as well as some of the more overt examples of personal behaviour on the part of the regional manager. The report makes several suggestions about improving the union's management practices, as well as giving a strongly worded recommendation that the management team acknowledge the racism in the organization, make a formal apology to René for the racism directed towards him, and develop a plan for creating a more equitable work environment.

Members of the management team, which includes René's regional manager and the director of member services, have met to review the investigator's report. The report makes them very angry. After a two-hour meeting, they decide to dismiss the report, citing the following reasons: that "the evidence of racism isn't strong enough. This is a progressive union that doesn't tolerate racism." In their e-mail note to René outlining their decision, they make several statements intended to argue against the investigator's report. They ask how writing memos about punctuality can be racist. They remark that performance issues must be dealt with, and that the regional manager was just doing his duty. They do agree that the regional manager needs to change his behaviour a bit, and that he should withdraw the "Aboriginal assignment."

René has had consistent backing from the internal staff union throughout the harassment complaint. Now he and his union steward, a White man named Tom, discuss going to the Human Rights Commission and making this situation more public in the community. They communicate this intention to the director of member services. The director is alarmed and asks for a meeting with René and Tom before doing "anything that would harm the union."

1. What inequities in power do you see in this situation? How is power being used to challenge or reinforce racism?

2. Where are the specific openings for action, to shift how power is working? At what points could you do something different as René? the regional manager? the director of member services? Tom the union steward?

DISCUSSION & ANALYSIS

How Power Is Working

1. **Systemic forms of racism look "normal" to White decision-makers.**

    The union's staff don't reflect its membership, with the result that the union cannot properly service its Aboriginal members, and likely its non-Aboriginal members. The only Aboriginal staff person is expected to compensate for this larger problem, while White staff reps go about their business. The manager responds to René's complaint with reprisals—insults, memos, isolation, increased performance monitoring, and damaging his reputation with the locals. None of these actions or situations are seen as examples of systemic racism or barriers to the union performing its stated purpose. The problem must be René.

2. **The onus of "proving racism" is on the Aboriginal person.**

    In a situation where systems with a racist impact are hidden, "racism" is interpreted as individual actions with racist intent. And the people deciding whether this is credible or not are the very people who will have to take responsibility. It's very difficult to "prove" racism in this context.

3. **Standards of "objectivity" don't apply to White people.**

    The independent investigator upheld the complaint of racism, citing a number of systemic problems like job assignments and performance monitoring, as well as individual behaviours of the regional manager. Yet with no criteria to assess whether racism was happening or not, the regional manager and director of member services decide that "the evidence of racism isn't strong enough." Their emotional response to a report that holds them accountable is couched in political rhetoric: "This is a progressive union that doesn't tolerate racism."

4. **Decision-makers ignore their conflict of interest and protect themselves and other decision-makers.**

    Neither the regional director nor the director of member services seems to notice there is a blatant conflict of interest. The regional manager, the respondent in the complaint, participates in dismissing the independent report that finds him culpable. Not only that, but the regional manager's questionable management practices continue to be ignored by the director of member services, except for an acknowledgement that "the manager needs to change his behaviour a bit and withdraw the 'Aboriginal assignment.'"

5. **"Progressive politics" and loyalty to the organization belong to the White managers only and not to the Aboriginal staff.**

   This is a "progressive union that doesn't tolerate racism." The director of member services becomes alarmed about the possibility that René and the steward's actions will "harm the union." In this version, the managers become the defenders of the organization, while René's challenge to racism in the organization becomes a threat to it.

6. **Management tries to move the focus from the racism upheld in the report to René's alleged performance problems.**

   There is no proof of performance difficulties. In fact, the huge assignment that the regional manager tried to give René would indicate trust in his competence. "Performance problems" became an issue when René raised questions about his assignment and suggested that racism was a factor.

TOOLS & STRATEGIES

Listed here are four key strategies to draw on when having a meeting with managers (or board members, union stewards, and so on).

1. **Ask questions that require decision-makers to account for their actions.**

   In response to the memo, René and the steward can ask

   - What criteria did decision-makers use to assess the report?
   - What criteria do they use to assess whether racism is operating or not?
   - Did they consult with anyone who actually experiences racism, to help them develop criteria for assessing racism and the report?
   - What evidence would be "strong enough"?

2. **Wait through uncomfortable silences.**

   Management may have no response to these basic questions about how they made a decision that had serious consequences. Their discomfort is not something to fix. It's a moment when people can really learn something.

3. **Focus on how the system works, not just on the behaviour of the regional manager.**

   Individual motives are rarely proved. As long as the discussion of racism in organizations is confined to the realm of one person's intent and actions, the organization does not have to look at how everyone is implicated in what is happening. (See point three under Tools & Strategies in "Training Will Fix It.") Here's a tool we sometimes use to expose how things are working. We call it the Triangle Model (see figure 2) and it can be used to show how individual behaviours, combined with systems and unexamined ideas within an organization, can negatively affect some individuals and parts of the organization while not affecting others at all. The steward, member, or facilitator can use this model to map the "facts" which are generally agreed to. So, for example, in a discussion where this resistance to acknowledging racism arises, he/she can say:

"But look at the ways things work here. René is monitored for every little item and is oversupervised; he gets memos that give him instructions when nobody else does; the regional manager talked critically about his performance informally with other people— a case of performance appraisal by rumour, while other people have a proper process for their appraisals.

"All of the systems that you would want to look at—hiring, supervision, appraisal, complaint processes, promotion, training—are all at work here. These shape who gets heard, whose ideas get taken up, who gets credited with the ideas, who's considered a troublemaker and who's considered credible. There are ideas floating around in the organization about Aboriginal people, about White people, about who's competent at what. Nobody wants to go there because that's under the table; all this is under the table. This is the stuff that makes these individual behaviours look normal in the organization. We'll never prove someone's intent to be racist.

"But look at the effects of these systems and ideas on this organization. They keep producing the same old results which are that, except for René, there are no staff reps who are Aboriginal and people of colour in the union. The few racialized staff working here are in admin support positions, and many of those are on contract. Permanent jobs are occupied by White people, and the management is all White. Who gets the most severe discipline? And check out how this affects the organization; the organization can't actually do its work. It's tied up in these unresolved conflicts; it relies on a few underpaid people to do all the connecting with community; and White people remain unable to recognize or challenge racism when it's happening."

4. **Get support.**

   In this case, the union steward is fully supportive and prepared to press the case further, including with the community. For René who is isolated inside the organization, community support is also vital, not just to pressure the organization to do the right thing but also for his own mental health and struggle to keep his job. It is, in fact, the threat of going to the community that galvanizes the managers to ask for another meeting. (See "Building Community Coalition and Capacity" in this section.)

Figure 2:
The Triangle Model

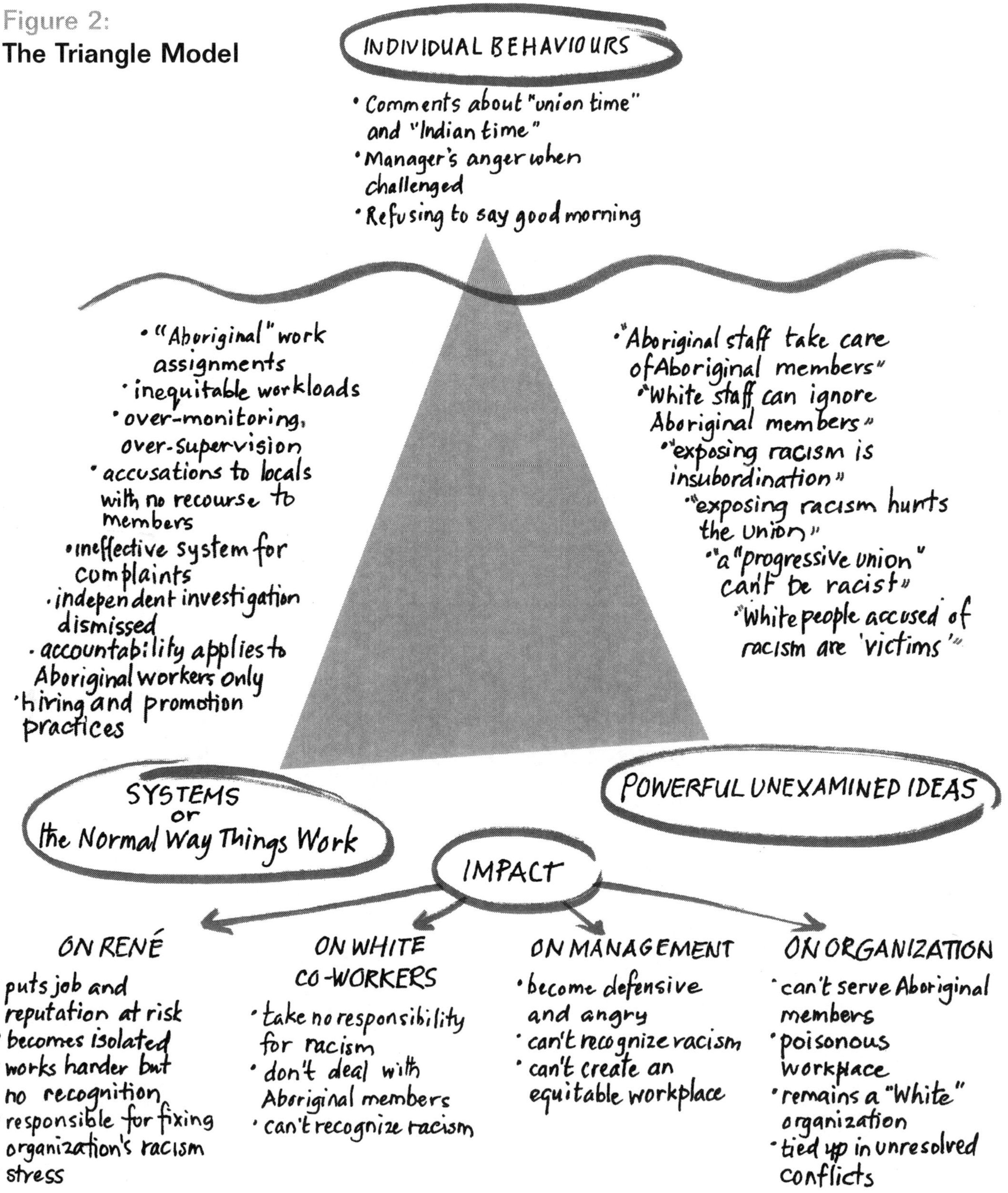

INDIVIDUAL BEHAVIOURS

- Comments about "union time" and "Indian time"
- Manager's anger when challenged
- Refusing to say good morning

- "Aboriginal" work assignments
- inequitable workloads
- over-monitoring, over-supervision
- accusations to locals with no recourse to members
- ineffective system for complaints
- independent investigation dismissed
- accountability applies to Aboriginal workers only
- hiring and promotion practices

- "Aboriginal staff take care of Aboriginal members"
- "White staff can ignore Aboriginal members"
- "exposing racism is insubordination"
- "exposing racism hurts the union"
- a "progressive union" can't be racist"
- "White people accused of racism are 'victims'"

SYSTEMS or the Normal Way Things Work

POWERFUL UNEXAMINED IDEAS

IMPACT

ON RENÉ
- puts job and reputation at risk
- becomes isolated
- works harder but no recognition
- responsible for fixing organization's racism
- stress

ON WHITE CO-WORKERS
- take no responsibility for racism
- don't deal with Aboriginal members
- can't recognize racism

ON MANAGEMENT
- become defensive and angry
- can't recognize racism
- can't create an equitable workplace

ON ORGANIZATION
- can't serve Aboriginal members
- poisonous workplace
- remains a "White" organization
- tied up in unresolved conflicts

KEEPING OURSELVES IN THE PICTURE

White stewards and allies get invited to collude in racism in a variety of ways. In this situation, anticipate that

- White managers' "legitimate questions" will be directed to the steward or White ally
- White allies will be seen as more objective than René
- anything that René says will be suspect because he's "biased"
- René is outnumbered by White people talking about him, as though he is the least capable person to talk about his situation
- René's legitimate anger, if expressed, will be seen as further proof that he's exaggerating
- any success at moving the conversation forward will be attributed to the agility of the White ally, in this case Tom the steward, and not to the huge efforts René has made to listen, accommodate, and push the organization to do the right thing
- in this restricted situation where René's options are so limited, Tom needs to take direction from René, and make it apparent to the managers that he is doing so (see Keeping Ourselves in the Picture in "Training Will Fix It")

Being the "Diversity Co-ordinator"

Most "diversity co-ordinators" are people of colour; most managers are White. People of colour are supposed to educate White people about racism. The chances of this are zero unless someone needs information quickly, like, "I need information about Aboriginal people by 3:00 p.m. this afternoon."

—Member of Focus Group, Calgary, August 25, 2003

Natasha is discouraged and angry. She reports to George, the director of personnel at a medium-sized school board. The two of them have just emerged from a principals' workshop she facilitated on "Managing Diversity." She asks to meet with him immediately afterwards, to sort out some issues. The workshop was mandatory, and the principals were resistant. One principal had said bluntly that racism was not an issue in their school; another had complained that the organization faced "really serious issues" and that this "workshop was badly timed." Another expressed resentment that there were lots of "assumptions about White people," and she for one was sick of being "guilted."

Natasha is surprised by a few things: the level of denial, frustration, and hostility directed at her by some of the principals; the silence of other principals she thought cared about equity; and the lack of any support or direction during the workshop from George. It is this that she wants to talk to him about. She had done a great deal of preparation for the session, including individual interviews with several principals to assess how racial equity issues affected their schools and daily work. She had met with the leaders of the Parents for Equity Coalition who had prepared a report they had researched, written, and presented to the board. Their report was entitled "Addressing Racism in our Schools." Natasha wanted to use her interviews and parts of the report for the workshop, and she had talked to George about the importance of communicating racial equity as a priority of the school board. His response was to make this half-day workshop mandatory, and he insisted that she call it "diversity" instead of "racial equity." She reluctantly complied by changing the title, but thought she had his support to examine ways in which racism affected students, parents, teachers, as well as principals. The report and her interviews confirmed that racism was a real issue. After the workshop, she feels isolated and unsupported in doing her job, and tells him so.

George replies, "I think it may be a problem with your expectations and your tone. You need to get people comfortable with your issues, and your insistence on the word 'racism' just raised hackles. I didn't want to close down the discussion by saying that equity was a priority. That would just have caused resentment. And we have other policy issues coming down the pipe from the Ministry of Education. The trustees are dealing with a financial squeeze and it looks as though we're going to have to lay off some people. The principals are preoccupied with keeping their best staff. I need their support right now. You do your job and I'll do mine."

She has been on the job six months to "implement the diversity plan." She has limited time because external funding is only for one year. Her job is the result of focused lobbying by the Parents for Equity Coalition. However, there are no equity policies or procedures, let alone a plan to implement them, and George is focused on the current crisis of finances and staffing at the school board.

She stares at him in silence. She wants to say (but doesn't), "George, we have a problem. Now you are evaluating me on the basis of a vague job description; you have never clarified how you're measuring my work; you haven't communicated to the organization what my job is, so yesterday someone called me the 'translator.' Yet every time the Parents for Equity Coalition visits the trustees to find out what's happening with this project, you call me in here and suggest I should be doing more. More what? I can't even get the superintendent of programs to invite me to the Diversity Committee meetings! We're not even talking about the impact on me as a racialized woman, of trying to do this work with White decision-makers when I have no authority. Now you're talking about layoffs, and you know who will be the first to go—the only Aboriginal teacher and the few teachers of colour who are on contract. Do you have any idea how that will affect racialized students and parents? Don't you think that there's a connection between how you're handling this crisis and issues of equity? We've got six months more funding for my time here. Why don't we talk about how you could use my expertise to deal differently with the realities you're facing?"

She wants to say something, even as she watches him check the time and reach for the phone.

1.   What inequities in power do you see in this situation? How is power being used to challenge or reinforce racism?

2.   Where are the specific openings for action, to shift how power is working? At what point could you do something different as George? a principal at the workshop? Natasha? a trustee? the Parents for Equity Coalition?

How Power Is Working

1. **Decision-makers do not take any responsibility for increasing equity.**

   Natasha reports to the director of personnel, but he expresses no sense of responsibility for advancing equity. Indeed, he is visibly uncomfortable with any discussion of racism. "You do your job and I'll do mine" is his response to her efforts to handle things better together. George did make the workshop mandatory for principals, but then refused to deal with the hostility of some principals at the session. In fact, he defended the principals' behaviour to Natasha and refused to grasp the impact of their actions on her. The administration has never communicated that equity is a priority, even when urged repeatedly to do so. Other staff remain ignorant of what Natasha's job is.

2. **The comfort of White people determines the words and approaches racialized people must use to address racism.**

   The director of personnel changed the title of the workshop from "Racial Equity at Work" to "Managing Diversity" so as not to offend the principals. Natasha based her workshop design on the report the parents prepared, which had resulted in her job, and on interviews with the principals themselves. And still, the discomfort of some White principals controlled the discussion at the session. When Natasha confronted George on his lack of support for her, he made her the problem. "I think it may be a problem with your expectations and your tone. You need to get people comfortable with your issues, and your insistence on the word 'racism' just raised hackles." In George's mind, racism is Natasha's issue, and she, as a racialized woman and the diversity co-ordinator, needs to help White people get comfortable with it.

3. **Potential White allies stay silent.**

   Even the principals that Natasha thought were committed to equity are silent in the session. In weighing their choices, they have somehow decided that the consequences are more severe for speaking up than remaining silent.

4. **Senior administrators make programming and staffing decisions with no attention to their impact on racialized staff, students, or parents.**

   Major decisions are being made by trustees, senior administrators, and principals on staffing and programming. Yet equity seems not to be a factor in their thinking. Parents have had to bring racism to the attention of the board, but once the diversity co-ordinator is in place, it's business as usual. George expresses great concern about the impact of board decision-making on White principals, but none about the impact on racialized students and parents, or Natasha.

5. **The administration pays lip service to the Parents for Equity Coalition, while appearing to be influenced by them.**

   Parents have mobilized to research, write, and present their report "Addressing Racism in Our Schools." They have had some impact. The board found outside funding and hired a diversity co-ordinator, and when the coalition visits trustees about action on equity, there is a momentary ripple through the organization. But the responsibility for appearing to advance equity falls on Natasha. It is her job to do enough to keep parents appeased, but not enough to provoke the hostility of White principals.

6. **Hiring policies have resulted in one Aboriginal teacher and a few teachers of colour, mostly working on contract.**

   Hiring practices keep resulting in the same homogenous workforce. The few racialized teachers working at the board are mostly on contract, and they will be most vulnerable to layoffs in the current financial squeeze.

7. **School board staff are not bound by any racial equity policies or procedures.**

   Natasha has been hired to "implement the diversity plan," but no policy, procedures, or plan exists. There are no guidelines outlining the board's employment practices; no expectations that staff will promote racial equity in the curriculum; no requirements that staff be accountable for racist behaviour or its impact on students, parents, or each other. In this policy vacuum, equity is the individual issue of parents and Natasha and not a commitment and practice of the board as an educational institution or employer.

8. **The diversity co-ordinator has large, vague responsibilities for "diversity" and little authority.**

   In this procedural vacuum, Natasha is hired to do unspecified things about "diversity" and to act as a visible indicator that the board listens to parents. There is no policy to implement and no political will to develop one. She is left to find openings and corners to do useful work with people who don't see equity as relevant to their work. Her job description is vague and the measures for her performance hazy. When she challenges George to play his role, he uses his authority to suggest that she is the problem—that if her "tone" or "expectations" were more reasonable, principals would respond better. This kind of performance appraisal is a veiled threat, designed to stop her challenge to him. She is being evaluated simultaneously for not doing her job and for how White people respond to her work.

9. **"Diversity co-ordination" is not a line item in the budget.**

   The school board has found external money for one year to pay a diversity co-ordinator, but Natasha does not appear to have a budget to run a program. While external funding can be helpful in kick-starting an equity program, it appears to have shaped the hasty job description and stated goal of "implementing the diversity plan," which does not exist. When external funding dries up, the board appears to have no provision in its own budget to continue the position or any other related programming. The financing of equity reflects its marginal status in this organization.

10. "Training" is still the main strategy for equity work.

It is not unusual for "diversity co-ordinators" to have chief responsibility for "training" White people who see no reason for training, do not want to be trained, and have no incentive or pressure to apply what they might learn in training. In this situation, "training" occupies a lot of Natasha's energy. The gains for racial equity are questionable and the negative impact on her is huge. She works outside the corridors of power, and the structure of her job seems designed to keep her there.

If the school board were serious about racial equity, Natasha could be working with administrators, principals, teachers, and parents in policy development, strategic planning to incorporate equity into decision-making, research of relevant practices which advance equity, or coaching of decision-makers and staff to integrate racial equity into their everyday practice. She could be using her time, with support, to ensure that equity guides the actions of the board.

TOOLS & STRATEGIES

1. Possible actions that could take place in this moment.

Natasha has already acted with integrity and has risked a great deal by

- staying accountable to the Parents for Equity Coalition in meeting with them and using their report in the workshop
- keeping racial equity on the workshop's agenda
- confronting George on his lack of support for her during the workshop

It's unclear what she will gain from continuing to speak her mind frankly to George in this moment, although she may choose to do that. She may opt to do the following, while weighing the continuing risks to her job, prospects for other employment, and her reputation at the board if/as she does so:

- develop strategies with the Parents for Equity Coalition and committed trustees to pressure the board for policy development and a plan that involves her and the parents
- push George to insist on her involvement in the Diversity Committee to see if it could be a vehicle for change
- meet again with the principals who have some commitment to equity and see what possibilities for action lie there
- make a proposal to George about how she could assist him to integrate equity into the current decisions he faces (see "Dancing on Live Embers: Transforming the Systems" in phase three of this section)

George has many options to advance racial equity, and so far he has chosen none of them. He could, for example,

- listen to Natasha in this moment, and apologize for his lack of support and the impact that has had on her
- make racial equity part of his work
- recognize his need to learn from Natasha and strategize with her on some immediate next steps for both of them
- use his weight with senior administrators to insist on the development of a racial equity policy, procedures, and plan
- work with Natasha and the parents to redo her job description to include clear goals and specify supports that Natasha can expect to receive
- communicate to principals that racial equity is a priority that will inform all the ways the board does its work

Supportive principals at the workshop can

- apologize to Natasha for their silence, acknowledge the impact it had on her, and agree to begin speaking up for equity at their schools and on the board
- raise the issue at the next principals' meeting and ask for specific board commitments to advance racial equity
- say what they will be doing at their own schools, in conjunction with Natasha and the Parents for Equity Coalition
- pressure George for his clear, unambiguous support in challenging racism at the board and supporting Natasha to use her expertise well

Supportive trustees can work with the Parents for Equity Coalition to

- explain how the board works to the Parents for Equity Coalition so that they can pressure the board more strategically
- lobby other trustees to (a) build support for a motion to develop a racial equity policy, procedures, and plan and to (b) integrate equity into budget decisions and strategic planning
- keep posing questions that hold administrators accountable for equity
- commit to keeping racial equity on the agenda (see the strategies used by elected labour leaders to keep equity on the agenda in "Working Inside/Out: Building an Anti-Racism Activism at the Canadian Labour Congress" in section three)

2. **Structure the job so that it can make an impact.**

   Anti-racism/race relations/equity/diversity/multicultural/human rights co-ordinators know that their job is just a set-up without some basic conditions to make it work (see "Dancing on Live Embers: Transforming the Systems" in phase 3).

Here is a list of things that need to be in place from many people who have tried to do this job well, as given to us by those who have tried:

- authority in the job which matches the responsibilities
- clear job description with indicators of how progress will be measured
- job functions that connect clearly to the existing "real" work of the organization—for example, work with principals to develop a tool for hiring more racially diverse staff based on merit, and work with trustees to integrate equity into the coming year's strategic plan
- support of and direct reporting lines to top decision-makers
- built-in procedures that ensure reporting/accountability to a larger community of activists who are pushing the institution (see "Working Inside/Out: Building an Anti-Racism Activism at the Canadian Labour Congress" in section three)

3. **Create policy that frames and supports the job.**

   Ideally, a racial equity policy, its procedures and plan guide the hiring of the co-ordinator. The policy backs the co-ordinator to support managers and staff in doing their jobs and implementing policy. However, Natasha's situation is not unusual. An organization gets outside money, hires someone, and has no intention of really changing anything. In this case, pushing to develop policy becomes critical. Here is a list of components that are essential for an effective racial equity policy (see, for example, the Sample Human Rights and Equity Policy in section five):

   - identifies racism and other forms of inequity as persistent realities with specified effects on employees, members/clients, and the organization itself
   - identifies the benefits of equity for all concerned
   - specifies what actions the organization will take and what scope the policy has
   - specifies how senior administrators, trustees, and so on are responsible for ensuring implementation
   - clarifies how people will be held accountable for advancing equity within their jobs

4. **Budget for real programming.**

   Outside money is always a help. But in a society where racism pervades so many of our daily practices, racial equity needs to be a substantial line item in the organization's budget. It should provide

   - properly paid, high-level staff
   - program money that equity staff have authority and discretion to spend for projects, research, additional expertise, development of tools and materials, gatherings and working sessions, work with community, and so on

5. **Make advancing equity an expectation in the jobs of senior people.**

   In this scenario, hiring the co-ordinator is a tactic to appease parents. But an organization serious about equity uses the co-ordinator as a resource. Her/his job is supporting politicians, managers, and employees to do their jobs in such a way that they advance equity. The co-ordinator can also help the organization benefit from community expertise. Some indicators of senior staff accountability include

- job descriptions that specify equity expectations
- performance appraisal measures that integrate equity (see "Building Blocks for Equity" at the end of this phase for suggestions on some of these measures)
- supervision policy that integrates equity (see the Sample Supervision Policy in section five)

6. **Strategic use of community pressure.**

People who do this work agree that well-orchestrated community pressure is essential for making organizations more racially equitable, because there is too much pressure inside not to "rock the boat." (See "Building Community Coalition and Capacity" for strategies used by the Coalition for Equal Access to Education in Calgary.) Inside change agents need to have the outside pressure from community coalitions and can use their insider status to advocate for greater community involvement by

- coaching coalitions on how the institution works, how decisions are made, how to best make their voices heard
- suggesting input from community coalitions at staff meetings, decision-making forums, and board meetings
- staying connected to community coalitions for one's own learning and development

Building Community Coalition and Capacity:
The Fight for Core ESL in Calgary*

Community capacity is essential to keep institutions in line, because there is always slippage. Why would any institution that has the power not to change do it?
—Amal Umar, Program Officer at Canadian Heritage

We are walking through the forest and come across a fallen tree. What would it take for us to move that tree? Tools? Resources? People to push us? Our bosses? Good weather? Our motivation? Now, what would happen if beneath that tree were our child? We would try to move that tree regardless. We, as the representatives of parents, community groups, and ESL learners, ask you to move that tree.
—Hieu Van Ngo, presentation to the Standing Policy Committee on Learning and Employment, June 3, 2003

This is a story of a community coalition that began in 1992 in the struggle for higher quality and more equitable English as a Second Language programming at the Calgary Board of Education. Unlike many other coalitions, the Coalition for Equal Access to Education continues twelve years later, strengthened by experience, tenacity, focus, and broadened community support. This Coalition has much to teach us about how to build community capacity and what an important role community pressure plays in holding institutions accountable for equitable programming. In this story, we are looking not at a shift in power within the Coalition but at a shift in power relations between itself, the Board of Education, and the communities of students and parents. This story highlights the important role organized community pressure plays in holding mainstream organizations accountable to all of their constituents.

Calgary and the Need for English as a Second Language Education

Calgary, Alberta, is a fast growing city, with an increasingly diverse population. In 2000, Calgary was the fourth largest reception centre in Canada for immigrants, experiencing a 23.4 per cent increase in immigration. In 1999, immigrants, people of colour, and Aboriginal peoples, respectively, accounted for 21.7, 16.5, and 1.8 per cent of the population of

---

* We draw on the extensive and thorough documentation of this equity struggle developed by the coalition and its co-ordinator Hieu Van Ngo; a master's thesis by Pearl Yip who was active in the coalition; two interviews with Amal Umar, the program officer at Canadian Heritage who has worked with the coalition from the beginning; documentation prepared by Canadian Heritage staff; and feedback to an early draft of this article from Coalition members. We also include interviews we conducted with Coalition members in Calgary between August and November 2005. They chose to remain anonymous.

Calgary.[2] Among the top ten source countries of immigration to Calgary in 2000, eight were countries that do not have English as an official language. Forty-five per cent of the immigrants arriving in Calgary in that year could not communicate in English or in French.[3]

Legislation in Alberta, in particular, the *Alberta School Act* and the *Alberta Human Rights, Citizenship and Multiculturalism Act*, mandates quality language instruction for English as a Second Language (ESL) students, but ESL programs in Alberta have been inadequate. This has drastically affected the possibilities for academic success for English as a Second Language learners. Studies suggest a drop-out rate of 61 per cent to 74 per cent for ESL students compared with the provincial average of 34 per cent.[4]

The Calgary Board of Education (CBE) faces many of the same challenges as other large school boards across Canada: a diverse range of students and families, less money, and more pressure for fiscal restraint. Its number of ESL students rose from 3,406 in 1991–92 to 9,666 in 2001–02, an increase of almost 300 per cent over ten years. In 2001, students who qualified for ESL supplementary funding accounted for at least 10 per cent of the total student population, but some researchers have suggested that the actual number of students with an ESL background is 20 per cent or higher.[5] The CBE became the focal point for the coalition when, in 1992, it drastically cut ESL programming. However, one of the interesting elements of the Coalition strategy is that it has managed to pressure the CBE while remaining in a supportive relationship to it throughout these twelve years. As the Coalition's 1995 brochure explains:

> There is no intent to discriminate the CBE from other school boards in Alberta. The CBE, however, is the largest school board in the province of Alberta and one of the five largest in Canada. The ESL issue raised from this school board represents issues of educational equity which must be addressed by urban school boards throughout Alberta, and indeed, throughout Canada.

English as a Second Language students in the Calgary system are as diverse as those living anywhere else in Canada. Three primary groups of ESL learners include refugee children with both limited English skills and academic backgrounds who have experienced war, family dislocation, and poverty; immigrant children with strong academic backgrounds and limited English; and Canadian-born children with limited English because it is not the language spoken at home.[6] Canadian-born children might include Hutterite children and Aboriginal children whose first languages vary and are not English.

Why ESL Is an Equity Issue

The Alberta government's funding framework provides money to local school boards for ESL students through both the Basic Instruction Grant and an ESL Supplementary Grant. The Basic Instruction Grant should cover ESL as part of its core programs. To a board of education this means each ESL student brings the regular $4,239 per year in allocation from the Basic Instruction Grant, and $718 per year from the ESL Supplementary Grant. However, when strapped for resources, boards have tended to allocate only the $718 for ESL programming, using the ESL portion of the Basic Instruction Grant for programming other than ESL. This means that, "overall, students in need of ESL support receive comparably less value for the educational services received because the form and level of instructional support does not address a critical component of their learning needs—namely, second language acquisition in English."[7]

But there are other systemic inequities which the Coalition has pointed out. First, the province's ESL Supplementary Grant to school boards only covered ESL students born outside Canada. During the 1995–96 school year, for example, that excluded 1,424 Canadian-born ESL students

Coalition for Equal Access to Education members, Edmonton, 2005

at the CBE.[8] Second, funding was limited to three years, a puzzling number since, "typically, ESL learners need a minimum of two years of specialized language instruction to develop basic interpersonal communication skills, and between five to seven years to develop cognitive academic language proficiency—a requirement for any academic success."[9]

Third is the age cap of nineteen. At that age, students no longer qualify for Ministry of Education funding to boards of education. "Older immigrant students, especially those entering junior or senior high school often need more time to catch up."[10] Fourth, ESL is not considered part of the core language curriculum, despite how crucial it is for students who need it. In the initial cuts to ESL by the CBE in 1992, ESL was listed under the heading "Programs and Services Funded above the Provincial Mandate."

Fifth, ESL curriculum teams were physically set apart from other curriculum teams in schools. This has had the effect of marginalizing the teachers and the students. Sixth, the teacher–pupil ratio of 18.5 to 1 did not apply to ESL, so cuts could be made without violating an agreed-to ratio. The ratio of students to ESL personnel (including teachers, assistant teachers, school aides) went from 35 to 1 in 1991–92 to 81 to 1 in 2001–02.[11]

It has been the Coalition's task to point out systemic inequities that look normal but have a damaging impact on ESL learners. And in exposing these inequities, the Coalition has had to challenge unexamined but powerful ideas that ESL students are a "drain" and don't pay taxes, and that non-ESL learners are the overburdened taxpayers who do not benefit from the presence of ESL learners. A CBE administrative memo of 1992 pointed out that the value of the ESL Supplementary Grant doesn't cover the cost of the ESL program, and that "esl costs the Board and local taxpayer $2.1 million." This suggestion that there is a *"we who are taxpayers"* and a *"they who are a drain"* is familiar even if it is untrue.

The Calgary Board of Education Had Information about the Problem

In the 1980s, the CBE had funded the assessment of immigrant children with money from outside funders. Parents and community activists had protested, saying that assessing the proper placement of immigrant children was core business and managed to pressure the CBE to pay for it from its core budget. In 1989, the Canadian School Trustees' Association conducted a study, supported by the CBE and other concerned boards. It warned that boards are facing a crisis in addressing the needs of children who were English as a Second Language learners. Finally, in 1990, the CBE produced its own report from the English as a Second Language Task Force. Forty-one recommendations proposed changes throughout the system, urging and outlining a process of planned change.

Using a Mobilizing Moment: The Coalition is Born

In 1992, the Calgary Board of Education cut 50 per cent of English as a Second Language (esl) programming while the rest of the system faced a 3 per cent reduction. Cuts were made to the number of ESL teachers, classes, and resources available. This funding decision increased the bleak likelihood of illiteracy, poor academic achievement, and high drop-out rates for English as a Second Language learners (about 15 per cent of students in urban jurisdictions in Alberta). A group of community advocates was ready. It seemed to them that the CBE believed that ESL classes were easily expendable and that the community wasn't organized to make trouble:

> The response that was required to sudden, impending cutbacks was immediate and could not wait for the educational institution to adapt its organizational policies and practices. Nor was there time for the education institution to reflect on the negative, long-term ramifications of its proposals. Their decisions would directly impact an entire generation of immigrant children, increasing their likelihood of leaving the public school prematurely, and placing in question their future educational achievement.[13]

Advocates felt that trustees didn't understand the impacts of their decision. "It is important to recognize that the people who do not need ESL are in the position to define ESL as core or peripheral ... ESL thus becomes optional because it is not essential to the people that most educational leaders represent."[14] People in the community—parents, teachers, and immigrant advocates—organized and prepared a brief that they presented to the Calgary Board of Education. In addition, this fledgling group organized two demonstrations outside the CBE's offices that received substantial and positive media coverage. The outrage of advocates was summed up in the placard of a Chinese-Canadian parent: No English, No Future.

Community interest in the issue expanded as a result of this group's actions, and the Coalition for Equal Access to Education was born. Initially, the Coalition was composed of individual parents, immigrant settlement organizations, and social service agencies. The groups involved included the Calgary Immigrant Women's Association, Calgary Immigrant

Narim Ismail Tejo

Members of the Coalition for Equal Access to Education, waiting to address the Standing Policy Committee on Employment and Education of the Government of Alberta, 2005

Aid Society, Calgary Catholic Immigration Society, Calgary Chinese Community Service Association, Council of Sikh Organizations, Vietnamese Canadian Association, Committee Against Racism, Committee on Race Relations and Cross Cultural Understanding, Oxfam Human Rights Initiative, Southern Alberta Heritage Language Association, Alberta/NWT Network of Immigrant Women, and the YWCA.

Keeping up the Pressure and Building the Coalition

The Coalition had much to do. Despite its lobbying work, the CBE continued its cuts. In1993, it decreased the number of certified ESL teachers, replacing them with ESL teachers' aides and assistants. In1994, it eliminated system-wide ESL programming and reallocated money from general revenues to follow each individual ESL student to his/her school. Individual schools did not have to account for how they spent that money. In 1995, the CBE gradually withdrew its commitment to use some of the Basic Instruction Grant designated for ESL, and in 1996, it required that all schools have parent councils to help determine

Coalition for Equal Access to Education members

each school's educational priorities. This seemed like a progressive move, but in the absence of provisions and resources to ensure participation by parents of ESL students, the parent councils were no more reflective of communities than the CBE itself. Funding per ESL student dropped from $1,515 in 1991–92 to $719 in 2001–02, a 47.5 per cent decline.

In response, the Coalition began holding workshops with immigrant parents and various community organizations to raise awareness about ESL, and to encourage parents' involvement in their children's schooling. These workshops focused on how the school system worked and on the importance of the parents' involvement in their children's school success. The Coalition hired a participant from the initial training to work with other parents, involving them in presentations and sharing their stories. She used the Coalition's manual, *Towards Active Parental Participation*, which is now available in Vietnamese, Chinese, Spanish, Arabic, and Punjabi, as well as English. The Coalition received $23,000 in private funding for the translation from a donor who wished to remain anonymous.

The Coalition also collected accounts from students, parents, and teachers about the deteriorating quality of education and how this was affecting ESL students. These stories are woven into the Coalition's reports and literature, ensuring that the voices of those most affected are heard and reminding supporters that those being discriminated against are working to build a more equitable system for all.

Quality research was also critical. While continuing to advocate with the Board of Trustees, the Coalition worked with the Calgary Civil Liberty Association to prepare a report on ESL as a human rights issue. The Department of Canadian Heritage provided some funding for the preparation of this report through its Human Rights Program. The Coalition researched and distributed customized background information and recommendations to the Government of Alberta, the University of Calgary, the Calgary Board of Education, and the community in the publication of *English as a Second Language Education: Context, Current Responses and Recommendations for New Directions*. "Dedicated to all children of Canada," this document is a vision, a thoroughly researched rationale, and a series of thoughtful, feasible recommendations for action by all levels of government. It said:

> The Calgary public education system is truly at the crossroads. It must either choose
> to create a new collective vision of fairness and quality learning for all students, or
> risk being part of the development of a subculture of defeat and marginalization, in
> which culturally diverse youth, denied basic language instruction, face life-long
> underutilization of human potential.[15]

Involving the Academic Community

Early in the Coalition's development, its members began visiting the University of Calgary on an annual basis to speak with graduate students and to encourage them to undertake thesis research related to issues of ethnic and racial diversity. Pearl Yip and Hieu Van Ngo, ongoing, passionate contributors to the Coalition's work, became involved at this time. As a result of these new connections, some members of the university academic community joined the Coalition. For example, a retired drama professor from the university edits all the Coalition's documents as a volunteer. Two researchers from the university undertook a study on drop-out rates among immigrant youth who lacked adequate ESL support (74 per cent) as opposed to mainstream students (33 per cent). The results of that research were quite dramatic, showing that drop-out rates were double for students without adequate ESL support. This research provided strong factual support for the Coalition's insistence on the need to reinstitute funding for ESL in Calgary schools.

Building Critical Relationships with Power

The Coalition held public information sessions that helped people to understand how provincial funding should work and to explain the impact of the CBE's decisions on ESL students. It maintained a steady correspondence with various players at the CBE, asking questions and putting forward proposals. Some of its requests for information about the numbers of ESL teachers and aides were not answered because the CBE itself didn't know the answer. This has led to ongoing communication between the CBE and the Coalition, because the Coalition's expertise on these issues is so useful to the Board.

The Coalition was also corresponding with the province, asking among other things, that the education minister audit the CBE's use of ESL funds. It was putting out position papers, such as the one in 1993 that explained the role of ESL teachers in planning individualized programs, monitoring students' learning, and working with other teachers to integrate students into mainstream classes. And it was raising questions about why people who taught ESL students were considered cheap labour. The bilingual aides who were being asked to perform certified teachers' duties were being paid much lower wages and benefits. For the Coalition, this was a significant equity issue. "Many bilingual immigrants who work or would want to work in education were once educators in their home country. Because of the lack of recognition of their foreign credentials, their work and skills as aides would be valued in Canada, but not monetarily. The move to de-professionalize ESL would thus effectively institutionalize an inequitable practice."[16]

The Coalition developed a strategy with which to approach the Government of Alberta and local Members of the Legislative Assembly (MLAs) about the issue. In addition to its letters to various provincial players, the Coalition began meeting with MLAs individually and in groups. These conversations were always accompanied by helpful briefing packages that informed the MLAs about the issues. As a result of the Coalition's interventions, the provincial government appointed a committee to deal with a number of educational issues, including the provision of English as a Second Language classes. The Coalition provided

Narim Ismail Tejo

Members of the Coalition for Equal Access to Education

the government with documentation showing that, although ESL was being provided for children born outside Canada, kids born in Canada to immigrant parents were not being served, regardless of their knowledge of English upon entry to schools. The Coalition was successful in convincing the province to lift the cap on ESL funding that was preventing the participation of Canadian-born children.

However, it became clear to the Coalition that the Calgary Board of Education didn't have the infrastructure to properly track the extent of eligible demand for ESL. At this time the Coalition proposed that the CBE needed to prepare an accountability framework for the provision of ESL and offered to help in preparing such a framework that included three key areas: adequate resource allocation, program standards, and achievement outcomes. Throughout this whole process, Coalition members were developing a very sophisticated knowledge of the policies and practices of schools and of the CBE.

Using Ongoing Mobilizing Moments

Even if you make gains, it doesn't mean they're permanent; you need to stay alert and advocates have to remain very vigilant. When the Calgary Board of Education tried to privatize the assessment of ESL students, the Coalition was ready. Up to a certain point, the CBE had been working with the Coalition. Then the CBE's leadership changed and a new superintendent came in. At the same time, a non-profit settlement agency approached the CBE offering to do the ESL work on contract.

The Coalition could have been side-tracked and attacked the community organization. However, this would have divided the community and drastically sapped the Coalition's energy. Choosing where to focus energy was a critical decision. As one Coalition member recalled: "I lost sleep. We organized demonstrations. We mobilized the community. We went to the Calgary Board of Education. It was a major, uphill battle, and we stayed with them." Another said, "It [was] like racism among us; it [was] like the non-profit sector eating each other. The community organization was very upset and felt betrayed by us, but we kept the pressure on the Calgary Board of Education, and we called for a public community forum to justify what they were doing." This required that the Coalition resist division among its members and focus on the goal—to insist that ESL education was the responsibility of the public education system.

In half a day, the Coalition mobilized the whole community into a public protest at the CBE. A few phone calls and everybody was there, everybody was angry, and their focus was politically astute—they did not concentrate on the community agency but turned the spotlight on the CBE. The community responded quickly because the focus of the community response was in place. According to Hieu Van Ngo, being issue-specific is key: "You really need to be very specific, otherwise it's just a network. And the goal needs to be specific. The very successful Coalition that we have here focuses on ESL like a dog with a bone and nothing else. So when this proposal to privatize the assessment of immigrant kids came in, we were leading the struggle. We were the forefront of it and we were able to bring the members together and stop it."

Hieu also argues that maintaining your focus is an important survival strategy: "Resources are scarce, and we are an issue-based Coalition. We can grow and change our activities but everything we do must advance our cause, and build the work. … We have to select our battles strategically and work where we can have the most impact on decision-makers. If we had tried to tackle both the public and the Catholic boards of education, our energies would have been too scattered to have any real influence.

"Maintaining our focus means that we are not stepping on our partners' feet because they are clear what we are doing, and they don't feel they have to compete with us. Right now we are not focused on adult ESL learners but on children in the school system. And while we must be aware and responsive to individual stories of hurt and discrimination, our focus is on the systemic issues that affect all ESL students in schools."

As Amal Umar points out, maintaining the focus also means remembering who should benefit. "When the Coalition started meeting with the Calgary Board of Education, trustees used to ask who these immigrant parents were. 'We haven't seen them. They haven't come to us.' One of the Coalition members finally said to one trustee, 'I want you to stay late tonight and meet some of the parents, because they are coming to clean the building.' The Coalition put faces on these parents for the decision-makers."

Building Diverse Leadership

A coalition needs an effective management committee as part of its leadership team. "You have to develop structures that are not elaborate, and that can make very fast decisions," says Hieu. "The Coalition is lots of people, but we do have a management committee. That management committee has the mandate to act whenever we see fit. If we have to go on CBC [Canadian Broadcasting Corporation], we don't have to consult with the whole membership. If the minister of education is coming to town the management committee doesn't have to talk to everybody; we contact four people by e-mail. You need that think tank where people trust each other and the rest of the community trust them to make good decisions."

Who gets on the management committee? How do you build the trust required for a small group to really act for a large group? The Coalition has tried to choose their management committee according to expertise. As Coalition members express it: "We need a good editor, we need a good strategist; we need a parent and a co-ordinator; and we need somebody who can read the financial statement." The trust takes years to build and you need "people with very small egos. It's good to have egos but they have to be healthy egos, not sick egos or you can't get the work done. People have interacted with each other over different things over the years; they have come to trust each other, knowing they're doing things for the right reasons. And ... they have produced results." It's this track record of working over the long haul that allows a large group of people to trust a small group of people to act in everyone's best interests.

A coalition needs many kinds of leadership. As Amal puts it: "You need community leadership; you need enlightened funders willing to invest money in it; you need people who can analyze the current political moment and are good on strategy; you need people who are paying attention to conflict, and can do conflict resolution; and you need sympathetic allies inside an organization who can use the coalition's work to push for change inside. " These forms of diverse leadership require many different kinds of skills, as Hieu Van Ngo points out: "Varied skills in small organizations means you are able to do the administrative work, raise money, build relationships with funders, decision-makers and community groups, conduct research, deal with the media, provide effective education,
provide technical and emotional support, mentor and encourage the next wave of leadership."

The leadership of the Coalition has developed respectful and strategic relationships with the Calgary Board of Education. In 2003, Alberta Learning set up a commission—the first since 1972—to review the education system. The Coalition worked with both the public and Catholic boards to propose joint recommendations, providing research and advice on practices that would benefit ESL students. Their joint effort with the commission resulted in funding for ESL students at the kindergarten level and strengthened the Coalition's relationship with these boards. As Hieu points out, leadership must include strengthening people's capacity to strategize: "We do more than criticize them. We praise them when they do something helpful for ESL students, and we advocate with them to the provincial government." Political analysis means identifying moments to act, what strategies would likely produce results, who should be the focus of the coalition's attention. It means agreeing on when to lay low and recognizing when things have gone too far.

A strategic leadership also knows when to allow new people to speak out. When the Coalition made its presentation to the Standing Policy Committee on Learning and Employment (which included the minister of learning and other Members of the Legislative Assembly of Alberta), the leadership agreed that parents and students would provide their stories and that staff and advisers would address the technical aspects of the issues— a collective way, says Hieu, to "engage both the heart and the mind." The group did role-plays of what could happen as a way to prepare the parents and students to speak with confidence, and they went as a group to the presentation. A parent involved with this effort recognized the importance of team work: "We chartered a van and we went out to Edmonton with everyone. It's important that the people are proud of their work, they own the work, it's their work."

Sometimes coalition work requires difficult decisions about who is best to speak. There's a risk of hurt feelings in order to advance the group's goals. To avoid this, an older Coalition member suggests that "you need to mentor the people around these issues, and at the same time bring everyone to a higher level. For example, if I'm suggesting that you not go to the ministry, it's not because you don't have the skills or the competencies, but I really think this other person would make a better impression because she is a visible minority, and we need that. The people who trust the leaders don't take it personally, but if people don't trust their leaders, then they are going to feel hurt. Leaders need to go out of their way to make sure that nobody is hurt and everybody is engaged, and involved in these decisions."

It is vital that leadership include young people connected to the community with skills they can put to good use. The Coalition's co-ordinator, Hieu, joined when he was a university student. He combined his academic work with the research needs of the Coalition. "Hieu has done a blueprint for ESL in Alberta," says Amal. "I mean the work is top-notch. With his research, the Coalition has been able to impact policy; there's a whole body of literature out there now that's very credible." Pearl Yip also began working with the

Narim Ismail Tejo

Coalition as a student. Her thesis, "A Case Study Analysis of the ESL Issue," analyzes how coalitions function based on her careful tracking of the Coalition's work.

Broadening the Coalition's Work: Thinking Strategically

Learning Different Organizational Cultures[17]

Coalitions are fragile things; they are a collection of people who normally might have very different interests and perspectives, coming together for a common purpose. Amal Umar emphasizes that one of the secrets of the Coalition's effectiveness is its ability to work successfully with diverse organizations—big and small. That requires learning about each other's organizational and sectoral cultures. "If we are going to create change and we want to bring these different stakeholders to work together, we need to respect and appreciate the diversity within these multi-stakeholders."

In her work as a program officer, Amal works with many organizations and sees the huge inequities of resources and surprisingly different ways the same things get done. "You have a one-million dollar budget in one organization, and the other has two thousand dollars. One has a whole three floors downtown and one works in the basement of the church. One has business plans and outcomes with consultants writing their proposals, the other is holding a fundraising raffle. One has three hundred employees, and the other has a half-time volunteer co-ordinator. And the people who are trying to do the change are the ones that have a part-time volunteer, who are putting the pressure on the big giants to change. The inequities are right there. Even the non-profit sector is not homogeneous. I think advocates have been very naïve and have not done their homework to appreciate the diversity in resources when they are organizing."

Narim Ismail Tejo

Hieu Van Ngo, Coalition for Equal Access to Education, talking to the media, Edmonton, 2005

Using Media Effectively

Using media effectively and ethically is another important strategy and practice. Making effective decisions is sometimes challenging, according to a coalition member: "Should we meet with the Calgary caucus, or should we go to Calgary Board of Education, or should we do a press release before we go. And we have to think, if we are going to the Calgary Board of Education in good faith, no, we shouldn't be doing a press release, because then, the Board has good reason to be worried about us. Maybe we should keep our top guns for later. And when we go to the media, what should we be saying? We shouldn't be bad-mouthing the Calgary Board of Education publicly. They are our partner, so we should be trying to engage them instead." There is an ethics for times of difficult peace and there is an ethics for states of emergencies, and sometimes it's war. For example, in the early 1990s when the CBE was starting to privatize the assessment of ESL students, the Coalition felt that a more direct, confrontational strategy was required. Another member recalls: "When it came to privatizing, it was war. You go to the media, and you say, 'They are privatizing our children's future.' That's the title [for the story]!"

The Coalition has worked successfully with the *Calgary Herald, Western Parents Magazine*, CBC Radio, *Fast Forward Weekly, Insight into the Government, Choices Magazine*, and the *Edmonton Journal* to disseminate its concerns and findings. Its work is cited as leading edge for other emerging ESL coalition work across Canada in a September 2004 series of articles about ESL students in the *Toronto Star*.

Moving with the Political Times

Over the twelve years of the Coalition's work, the political moments have changed many times. This demands attention and flexibility on the Coalition's part. For example, in 2003, Alberta Learning increased the ESL Supplementary Grant from $736 to $1,028 for each student for the 2004 and 2005 school years, with a further $351 per year for each refugee child. This increase is something to celebrate as one of the outcomes of the Coalition's work. But Alberta Learning no longer requires boards of education to account for how they spend that money. This makes it much harder to determine whether the boards are actually using the ESL supplementary grant for ESL programming.

When boards of education are not required to report, the Coalition's access to such information must come through its relationship with the board and with the parents who ask questions at the board level. The Coalition has intensified its work with parents to equip them to raise questions in their schools and at the CBE as a strategy to hold the CBE accountable for this new money.

Round Tables and Cross-Sector Symposium

In 2001, the Coalition produced its blueprint for effective education, which it has used to stimulate discussion with different sectors. In 2003, the Coalition led a collaborative project called "Toward Innovative Vision for Quality, Equitable ESL Education" that involved a series of eighteen sector-specific round-table discussions in Calgary and Edmonton, with 250 people attending. A summary of the proceedings was produced followed by a cross-sector symposium in May 2003 where 143 people came together to develop strategy.[18]

The cross-sector symposium included members of diverse communities, agencies, schools and school boards, provincial and federal departments, as well as parents. Their final strategy focused on seven areas of activity:

1. comprehensive, effective programming and curriculum
2. mobilizing and advocacy
3. responsive resources
4. guidelines for monitoring ESL instruction and outcome measures
5. cultural competency
6. capacity building, and
7. collaboration, co-ordination, and networking

These key activities will be used to ensure that quality, equitable programming benefits all children. For example, "cultural competency" refers to the need for all people working in organizations to have equity skills that recognize discrimination and that support and build equitable organizations. "Everybody needs to be culturally competent to do this work, not just minorities. The whole organization whether they are hiring White people or Black— everyone needs to be culturally competent," explains one Coalition member. The Coalition has produced a "Cultural Competency Tool Kit" to support schools in this integration work. Orders for the kit are coming in from other boards and other provinces as cuts to ESL programs provoke more parent organizing in urban centres across Canada.[19]

In June 2003, members of the Coalition, accompanied by parents, community representatives, and educators, presented the strategy emerging from this process to the provincial Standing Policy Committee on Learning and Employment. The members then met with representatives of Alberta Learning to discuss the recommendations they were putting forward. The Coalition received plenty of media coverage throughout May to July 2003.[20]

In its written submissions, the Coalition identifies its plans for expanding its work in the future. It is committed to the following roles in the coming years:

- raising awareness among community, education, and government sectors as well as the general public about ESL issues, and the roles each can place in improving ESL education
- providing training to community, education, and government partners
- facilitating dialogue among stakeholders to build quality, equitable ESL education
- supporting community, boards, and governments in implementing strategies in the seven areas of its strategy
- conducting action research

- monitoring and providing feedback to ensure that policies and practices serve the needs of ESL learners
- facilitating active participation of parents[21]

As a superintendent of the Calgary Board of Education acknowledged at the 2003 symposium: "The Coalition is truly a critical friend. They both support and challenge our work with ESL learners."[22] And as more and more parents become knowledgeable about how the school system can serve their children better, the Coalition is ensuring that their voices are heard. Andrea Marquez, a parent representative presenting to the Standing Policy Committee, brought the point home: "We don't want our children to be second-class citizens of Canada. We want our children to be well educated in order to make a great contribution to the Canadian society's development."

This ongoing work will require long-term funding, a responsibility Amal continues to handle: "My job is to facilitate access between the people and their tax money. There are no power dynamics. It's just pure access." The budget began at $7,000 in the first year. It's now over $100,000 and comes from a diverse funding base. The Coalition can get enough money now because it is a "success story," and people want to fund its work. Amal is very practical where money is concerned. She's a funder herself, and she sees the value of enlightened funders. To support progressive funding and to ensure maximum benefit with scarce dollars, Amal has participated in "funding tables" where people with access to different pots of money can talk about how to support projects such as the Coalition. Amal has built trust with community-minded funders by getting involved in their issues, volunteering to strengthen their anti-racism work, building relations of mutual support. "I'm very genuine when I say it will make you look good and it falls under your mandate; this is an equity issue and you are involved in equity and social justice and helping this work along. I'm very clear at analysis. Racism is a Canadian Heritage priority. My aim is to make it everybody's priority."

Broadening the Base

The Coalition began over twelve years ago as a way to influence the Calgary Board of Education's policy and practices on ESL. Now it's working to influence the quality and equity of ESL education province wide. Its success depends on convincing more and more people that this is important. "The Coalition must engage the wider community, and they need to develop the strategies for that engagement," says Hieu. "We don't have to violate our principles or moral and ethical values, but we really need to do our homework because we can miss the boat in a few instances. When we're talking about a city strategy, we're not just talking about developing the community. We have to be also talking about bringing those leaders in these communities together to influence the other major leaders in the city, to influence the agenda of the city. A coalition must influence policy. If it is talking about addressing systemic discrimination, it is talking about global issues, and it needs to do the work to produce results. People don't want to be empowered just to feel good about themselves. They want to be empowered to produce real change."

In this regard, the Coalition for Equal Access to Education is most proud of its work in mobilizing and equipping parents to be effective advocates for their children. "We have developed tools so that groups can do the training themselves," says Hieu. "It's as if the Coalition has written a paragraph, one good sentence at a time. The paragraph continues to expand, but every new sentence supports the central idea—the right of every child to equitable, quality, publicly funded education."

Celebrating Successes

Throughout its twelve-year history, the Coalition has made occasions to celebrate its work and the enormous value of people coming together to create justice for themselves and others. Its members have successfully

- ☐ lobbied the Alberta government to lift the cap on funding for Canadian-born ESL students

- ☐ influenced the Alberta government to lift restrictions on the number of students qualifying for ESL support

- ☐ persuaded the government to lift the three-year funding cap

- ☐ convinced the Alberta government to raise the ESL Supplementary Grant by 30 per cent with added money for refugee children

- ☐ had ESL raised in legislative debates

- ☐ secured funding for ESL at the kindergarten level

- ☐ established a strong presence at the Calgary Board of Education

- ☐ established a sound relationship with the senior leadership of the Calgary Catholic School District to address the ESL challenge

- ☐ kept ESL issues visible in the public domain

- ☐ enabled more parents to be effective participants in their children's education

- ☐ developed expertise and capacity to bring diverse organizations and players together and to focus on common goals

BUILDING
BLOCKS
FOR EQUITY

A Summary of Common Characteristics of Phase 2, Getting Beyond Training*

Decision-making

We think about who's deciding, how they are deciding, and what the results are.

➤
- Decision-makers are under pressure from members (and funders for social service agencies) to be more diverse and to have an equity policy.
- The leadership has hired a consultant to develop a policy.
- Leadership/management is aware that equity is an issue and has raised money and hired an equity co-ordinator on contract to deal with it.
- Leadership/management is willing to acknowledge it does not look like or fully represent its members and the people it serves.
- There is a belief that training may be the answer (see "Training Will Fix It").

What gets missed?

- The leadership is just beginning to listen to a growing pressure that the organization is not equitable (see "Building Community Coalition and Capacity").
- The equity co-ordinator has huge responsibilities for equity throughout the organization and no authority to ensure it (see "Being the 'Diversity Co-ordinator'").
- Employment equity practices are still confused with "quotas" and a stated concern about "reverse discrimination."

Communicating

We look for who communicates what, who's supposed to listen, where the silences are, who gets what information, whose information is valued.

➤
- Statements regarding respect and dignity are posted in the workplace.
- The organization uses words like "diversity," and "cross cultural" to name issues so it doesn't alienate anyone, in particular White people.
- Some key documents will be translated into two or three priority languages of members and clients.

What gets missed?

- While translation of documents is a good start, the organization does not, in fact, have staff or a structure for working in those languages.
- Words like "diversity" and "cross cultural" mask the racism that is happening; and they are no help for addressing the crises which keep erupting.
- The few staff and the members and clients from target groups— women, people with disabilities, people of colour, Aboriginal people, gay/lesbian/bi-sexual/trans people— see the organization as White, male, straight and able-bodied, and resistant to change.

Expertise

We're interested in what and whose expertise is sought, valued, paid for, and used. We seek to continually widen the expertise from which the organization can benefit.

■ Informal use of staff who speak other languages when clients or members need it.
■ Use of the equity co-ordinator and her contacts in the community, particularly for funding applications that require community support.

What gets missed?

■ Staff are encouraged to use their language skills with clients when necessary but reprimanded when they speak it with each other.
■ Advocates for equity are marginalized and seen as "single-issue" people or "trouble-makers" (see "'Proving' It's Racism").
■ Conflicts are blamed on equity advocates and not on the organizational barriers to equity (see all three situations in this phase).
■ The organization has no plan to develop expertise of all of its staff to recognize inequities and address them in the workplace.

Networks/connections

We look for what and whose contacts and networks are sought, valued, paid for, and used to hire, promote, train, develop programs, and evaluate. This is the opposite of the "old boys club."

■ The organization is talking to a few sister organizations, through its equity co-ordinator, to get copies of their equity policies and to find out who to use for training.
■ The organization is trying to recruit/encourage election of one or two racialized board members, stewards / volunteers.

What gets missed?

■ Learning from other organizations is a good first step. But phase-one organizations need to involve their own staff in discussion and development of new policy and practices if they want action to result.
■ Training is still seen as an answer to a problem that hasn't been defined (see "Training Will Fix It").
■ The organization is not yet talking with the communities who are pressuring it to change and could teach it how to do so (see "Building Community Coalition and Capacity").

Resources

We're interested in who allocates time, energy and money to what; who benefits from the allocation of resources; who influences the allocation.

The equity co-ordinator is on contract for as long as external funding is available; her salary is mostly covered by government/foundation grants.

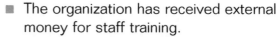

- The organization has received external money for staff training.
- The organization has budgeted for consultants to develop an equity policy and to help it deal with a situation that has blown up in one of its workplaces.

What gets missed?

- Employees using languages other than English are not paid or formally recognized for it.
- Equity is still not a line item in the budget. Equity staffing and work is dependent on outside funding (see "Being the 'Diversity Co-ordinator'").
- As yet, no attention is being paid to creating internal capacity for racial equity.

* This tool is adapted from the theoretical work of Jojo Geronimo and Marlene Green for the Ontario Anti-Racism Secretariat, 1993–1995.

Phase 2:

Getting to How Things Work

In phase two, the organization has moved past denial and is engaged in some anti-racism activity. It may even have a reputation for being very multicultural and accessible. There may be at least one director who's known for creating a really inclusive department or division. Difference and diversity are openly valued inside the workplace and shape the public perception of this organization in the larger community. The organization talks about and, in some cases, actually hires racialized people. The mission, mandate, equity policy, and the work of the agency's equity committee all attest to this organization's desire to be equitable.

However, something's not working. Many of the new racialized employees are seen by White people as "employment equity hires." They're concentrated in a department that "does outreach and organizing with the community." Some of the newly hired people themselves feel "lucky" to have a job and may not feel confident that they were hired because they are competent and the organization needs what they can do. It's not clear how people of colour and Aboriginal people are benefiting from the organization's many policies and stated intentions. However, a few White staff have developed reputations for being equity champions, and they are asked to speak at conferences on "equity initiatives" in their organization.

Unaddressed tensions simmer in the organization over recognition, promotion, and reprisals for speaking out about inequity. The management team is still all White, not because they don't want to diversify but because "there are no qualified candidates who could have moved into the job quickly enough." The organization may have "done anti-racism" before, by which it means that it hired outsiders to conduct anti-racism training that was "difficult for a lot of people. Nothing much came of it." There is a general feeling that "a refresher" in equity and diversity would benefit employees.

Does this sound familiar? Well-meaning governments, agencies, and unions who care about equity are somehow not able to translate this language of equity into substantive action. And yet the challenges of implementing racial equity have been documented for years.[1]

We include three situations to illustrate this phase. "Who Deserves the Job?" examines the unequal effects of typical systems of hiring and the lack of any forum to take up people's confusion about equity and hiring. "Bargaining for Equity" explores how "normal" ways of collective bargaining in unionized workplaces can benefit mostly White workers, and highlights the struggles of newly emerging racialized leaders to make their voices and

issues heard. "Who's Afraid of the New Executive Director?" probes the differential assessments and expectations of racialized leaders and the challenges they face in using their authority and expertise for the good of the organization.

Our true story for this phase draws inspiration from the work of Hazelle Palmer, an African-Canadian woman who is the executive director of a community organization, and Rainer Soegtrop, a White male senior manager of a large housing corporation. Both are passionate about advancing racial equity in their organizations and share with us a range of creative strategies. They are skilled anti-racism leaders who reflect on their work with wisdom and humour.

This section finishes with "Building Blocks for Equity" in which we summarize the possibilities and challenges faced by organizations in phase two of their transformation.

Who Deserves the Job?

There have been mutterings in the hallways and meetings for weeks. No one comes right out and says it, but everyone's talking privately about the hiring of the receptionist. A White, English-speaking woman has been filling the position on a temporary basis for months, and now there's funding to make the position permanent. At the monthly general staff meeting, the executive director announces that hiring for the position will take place in the next month. One staff person asks why the organization doesn't just make the temporary staff person permanent.

The executive director explains that the organization still needs to put a process in place so that it's fair, and that a committee will make the final decision. Suk Yin, a recently hired Vietnamese worker explains that the Vietnamese clients that she serves are afraid to call because they are not fluent in English. She wonders whether language fluency in Vietnamese or another "newcomer" language wouldn't be a help for the position. An awkward silence follows.

Then someone says, "What about the Aboriginal people? We don't serve them. Or how about Tamil clients? There are lots of communities that need our services. We can't hire someone from each of those communities." Someone else says, "I think we should just hire the best person for the job." Another person says, "We've already done so much for the Vietnamese community. Isn't it someone else's turn?"

Another awkward silence ensues. The executive director says, "I think it's too late to fiddle with the job description now. The hiring committee's starting interviews next week. We'll keep you posted. We've got a tight schedule today, so let's move on to the next agenda item."

In the hall after the meeting, three staff are overheard talking with irritation about the idea that language should be a factor in the hiring of the receptionist. "They may as well tell White people not to apply." "Yeah, you know, we've come so far and done so much, and it's never enough." "The fact is that we need a good receptionist and Nellie's been doing the job. Why wouldn't we hire her?" "It would really hurt her if she found out about these comments. And she can't afford to lose this job."

Suk Yin is leaving the building with Krishna, the office administrator. Krishna says, "Well, you tried." Suk Yin replies, "Did you hear that? They've 'done so much for the Vietnamese community'! What do they mean by that, that they've done us some big favour by hiring me?" Krishna said, "Yeah I know. I tried to say something but I'm so tired of hearing the same old excuses. They act like we're just flavours of the month. Which one will it be this month?"

In the kitchen, Sam and Mohammed are making coffee. Sam says, "I think Suk Yin had a point. What do we do about clients who have difficulty communicating in English?" Mohammed replies, "Maybe she had a point, but she should be careful how she says it. She sounds a bit angry when she talks, and it makes people uncomfortable. These things take time." Sam says, "She was advocating for her clients." Mohammed replies, "Yes, but not everything is about racism."

Two months after Nellie has been confirmed in the position, the tensions around her hiring remain unresolved. People continue to take positions about it. Some people use it as an example of what's wrong with employment equity. Others refer to it as an example of how they continue to experience racism, even in their efforts to challenge it. The references are always coded, and there's never an open discussion about the flawed hiring process or about the divisions it has created among the staff. In a department meeting with the executive director present, the manager raises the issue of a new staff opening and the possibility of developing new job requirements. People look at one another, but nobody says anything.

1. What inequities in power do you see in this situation? How is power being used to challenge or reinforce racism?

2. Where are the specific openings for action that can shift how power is working? At what point could you do something different as the executive director? Suk Yin? Sam? Mohammed?

How Power Is Working

1. **Only outreach workers have language requirements in their job descriptions.**

   Language requirements (other than English) are only written into "outreach worker" job descriptions. Outreach workers, often racialized people, are expected to work in both English and the language(s) of "target communities." Other job descriptions, such as receptionist, have not been reconceived to take these requirements into account. English is still viewed as "normal." "Community languages" are still conceived of as "special needs." This confirms English as the most important language of the organization and entrenches the burden on "outreach workers" to serve those communities on the organization's behalf.

2. **The hiring process is unclear.**

   What are the routes to getting a permanent job in the organization? If a key route is through temporary or contract positions, then this needs to be explicit. Currently, the status of temporary workers is unclear. Ensuring equity would require a re-examination of contract and temporary positions to ensure the requirements advance the organization's equity agenda.

   It's not clear from this case whether the executive director has made some informal arrangement with the temporary person that if money became available, she would be hired as permanent staff. However, several staff people believe this is the case. The absence of a transparent process calls into question the merit of the receptionist's own qualifications and may impair her ability to do her job. Unclear hiring processes do not benefit the reputations of any worker.

3. **The people who are the least informed about what the clients need construct the jobs.**

   There has been no open discussion of what the organization needs from the job of receptionist. Workers who are closest to the most marginal communities that the organization serves have no formal avenue to raise questions or contribute to the design of the job or the process of hiring. Thus, the organization cannot benefit from their insights.

4. **It's the outreach workers who have to raise the issues.**

   In the absence of any structured discussion about how the organization needs to advance equity, the least powerful workers in the organization are left to raise the issues. Since these workers are the only ones taking care of equity on behalf of the organization, their challenge to the larger staff to think about these issues is resisted. When people with power do not listen to the questions and challenges of racialized workers, their avoidance reinforces the already prevalent idea that only racialized workers benefit from equitable processes and that White people lose in the fight for equity. It also reinforces the idea that this is all that racialized people care about.

5. **Arguments against increased equity are unchallenged and look plausible.**

In the staff meeting, three people in a row raise concerns about language requirements for the receptionist. Their questions all sound like concerns about ensuring "real" equity and yet, whether intended or not, result in blocking it. ("There are lots of communities that need our services. We can't hire someone from each of those communities." "Hire the best person for the job." "We've done so much for the Vietnamese community. Isn't it someone else's turn?")

None of these remarks is discussed or challenged in the staff meeting. This has a tremendous impact on Suk Yin and on other racialized workers who, by association, feel degraded by judgements about "the best person for the job." Perhaps they were hired because they belong to a particular community and not because of their expertise. Are they expected to be grateful because the organization has "done so much for the Vietnamese community"? There is no forum in which to pose these questions, to challenge the implicit implications, or to expose how these judgements affect racialized workers in the room.

Whether intentional or not, the absence of a challenge and the confirmation of the receptionist's job gives these ideas increased plausibility. This increases the difficulty for staff who want some discussion of these ideas and who hope the organization will do things differently next time.

6. **Racialized people feel at risk.**

Mohammed expresses anxiety about how "angry" Suk Yin sounds. There is already a prevailing notion that people of colour are "angry" and "demanding." He fights for a broader image of himself in the organization; an image that is more than just someone always concerned about racism.

TOOLS & STRATEGIES

The following suggestions could be used by the executive director at the all-staff meeting, or by a manager chairing a team or department meeting, or by a facilitator who finds herself/himself guiding this discussion.

1. **Ask for specifics.**

   Coded conversations about a situation that everyone knows a little about do not help clarify the situation and only increase unease and silence. Here are some questions that might help clarify the situation:

   ■ Does everyone know the situation to which Angel is referring? Just so we can all participate, could we clarify which situation that is?

   ■ Why do you not want to name names when everyone here seems to know exactly the situation to which you're referring?

   ■ If you're worried about "getting into trouble," just recount what you heard and saw, without giving any assessment of it.

2. **Name the reality that there are tensions and discomfort in the room.**

   There are different ways to do this.

   ■ Sometimes it's more effective to ask, "What's happening in the group right now?"

   ■ At other times, you might risk putting yourself in the picture to make it safer to talk about what's going on. You might say, "My stomach is feeling tight and tense, as though there's a lot we're not saying. It's all sitting like glue in the middle of the room. Is anyone else feeling uncomfortable? Yes? Do you have a sense about what that's about?"

   ■ Still another way could be to connect the difficulty of talking about equity to the situation in the moment by saying, "It seems that what is in the way right now are the very things that you've said get in the way of talking about equity. Does anyone want to say anything about that?"

3. **Identify, matter-of-factly, the differences of opinion in the room.**

   One of the reasons that tensions about equity go underground is that people are afraid that a disagreement will leave them permanently divided, when they have to keep working together. Advancing equity requires increased comfort, willingness, and skill to name and examine differences in perspective. To point out these differences, for example, you could say: "Peter, you feel that it was inappropriate for Suk Yin to raise the question of language requirements at the staff meeting because the hiring process was already underway. Corolla, you feel Suk Yin had no choice because she was concerned about her clients' access to the organization, and she had a responsibility to see what she could do about it. You both agree that this meeting was not ideal, but for different reasons."

Reassure people that this tabling of differences is helpful and an important component of equity work.

4. Distinguish between personal opinion and systemic issues.

The Triangle Model is a good tool to use here (see figure 3), because it helps people analyze the components and dynamics of a situation in a more detached way. It depersonalizes the situation. A conversation using the triangle might look something like this:

"We've been talking about these individual behaviours (write a few of them at the top), but what's really happening?" You might identify a few obvious systems. "For example, we have language requirements, but only in 'outreach jobs' and 'outreach workers' are expected to serve racialized communities, but White workers are not. There are a few powerful ideas that are operating here, whether we like the sound of them or not. One is that 'hiring a Vietnamese worker equals serving the Vietnamese community.' There's another idea that we really need to talk about, which is that 'people of colour are hired because of their language skills; White people are hired because of their competence.' But we haven't named the competencies. And what's making this really difficult is that some of us fear that if we talk about the inequities between us, it will further divide us."

Stress that these ideas are not ones that anyone subscribes to publicly; they are the ideas that appear to underlie the actions or lack of action (see below for an analysis of the situation). Ask people to name the impacts on different players and on the organization. What are the powerful ideas that are supporting the way things are working?

Discuss the connections between these different points on the triangle and any insights emerging about why the whole situation was so hard to deal with.

5. Identify places to intervene now.

Stay with the visual of the triangle if it's helpful. Given that the situation happened a while ago and that it's still simmering informally, where is it possible to intervene now? Identify one or two practical things that this group can do to make a difference. (See "An Equity Lens for Reviewing Policies, Programs, and Materials" in section five, and Evelyn Murialdo's ideas for speaking out in organizations in "Dancing on Live Embers: Transforming the Systems" in phase three.)

Figure 3:
The Triangle Model

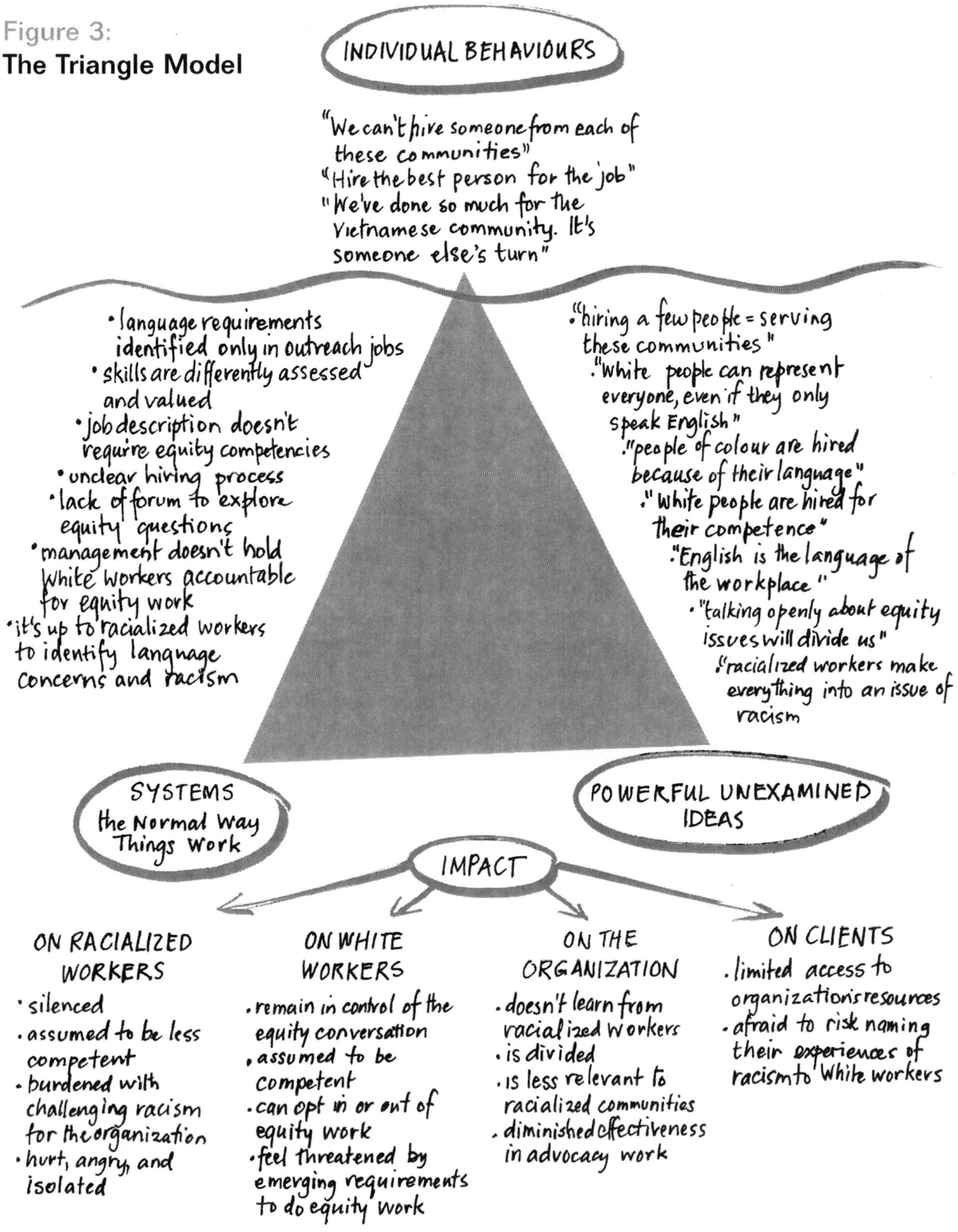

INDIVIDUAL BEHAVIOURS

"We can't hire someone from each of these communities"
"Hire the best person for the job"
"We've done so much for the Vietnamese community. It's someone else's turn"

• language requirements identified only in outreach jobs
• skills are differently assessed and valued
• job description doesn't require equity competencies
• unclear hiring process
• lack of forum to explore equity questions
• management doesn't hold White workers accountable for equity work
• it's up to racialized workers to identify language concerns and racism

• "hiring a few people = serving these communities"
• "white people can represent everyone, even if they only speak English"
• "people of colour are hired because of their language"
• "White people are hired for their competence"
• "English is the language of the workplace"
• "talking openly about equity issues will divide us"
• "racialized workers make everything into an issue of racism"

SYSTEMS
the Normal Way Things Work

POWERFUL UNEXAMINED IDEAS

IMPACT

ON RACIALIZED WORKERS
• silenced
• assumed to be less competent
• burdened with challenging racism for the organization
• hurt, angry, and isolated

ON WHITE WORKERS
• remain in control of the equity conversation
• assumed to be competent
• can opt in or out of equity work
• feel threatened by emerging requirements to do equity work

ON THE ORGANIZATION
• doesn't learn from racialized workers
• is divided
• is less relevant to racialized communities
• diminished effectiveness in advocacy work

ON CLIENTS
• limited access to organization's resources
• afraid to risk naming their experiences of racism to White workers

KEEPING OURSELVES IN THE PICTURE

Executive directors, managers, and facilitators will experience different traps and risks in responding to this situation, depending on their racial identities.

For the racialized manager/facilitator:

- White employees can see the racialized manager/facilitator as having a "chip on the shoulder" about equitable employment practices. In the prevalent notion that only racialized people benefit from equity, his/her expertise may be resisted by White people.
- She/he may be cautious about sharing personal experience of racism and may choose to draw on her/his experience of privilege in other forms of oppression (heterosexism, for example) to shift the notion that racialized people only speak about racism and always see themselves as victims.
- She/he plays a particular role in ensuring that racialized people in the room get heard, not just as people with emotional experiences but as workers with a legitimate analysis that is supported by evidence gathered over decades of experience (see section one, "What is Racial Equity Work?").

For the White manager/facilitator:

- White participants may look to White equity advocates to understand and support their efforts to think through various aspects of employment equity. In such situations, the White advocate needs to be able to distinguish when her/his intervention takes away from the expertise of colleagues of colour and when it supports them.
- Sometimes a White manager/facilitator can use her/his whiteness to reassure White people to admit they don't know something and to get help in exploring some questions.

In these cases, her/his job is to:

- offer personal experience as a White person learning about racism, to make it easier for other White people in the room to admit that they're learning
- reinforce racialized colleagues as teachers on the subject of racism, which she/he can do by
- returning to questions and points that a racialized colleague has made: "Tim asked earlier about … Can we hear some more about that?"
- telling a brief anecdote about some aspect of equitable employment that she/he learned from Tim or some other racialized colleague
- summarizing what she/he has learned from workers of colour or Aboriginal workers in the room
- identify and stress the benefits of increased equity to all workers, including White workers (for example, their clients get better service; they can learn how to do their jobs more effectively)

Bargaining for Equity

The first meeting of Local 65's new Bargaining Committee has just finished, and Joanne is already discouraged. She shares her frustration with Mahmood, whose first round of collective bargaining was three years ago. "How did you stand it last time? We're eight people who know the union, know the employer, and we can't agree on the basic issues affecting the membership! It's all about better wages and pension plans for the people who've been there the longest, and guess who's left out … again?"

Mahmood grins. "Calm down, and pace yourself. At least now the White people have two of us to deal with on the committee. We need to pull along a couple of them like Doug, who could be a real ally. We'll get down to the real stuff tomorrow."

Joanne swallows her frustration. She couldn't get the White people on the committee to listen to her, and she couldn't get the younger, racialized part-time workers to take the union seriously. She hadn't even been able to convince most of them to fill out the bargaining survey, which laid the basis for the Bargaining Committee's priorities. She had interviewed a number of people on the night shift who hadn't even received a survey, and talked to some on her own shift who told her the survey was a waste of time. The questions were all geared to the assumed interests of the older full-time employees. They agreed to talk to Joanne about their issues, but expressed doubt about the upcoming bargaining.

One worker said, "The union isn't going to do anything for us. It's just going to take care of the White boys who run it." Another complained, "None of the questions on this survey fit me. I kept checking the 'other' category, but there was no space to say why I was checking it."

On the second day of committee meetings, Joanne comes prepared. She has typed up the list of issues identified from her interviews and she leads off at the start. "Can we bring in the issues affecting all our members, not just the few activists who show up for union meetings? Most of the people of colour and the few Aboriginal folks like me are concentrated in the temporary and part-time jobs. The majority are under thirty-five years old; they never know how many hours they can count on and they have families to raise. That means some of them have to take other jobs to make ends meet. Some of them have been there for five or more years and they're still on temporary contract; they want some job security. We need equal hourly rates and access to the same benefits for these workers. Otherwise it's in the employer's interest to keep hiring more and more part-time people, keep their hours irregular, and never make them permanent. I think …"

Jamie, the committee chair, interrupts Joanne. "No offence, Joanne, but this job takes real experience, and you're new at this. The bargaining survey gives this committee a mandate from our membership—an eight per cent catch-up raise, better pensions, some clean-up on the health and safety issues, and some job security. We need to strengthen our no-contracting out clause. Does everyone agree?"

Joanne starts to say, "But the survey didn't ask part-timers about their issues," but she feels silenced by Jamie's tight face.

As Jamie looks at each of the six White people in turn, one of the White women nods, the other says nothing and looks anxiously at Joanne. One male member says, "Absolutely." Another is checking his cell-phone messages. Jamie is finishing his round and settling his gaze on Doug, when Mahmood says, "I think Joanne's got a point. Our part-time membership has increased by twenty per cent since the last round of bargaining. That's where the majority of people of colour and Aboriginal workers are. Many of them are women. We haven't paid attention to them and they're ticked off with the union because they don't see what they get for their union dues."

Jamie reacts angrily. "What are you saying? That we're racist? That we don't care about women workers? We've built this union from scratch. These part-time workers have got

union protection because we fought for it." There is silence.

At this point Jamie looks at Doug for support. Doug says casually, "What's got your shirt in such a knot, Jamie? We've got a problem here, and you know it as well as Mahmood and Joanne do. Many of the full-time folks are retiring in the next five years and we're busy trying to get as much money as we can to retire on, but we haven't done anything about ensuring that this local will survive. Where's the new leadership we're bringing along? Why should part-timers support us if we have to strike on issues like pensions? We're becoming split on racial lines, and we're asleep at the wheel." Silence.

Jamie is clearly frustrated. "Doug, I thought you had more sense. This is not the time to go all out for part-timers. The employer will never go for it. And it will totally jeopardize the rights of full-time workers who've struggled to keep this local intact. And as for the split along racial lines, many of these people that you're so anxious to defend have never been to a union meeting, never walked a picket line, and won't be there to stand with us when we're in trouble. Let's get on with the work this committee has to do!"

---

1. What inequities in power do you see in this situation? How is power being used to challenge or reinforce racism?

2. Where are the specific openings for action, to shift how power is working? At what points could you do something different as Joanne, Doug, Jamie, other committee members?

Discussion & Analysis

How Power Is Working

1. **The racist structure of the workplace is not explicitly recognized or challenged by the union leadership.**

In this workplace, the hiring, promotion, terms, and conditions of employment have all been shaped by racism. While the employer has hired racialized workers—both workers of colour and Aboriginal workers—those employees are concentrated in temporary and part-time positions, and many staff the night shift. They are paid less for comparable time worked, have less benefits and insecure hours of employment. Some workers have remained on contract for five or more years without being made permanent. Some older union activists argue that newer hires have always been treated this way "whatever colour they were." But for the past while, this classic divide between new and old employees has been racialized, and the union has colluded in these dynamics of exclusion by maintaining its focus on the concerns of veteran members.

The racist impact of the employer's hiring and personnel practices is heightened by the age of racialized workers in this organization. Most are under thirty-five, with young families, and are struggling with more than one job as well as the care of children. The insecurity directly affects their quality of life and that of their families.

This employment structure also affects the health of the union. Workers who are preoccupied with survival, and fearful of losing what little employment they have, need compelling reasons to find time for the union. They work on shifts during times when stewards are unavailable to them. The absence of union action against racism in this workplace widens the gap between White and racialized workers. It reinforces racialized workers' sense of alienation from the union and confirms White workers' feelings that racialized workers don't care about the union.

2. **The survey reaches only the White permanent full-time members.**

The survey, with its questions about bargaining priorities, is a key union tool for (a) identifying the key concerns of the membership; (b) engaging members in a conversation about bargaining and how it can improve conditions for all workers; (c) guiding the Bargaining Committee's priorities. In her conversations with part-time workers, Joanne has discovered that the night-shift employees did not receive a survey. Many part-timers who did receive one had no one to talk to about it, nor did they have any reason to believe that if they did fill it out that it would have any effect.

The questions on the survey anticipate the concerns of full-time permanent workers but not part-time temporary employees. Thus, the union's own survey reinforces these divisions shaped by racism. It communicates that White workers' concerns are important and racialized workers' concerns are not. This impression is compounded by the system for distributing the survey and getting feedback. If the distribution system relies on union stewards who are full-time day-shift workers, then the survey does not reach or gather the concerns of racialized workers who are part-time and temporary. The process of creating, distributing, and gathering the results of the survey mirrors the inequities in the workplace itself.

In this situation, Joanne's efforts to interview and record racialized workers' con cerns represent an individual effort. They are not part of the action plan of the Bargaining Committee. In fact, Joanne's knowledge highlights the divisions in the committee itself.

3. **The concerns of racialized workers are not seen as union issues.**

The issues Joanne raises are seen as her issues, not the issues of union members. Her work to engage more union members is not seen as an important contribution to the committee's effort to identify what its members want; it is dismissed as the inappropriate actions of someone new to bargaining.

4. **White people are seen as union builders, and racialized people are posed as the threat to the union.**

The chair is explicit in his reasons for defending the concerns of White permanent workers as the priority. "We've built this union from scratch. These part-time workers have got union protection because we fought for it." In such a statement, the "we" are clearly the workers whose priorities count—White full-time workers. "These part-time workers" benefit from the struggles and courage of the veterans. Such a statement completely dismisses the contributions of racialized workers to the union, workers such as Mahmood and Joanne.

But Jamie goes further in responding to Doug's challenge. Jamie acknowledges the racial split in the union and blames it on the most vulnerable workers themselves. He explains this by suggesting that White workers defend the union and racialized workers are a threat to it. "And as for the split along racial lines, many of these people that you're so anxious to defend have never been to a union meeting, never walked a picket line, and won't be there to defend us when we're in trouble." The racial divide is an unchallenged fact that means "we" need to defend the union from "them."

There is no effort to look at how the union's own practices exclude or push racialized workers out. Nor is there yet a sense of how racism undermines the union's current efforts to mobilize its members or build solidarity among them.

5. **The chair marginalizes the voices of racialized Bargaining Committee members.**

There are promising signs that some of the White people on the committee, along with Joanne and Mahmood, are thinking more broadly about the union membership and its interests. Doug speaks quite pointedly against Jamie's arguments; the two White women look uneasy about their agreement with Jamie. At this point in the process, the more challenge he gets, the more Jamie asserts his agenda. He uses a variety of ways to try to maintain control:

- he interrupts Joanne when she tries to introduce the perspective of racialized part-time workers
- he patronizes her by suggesting that her arguments are shaped by her inexperience with bargaining rather than her expertise and knowledge of many of the union's members
- he silences Mahmood by focusing on whether Mahmood is accusing White people of racism, rather than examining the evidence of racism that Mahmood is raising
- he uses his irritation and anger to intimidate Joanne and the other women who might speak
- he turns the conversation away from the threats to the union that Joanne, Mahmood, and Doug are raising—the racially divisive practices of the employer; instead, he chooses to pinpoint the union's most vulnerable members as the threat to union health

6. **There is no effort to ensure that new union leaders will reflect the changing membership.**

   For the first time there are two racialized members on the Bargaining Committee. But the scenario does not make it clear what struggles the racialized workers went through to produce this result. Most of the current union leadership is White and will be retiring soon. Indeed, the chair's treatment of Joanne may make her less willing to remain involved in the union or to take a position of leadership in the future.

Tools & Strategies

Collective bargaining is an important opening to workers who are union members. It is a time when many people pay more focused attention to their conditions of work, their employer, and their union than they normally do. It is a moment for the union to build connections with all its members, to demonstrate its relevance to all workers, and to strengthen real solidarity among its members. And, it is a real opportunity for both union and employer to advance racial equity in conversations with each other. In this scenario, even with the current tensions, there are many openings for shifting direction. How can advocates for racial equity make this apparent in the bargaining process?

In this scenario, there are three general possibilities: Jamie continues resisting and bullying and the rest of the committee collapses and lets him run things; Jamie continues his behaviour but the rest of the committee begins to organize and take over things; Jamie begins to listen and, together, the committee starts to analyze the situation in a different way and to develop a different strategy. What happens depends on any or all of the following possibilities. The committee can:

1. **Shift the control and focus of the meeting.**

   Doug can

   - raise questions about why Jamie is allowing assumptions about the employer to dictate the union's bargaining priorities
   - remind Jamie of past bargaining efforts, where unlikely gains were made because people were committed to the issues
   - persist in reminding Jamie that the Bargaining Committee represents all members, and that a local that only protects the interests of a few soon becomes irrelevant
   - ask why the union would collude with the employer in targeting its most vulnerable members, and ask how such a focus is union-building
   - insist that Jamie and the other White people on the committee listen to the experience and knowledge of Mahmood and Joanne as the committee begins to shape its strategy
   - challenge Jamie because of their shared history, even as he models a different stance towards racialized workers in the union
   - thank Joanne for the extra effort she has made to contact the most vulnerable and least connected members, and insist that she shouldn't have had to do that on her own time and initiative; the Bargaining Committee should have a strategy to reach all its members

   Joanne can

   - raise questions about the survey; she can ask why the survey's questions only anticipate the concerns of full-time permanent members
   - ask how a steward structure that is only connected with this portion of the membership can reach the part-timers

   The anxious White woman can

   - say she's uneasy, she doesn't know what to do, that she doesn't like Jamie's treatment of Joanne or of another woman on the committee, and that she wants more respectful discussion and dialogue
   - mention her own experience as a part-time worker (if she has been one), and express solidarity with the conditions racialized workers currently face
   - say that she is learning from what Joanne and Mahmood are saying, that the union has to do more to address racism

   Jamie can

   - stop and ask himself why he's so upset
   - acknowledge that he feels connected and accountable to the full-time veterans and not to the racialized part-timers
   - ask for help (not a rewarded activity in most organizations)

2. **Analyze how racism shapes the structure of this workplace.**

   This committee can begin with a "mapping the membership" exercise, sometimes called "social mapping." They can involve the stewards and some informal leaders to find out names and numbers of members who are full-time and part-time; those who have less than five years employment; whose contracts remain temporary; who work on the night shift; who have dependents; whose first language is other than English and French; who are racialized; who require physical accommodation; who are thirty-five years or younger; who are women; who self-identify as gay, lesbian, or transgender people. The analysis should show concentrations of workers with particular identities in specific jobs, the status of those jobs, and the shift. It should reveal which components of the membership are served by stewards and which components are receiving no union service.[2]

   The committee can also analyze the grievances and complaints to identify where workers have complained about overt expressions of racism, and where satisfactory resolutions did or did not occur. This will force examination of inequitable treatment by the employer, the adequacy of current steward representation, and the effectiveness of any complaint or harassment process that exists.

3. **Restructure the bargaining process to reach racialized workers.**

   Joanne has already demonstrated a way to reach racialized part-time workers. The Bargaining Committee can decide to:

   - build on what Joanne has done and gather more systematically the concerns and issues of racialized part-time workers
   - train stewards and/or other informal workplace leaders to administer a new survey and gather the information[3] for the committee
   - summarize the key issues and circulate these to all members to stimulate discussion
   - identify the common ground between part-time and full-time workers in order to consciously bridge the current racial divide—for example, all workers want some kind of job security (which may look different for part-time and full-time workers); all workers want to be free from harassment and bullying on the job site; all workers can gain from enhanced benefits, including family and compassionate leave and flex time

4. **Do an "equity audit" of the collective agreement.**

   The Canadian Auto Workers Union has prepared a useful tool called a "Collective Agreement Equity Audit." Its guidelines can help committees review their collective agreements for
i.	effective anti-discrimination and anti-harassment clauses
ii.	accommodation and disability provisions
iii.	privacy
iv.	leaves of absence
v.	human rights training and personnel
vi.	benefits, pensions, wages, and hours

In addition, the Communication, Energy and Paperworkers Union of Canada's publication *Bargaining Equality: Joining Hands in Solidarity* (available online) is full of model collective agreement clauses on employment equity; rights for gay, lesbian, bisexual, and transgender workers; part-time work; hours of work; family leave; and child care.[4]

5. **Change the survey and its distribution.**

   Joanne and one or two other people on the committee could redesign the survey under headings which are common to many members—job security and hours, language that benefits families including elder dependents, and so on. The specific questions could not only be inclusive of all members but also educate members about one another's issues simply being posed. Different modes of distributing the survey and collecting the data have been mentioned above.

6. **Set up a Campaign Committee to support the Bargaining Committee.**

   A Campaign Committee could stay in touch with all constituencies of the membership and provide ongoing feedback to the Bargaining Committee. It could also use the energies of uninvolved members. Here is a place to mentor new activists who have links to racialized members, and to learn from them.

Who's Afraid of the New Executive Director?

The Maple Leaf Centre was opened in 1974 to assist new immigrants, poor people, and Aboriginal people develop skills they needed to find work. The first executive director was a White woman selected by the founders because she was a member of their community (a local Christian church). The next two executive directors were also White women, both of whom had been recruited through word of mouth and the informal networks of the board of directors. When the third executive director resigned in 2001, Matthias Fanon, the program co-ordinator at Maple Leaf Centre, applied successfully for the position. Formerly a university professor in Haiti, Matthias had become a refugee and made his way to Canada. Fluent in French and English, he had been hired as an intake worker at the Maple Leaf Centre twelve years earlier. He soon became a program worker, and eventually the program co-ordinator.

As the executive director, Matthias is surprised to find that the board of directors has different requirements of him than they have had of the previous executive directors. Whereas previous EDs had presented quarterly financial statements to the board, Matthias finds that the chair, Martha Stewart, asks for an update on the organization's finances at odd times, sometimes only a few weeks apart. When it is time for Matthias to have his first performance appraisal, he expects to meet with Martha and Aleesha, the chair of the Personnel Committee, as this has been the practice with the previous EDs. Instead, he is asked to meet with the chair and two other board members, neither of whom are on the Personnel Committee. When he asks about this change in process, Martha says simply that the board had made different arrangements due to a scheduling conflict. Matthias later learned that Martha never contacted Aleesha, a Jamaican woman and the only person of colour on the board, about Matthias's performance appraisal and the related meetings.

Some of the staff who got along with Matthias in the past now appear to resent the fact that they have to take direction from him. A White man and White woman complained to Martha that Matthias was an incompetent ED because he denied their requests for vacation. When questioned by Martha, Matthias points out to her that he has been following the agency's personnel policy regarding vacations in much the same way as the previous ED. Martha cautions him to be more attentive to the morale of the staff, and then insists that Matthias grant the two employees their request.

Since Matthias has become ED, more people of colour have applied for jobs at the Centre, believing they would have a better chance of being hired by someone who was an immigrant of colour. At the same time, some White staff view the hiring of any person of colour with suspicion, alleging Matthias is "favouring" people of colour. When Premala, the new program co-ordinator, points out that the hiring committee consists of a board member and a volunteer as well as the ED, these same staff argue that Matthias is "intimidating" and that the others are probably afraid to disagree with him. Besides, Premala (a South Asian woman) has herself been recently hired by Matthias, and of course she would defend him.

Community agencies serving Haitians and other immigrants have high expectations of Matthias and the Maple Leaf Centre. They assume he will create more opportunities for people to attend already full ESL classes or the equally popular computer training classes. When he explains that government funders are reducing grants and are becoming strict about who is eligible, Matthias is accused of "forgetting his roots." He is harshly criticized by some members of the Haitian and African communities.

On the night of the monthly board meeting, Matthias arrives at the agency twenty minutes late. Many board members glare at him as he enters, and one person says, "The board doesn't run on 'island time.'" Matthias attempts to explain that he had been stopped by a police officer on his way back from another meeting. One of the board members asks what he did to warrant being pulled over. Matthias states that he is regularly pulled over by the police near the agency because they are suspicious of an African-descent man driving a new car in that area. While many of the board members look sceptical, one White person comments that she had read something about racial profiling in the newspaper recently. Aleesha says that her son is often pulled over by the police when he drives home from his night class. Martha tells Matthias that he needs a time-management course, and asks the board to review the minutes from the previous meeting.

1. What inequities in power do you see in this situation? How is power being used to challenge or reinforce racism?

2. Where are the specific openings for action, to shift how power is working? At what points could you do something different as a White board member? As a White staff person? As a racialized board member? As a community group?

How Power Is Working

1. **Racialized executive directors must manage the organization while experiencing racism on the job and in society.**

   White people hiring mostly other White people through informal networks is rarely questioned. It is viewed as common business practice. A racialized person hiring a person of colour is often seen as evidence of favouritism and/or the "lowering of standards." (For more on the experience of racialized executive directors, see "Hazelle Palmer: An Executive Director with a Vision" in the true story below.) In this situation, White staff assume that people of colour are being hired because Matthias is hiring "his own people" and not because they are the best candidates for the job. No one questions the ways in which previous White executive directors (and possibly other staff) were hired. This view persists even when there are hiring processes in place to ensure decisions are made fairly and involve other people (as in the Hiring Committee).

2. **Different rules and more stringent practices are put in place to monitor the behaviour of racialized people.**

   Matthias is subjected to greater scrutiny than previous executive directors. Racialized people are monitored particularly carefully when they handle money. Negative stereotypes about people of colour and money abound—for example, "Asians are cunning with numbers and not to be trusted," or "African-descent people aren't used to having money" or "are financially incompetent."

3. **Racism shapes common assumptions about who is objective and who can be trusted.**

   Martha appears to believe that White people will fairly assess other people (both White and racialized) in a performance appraisal process. She doubts that Aleesha will be able to fairly assess Matthias since they are both of African-descent, which excludes her from the process.

4. **Racialized people who become executive directors have their authority questioned by White staff and by White board members.**

   Martha and White staff members contest Matthias's right to hold the two White staff accountable. Martha undermines Matthias's authority by instructing him to ignore agency policy and give the White employees the vacation days they requested. In most governance models, the board is supposed to remain uninvolved in the daily operations of the agency. Martha's actions are an inappropriate use of her position and power as the board's chair.

5. **Greater expectations are placed on racialized executive directors by their communities of origin and by other communities of colour.**

   Community agencies place greater pressure on Matthias to provide their clients with access to ESL and computer classes. Racialized people often expect executive directors of colour to ensure that they will not be discriminated against if they apply for jobs at the Centre and that more racialized people will be hired. They might also count on him to "open the doors" of the Centre, especially if it was previously a predominantly White organization.

6. **Racialized executive directors are sometimes penalized for the racism they experience.**

   When White board members remain unaware of how racism is affecting the executive director's efforts to carry out his responsibilities, they dismiss critical information and wrongly assess him. So Matthias is chastised for his late arrival rather than provided with support to deal with the racial harassment by the police.

   If White board members do not actively anticipate the ways in which their White privilege and power shape their interactions with the racialized executive director, their behaviour (unintentionally or not) will have a racist impact on him. As a result of the greater scrutiny and differential treatment by White board members, Matthias may receive poorer assessments and be deemed less competent than his White counterparts.

7. **White people who do try to challenge racism are ignored, especially when they are in the minority.**

   White allies may also not be clear on how best to intervene, particularly if they are uncomfortable with the content of the dispute, for example, racial profiling by police. While White people who name racism often have more credibility than racialized people, they too can be dismissed by others, particularly if they are the lone voice in the room.

8. **Racialized people who attempt to challenge racism aimed at the executive director are dismissed.**

   Identifying racism can be risky for racialized people. They may be criticized for their efforts to bring racism to the organization's attention: "they always side together," or "they see racism everywhere," or "the ED hired them so of course they would defend him."

TOOLS & STRATEGIES

1. **Have frank conversations about past and present biases in the hiring of staff.**

   What hiring practices have produced predominantly White staff? Many organizations have a history of hiring people who are from the same country or ethnic group in Europe, or who are connected through friends. For example, over twenty years ago, only Orangemen (originally from Scotland) were hired in certain municipal and provincial organizations in Toronto. Even today, in some companies, staff hire each other's relatives and friends. How recently have you, or someone you know, "put in a good word" for a friend who is applying for a position in his/her organization?

2. **Critique prevalent myths about employment equity and other efforts to create fairer hiring processes.**

   Employment equity is about merit. It is not about lowering standards. It is about ensuring systemic racism, sexism, and other forms of discrimination are identified and addressed in hiring systems. It is an attempt to create fair access to jobs for people who have been historically disadvantaged by the types of practices described above.

3. **Ensure clear procedures and processes are in place for the hiring, supervision, and performance appraisals of the executive director.**

   It is critical that this information is made available to all board members, the executive director, and any other relevant stakeholders. The entire board should discuss any deviations from the procedures.

4. **Review the performance appraisal tool.**

   What performance tool is being used to assess the executive director? Discuss ways to build in discussions that focus on how racism is affecting the person in the role. Develop strategies to address the racism that is identified and to provide appropriate forms of support. (See the "Sample Supervision Policy that Integrates Equity" in section five for suggestions on how to do this.)

5. **Consider creating a complaint mechanism for the executive director.**

   A complaint mechanism must be in place for the executive director who believes he/she has been unfairly treated by an individual board member or committee of the board. This is difficult to do and will probably require discussions with the agency's lawyer as well as board members. However, it is important to establish some protection for the executive director. The procedure does not need to be complex; it could include the creation of an ad hoc committee of the board to hire an external investigator and to receive the findings of the investigation.

6. **Create support networks for a racialized executive director.**

   The executive director is often isolated since she/he holds a unique position in the organization. Support networks for the executive director, and for the racialized executive director in particular, are essential. The organization should recognize participation in this network as a legitimate part of the executive director's work. It is a place to share strategies, develop partnerships, and gain support.

7. **Clearly identify roles and responsibilities.**

   The executive director's job description should clearly identify roles and responsibilities, and should be communicated to all board members.

8. **Specify limitations.**

   The "Executive Director's Limitations" (a document outlining the scope of the ED's authority) should be developed by the board and reviewed every two years and when there are substantial changes made to the ED's job description. Once these limitations are established, the board should abide by these definitions. The ED must have the confidence to act without fear that the board will interfere in the areas that have been identified as the ED's responsibility.

9. **Develop a governance policy.**

   The organization should also develop a governance policy that defines the type of governance model that is in effect and that describes the roles and responsibilities of the board. This is a useful tool for distinguishing the responsibilities of the ED from those of the board.

10. **Incorporate equity into board job descriptions.**

    Revise board members' job descriptions to include knowledge and skills for creating racial and other forms of equity. The board should understand clearly its role in approving an anti-racism policy and monitoring its implementation, and ensure that professional development for board members integrates anti-racism into the board's roles and core responsibilities.

11. **Create an Anti-Racism Committee.**

    Create an Anti-Racism Committee that connects racialized people and White allies who want to challenge racism in the organization. A committee that includes board members and staff will ensure that people at all levels of the organization can share information, strengthen their skills, and advocate for change.

12. Mandate racial equity.

Connect racial equity to the mission and mandate of the organization, and to the role of the executive director. The Maple Leaf Centre serves people who experience racism in addition to other barriers to employment. An executive director who directly understands the impact of racism on immigrants and on racialized people seeking employment brings this knowledge as additional, relevant qualifications to the role.

A TRUE STORY Using Organizational Authority to Shift Power: Anti-Racism Leadership & Strategies

In the course of doing this work together and separately for over a decade, people constantly ask us about examples of organizations that have developed "best practices" in the area of anti-racism. People are hungry for a list of "Dos and Don'ts" that they can follow in their own organization, or at least use to challenge others who are not doing enough. In this section, we have tried to capture moments in the life of different organizations in which people have tried to make effective interventions to challenge racism and build greater equity. Much of what needs to happen is a revision of the formal and informal practices of an organization, and we spend a lot of time rewriting human resource manuals, revising policies, job descriptions, and program guidelines, as well as developing new procedures.

There is a danger that with this focus on the "systems" of an organization, we neglect the importance of the political will and commitment of individuals who can use the power and the resources at their disposal to advance anti-racism work. We are also concerned that in this section, the critique of organizational leaders (management and union) might lead people to conclude that people with organizational power only impede anti-racism organizational change. The good news is, of course, that there are people who use their authority well to challenge racism in the systems of their organizations and to ensure staff have appropriate opportunities to unlearn racism.

In this true story we introduce you to two people who have grappled with both personal and organizational challenges in order to determine how best to use their organizational authority to promote anti-racism work. Their successes as well as the challenges they have experienced over time have led to some hard-earned wisdom about the effective uses of their authority to sustain this work and to shift power.

Hazelle Palmer and Rainer Soegtrop are senior managers in two very different organizations. Hazelle is the executive director of a unique community health centre, and Rainer is a vice-president of a large social housing institution, both in Toronto. They are held accountable to their organizations in different ways, work in places with very dissimilar cultures, and their organizations serve somewhat distinct client populations. They are also of different gender and race, and this too shapes their experience of the consequences of championing anti-racism initiatives.

We asked Rainer and Hazelle a number of questions about their leadership roles and their strategies for doing anti-racism work in their organizations. Their answers, from which we quote extensively, form the basis of this true story.

HAZELLE PALMER: An Executive Director with a Vision

Hazelle Palmer is the executive director of Planned Parenthood of Toronto (PPT). PPT is "a community-based, pro-choice agency committed to the principles of equity and to providing accessible and inclusive services that promote healthy sexuality and informed decision-making to the people of the City of Toronto. PPT is affiliated with the Planned Parenthood Federation of Canada and is a community health centre that offers a variety of medical information, education, and outreach services in primary and sexual health care."

Organizational Context

The mission statement of PPT, quoted above, conveys just how central equity is to the organization's values and services. People's right to the information and services they need have been central to the organization from the beginning. The decision to be "pro-choice" was a political one when the organization was formed in 1961. At that time, the dissemination of information on birth control was illegal in Canada, and it was only after a massive campaign by PPT and others that the criminal code was amended in 1969.

PPT now runs a number of community-based sexual and reproductive health programs for women and youth in the City of Toronto that promote healthy sexuality and informed decision-making. Volunteers, in particular peer volunteers, play an active and key role at Planned Parenthood of Toronto, providing information on sexual and reproductive health directly to clients with support from PPT staff. The agency also offers a full range of primary and sexual health-care services to youth aged thirteen to twenty-five. An innovative telephone information service offers teens a confidential and anonymous way to acquire sexual health information.

Hazelle places a great deal of emphasis on PPT's philosophy of choice. It is not something she takes for granted as there is an active anti-choice movement in Canada. She comments, "The anti-choice movement equates pro-choice with abortion. But being pro-choice means supporting a woman's choice, whether it is to have a child or not. We need to break down the stigma attached to teenage pregnancy so that young women can make the choice they want to make. It also includes having access to sexual health and the freedom to be sexually active and safe. It's about people's right to advocate for their rights and freedoms."

Factors Supporting Anti-Racism

A lot of work in the area of anti-racism and anti-oppression has been done with the staff of PPT. In 1998, when Hazelle joined the organization, there was a perception that PPT served mostly White, straight, middle-class university students or women. Over the years, the organization made strong commitments to providing services that were accessible and equitable to youth, people with disabilities, gay and lesbian people, and to transgender and transsexual communities.

In staff discussions about supporting people's right to choose, there have been important agreements reached about supporting people's right to self-identify and to have access to services that are appropriate to their sexual and other life choices. Anti-racism and anti-oppression work is placed in the context of this tradition of defending people's rights. "We start with people's passion for the work, for issues in communities about rights, about being able to have a choice. We then connect the anti-discrimination policy to people's rights in these areas, and their right to address experiences of not being treated well or being denied a choice," Hazelle explains.

Staff who work at PPT are often drawn by the agency's commitment to creating an inclusive and equitable work and service environment. Hazelle is proud to say that PPT has a reputation "of being very youth positive, sex positive, and gay positive … I hear staff say, 'I love working here because I can be who I am here, I can be out here.' It makes a difference." There are real connections between the mission of the organization, the reasons people are drawn to work there, and anti-oppression work.

Factors Working against Anti-Racism

The board is committed to being pro-choice and to ensuring that services are accessible to youth, and is open to doing more work on how racism affects access to services and employment in the agency. At times the board has chosen to use the language of diversity to have discussions about difference in the organization. For some, diversity means sexual identity and sexuality, for others it implies having different professions represented among board members, and there are those for whom it signifies dealing with the impact of racism. The ambiguity of the language has meant that the more difficult discussions about racism and inequity have sometimes been deferred.

In addition, some of the anti-racism work done with staff in the past has been less than effective. Past staff training focused on people's attitudes and did not address organizational systems or power. Unfortunately, the conversations became focused on interpersonal tensions between people. These sessions became the forum for people to vent about unaddressed issues and conflicts in the organization. Huge silences developed and nobody wanted to talk about issues of discrimination and racism.

How Social Identities Affect Organizational Authority

Hazelle is an able-bodied, Black woman who was born in England and grew up in Montreal. There are particular challenges to being in a position of organizational authority in the body of a woman of colour. Hazelle describes her experience in this and other organizations as one of being constantly tested and subjected to offensive comments. For example, a co-worker once asked Hazelle, "Why do you people leave your country when it's so cold here?" Hazelle's reply was, "Oh, did Quebec separate over the weekend? Why didn't I find out about it?"

Hazelle joined PPT in 1998 as a communications manager and was the only racialized person on the management team. From the first day on the job, co-workers who were surprised at the quality of her work were constantly testing her. Just prior to becoming the executive director, Hazelle experienced racism from a former member of the board. "I had gone to a board meeting to make a presentation on a particular issue. I ended up fielding a lot of questions from one particular member that I found inappropriate. She wouldn't look at me as she spoke, but looked at everyone else as if I wasn't there. I thought it was very disrespectful and I left the meeting extremely upset. As I thought about it, I began to remember other things that had happened but that I had simply accommodated just to get through the day. I remembered the number of times I interacted with this board

Jamie Slater

member, and she would either walk away from me or turn her back on me and behave in ways that were unprofessional. I wrote the Executive Director a letter that stated clearly the impact of her actions. Her comments during the meeting had the impact of raising questions about my qualifications to do my job."

The situation was not handled well by the organization, and after an unsuccessful effort at mediation, the matter was dropped. In considering the offer of the interim executive director position, Hazelle had to reflect on whether this incident would affect how she would work and communicate with the board. Since then the board has been successful at increasing the racial diversity of its members and has worked with Hazelle to establish a healthy working relationship.

As the executive director, Hazelle has a responsibility to promote the organization within its sector, with funders, and with the broader community. Here, too, Hazelle finds she is treated differently from others because of her social identities. She describes some typical moments during meetings where there are often few racialized people. "At times it is like you are under a magnifying glass. If you talk to another African-descent person, people notice. They think, 'Oh, they must be friends. I wonder what they're talking about.' It's discouraging because we are working in a sector that is progressive and community based, that works from a community development and anti-oppression framework."

Hazelle describes the effect moments like these have: "It's like being tested and being watched. I went to a meeting last year and I was the only person of colour (not the only Black person, the only person of colour) there. It was mostly executive directors and board chairs, and it was a gathering that brought people together from all over Canada. It was pretty isolating in the room. And yet anti-racism and equity are still not on the agenda of this organization. The response when I commented on this to someone in the room was 'Why don't you raise it?' I'm tired of talking about it. Where is the commitment of the organization?"

There are also particular expectations of senior managers of colour from racialized communities. People in the communities expect that racialized managers will open the doors of the agency to other people of colour seeking employment or looking for appropriate services. It is in some ways a legitimate expectation since a community development approach aims to make the organization a resource for all communities. However, there are times when racialized people are more demanding of executive directors of colour, either as employees or as service recipients. There are no similar expectations of "loyalty to the community" made of White executive directors. This adds to the stresses of an already demanding position in the organization.

Some Risks Connected to Promoting Anti-Racism Organizational Change

Making anti-racism organizational change a priority can be particularly difficult for a Black executive director. There's a risk that anti-racism becomes identified as the executive director's personal issue rather than an area important for the organization to pursue. "It can be seen as a personal agenda that I am imposing. If there isn't support from staff and from the board, I can be seen to be creating rifts in the organization in order to pursue a personal interest. So it's particularly important for me to ensure there are policies in place, and systemic reasons for doing this work."

Hazelle is also vulnerable to the common stereotypes about Black women who speak up about racism. "If you challenge issues around anti-racism in particular, you could be considered 'an angry Black woman,' a disruptive influence. People say you're taking advantage of people's fear of challenging the executive director, or of their fear of being called racist. A worker might say, 'I can't challenge this because my ED is Black.'"

Things are further complicated because people within the organization focus primarily on Hazelle's organizational authority and may dismiss the fact that she can also be subjected to racism and sexism. "People seem to think that I walk around with the authority of an executive director in the world. They don't realize that the power and authority is localized; it's true within PPT but as soon as I walk out of the door to go to the store, I become a Black woman, with all that entails."

Another challenge faced by racialized executive directors is that people assume they are experts on anti-racism. "Everyone looks to you to figure out what to do when an issue arises. You're not allowed to be just as confused about the situation. I think if I was a White executive director there would be more ownership by others—'What do we do about this?'—rather than everyone looking to me. I'm not an anti-racism expert. When was that supposed to have happened—at birth?"

Acting Strategically

Use the Policy as a Process for Linking Anti-Racism to the Core Business of the Organization

The organization was pressured to develop a policy on discrimination and harassment by one of its primary funders. Rather than simply crafting a policy on paper, PPT connected the anti-discrimination process to people's passion for equity in communities, for protecting people's rights, and for their right to make their own choices. The policy was seen as an important vehicle for ensuring that people would be able to address any experiences of not being treated well or being denied a choice.

Use a Community Development Model

Hazelle describes PPT's community development model in this way: "You can overload staff with initiatives—now we're doing this, now we're doing that. The adoption of the Community Development Model was really a good initiative for the organization because it brought back working with the community in a different way. It moves the organization away from parachuting into communities and telling them what to do and how to do it. Instead, we become a resource to the community to build their own tools to empower themselves."

The organization chart for PPT places the agency in the middle of Toronto's communities (see figure 4). At one end of the chart are the communities from which the board members are recruited and to whom the organization is accountable. In the middle are the staff of PPT, providing programs and services to the diverse communities of Toronto. On the other side of the chart are volunteers and partners that are also from the various communities. "At the end of the day," Hazelle says, "what you really want is for the communities to be able to direct all of the programming that you do, and you want to be able to pull them in to act as resources. They are at both ends of this process."

PPT used a large visual representation of a community development continuum that was placed on a wall and made the focus of discussion for staff. It was a way of developing a program planning model (see figure 5). "We wanted to move away from having the organization parachuting into communities and telling people what to do, and why we are the ones who should do it for them. Instead, we should be a resource to the community to build their own tools and to do things themselves. What we did over a series of meetings is have people use this continuum to literally locate themselves on the chart. It led to really interesting conversations between people about their work. A physician may think of herself as doing direct service work with hardly any work in the community. But if she sees herself as part of a team, then the health promotion staff on the team bring things full circle. It's in the community and can bring back learning from the community that shapes the services we provide. Everybody got a different sense of where people were on the continuum. People gained a new respect for the work and the contribution people make to the organization. We also began to understand the connection between how we really reflect a community and how that makes us more responsive to the community."

Figure 4: PPT's Community Development Model

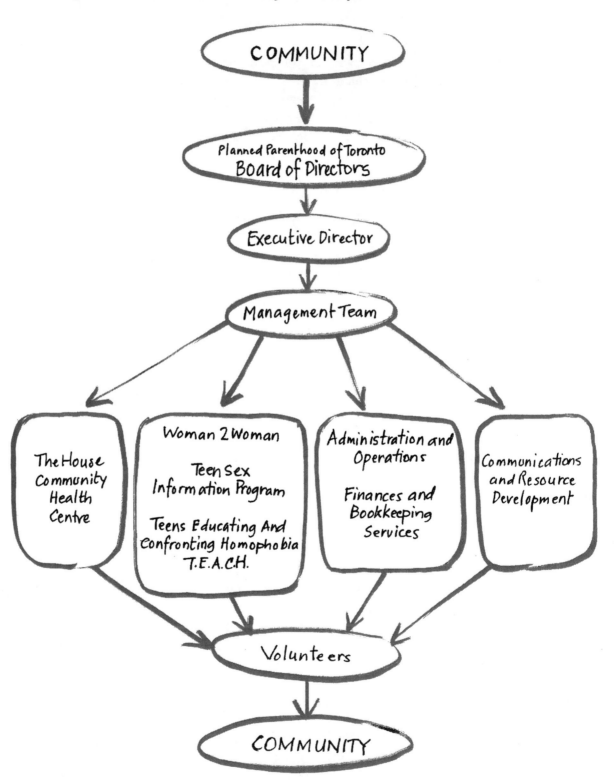

Figure 5: The Community Development Continuum

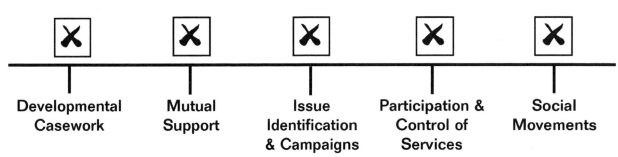

| Developmental Casework | Mutual Support | Issue Identification & Campaigns | Participation & Control of Services | Social Movements |

Developmental Casework is described as "providing service on a one-to-one basis." It is distinguished from the traditional approach to service delivery in that it "aims to develop the capacity of individuals to make informed decisions and advocate for their own needs," rather than making the individual dependent on the service provider.

Mutual Support, as the title suggests, aims to connect the service recipient to others who have similar needs and with "strengthening the natural relationships that a person has with family friends and neighbours."

Issue identification and Campaigns is a process that brings "together the various 'natural networks' and individuals sharing a common issue to take some joint action." In the previous two stages, people deal with issues on a personal level. At this point in the continuum, people become involved in campaigns at a social, political, or community level; this point "marks the transition from participation for survival to participation to achieve change."

Participation and Control of Services suggests that at this point people "attempt to exercise greater control by joining groups or forming new organizations." They may join a committee, a board of directors, or a community advisory group. Service providers must create ways for community members to really influence the way the organization operates.

Social Movements are a way for people to seek "fundamental change in decisions that affect their lives and in the way those decisions are made. The focus could be government of another major institution that exercises a great deal of control over people's lives. The strategies may involve community organization, discussions, presentation of briefs, use of media, protests or any one of a number of techniques."

This model is not intended to represent a linear process. People "can be at different points in the continuum on different issues." Diana Ralph, a researcher involved in community development for many years, comments that "we would be making an ethnocentric and patronizing assumption if we were to think that white middle-class staff can or should develop 'poor' people." She adds that few people move smoothly through the points on the continuum, and that some people are drawn in to social movements before they access services.

Source: Adapted from Jackson et al., "The Community Development Continuum" in Ontario Prevention Clearing House, *The Community Development Resource Package.*[5]

Jamie Slater

The values of the organization also reinforce an anti-racism approach to the work in which PPT serves the full range of communities and is removed from the position of expert. "We're doing many more consultations and needs assessments which results in more diverse and responsive programs. We don't get caught in the trap of trying to identify 'target populations.' This approach allows people to decide how they want to fit into our organization. Our values include being client centred, equity seeking, inclusive, and accessible to all communities. We also want to provide holistic health care that tends to the physical, spiritual, and emotional well-being of the people who come here for services. Anyone should be able to come though the door and be comfortable here as an employee, a volunteer or a client."

Integrate Anti-Racism into Employment Practices

"The way we do things, from the job postings to the interview questions that we ask, are a way for us to gauge where people are in their understanding of equity and community development. We want to know where we need to start with those staff when they join the organization. In the interviews, people are asked to provide definitions for some terms that are fundamental to the mission and values of PPT. Some of the terms asked about include 'sex positive,' 'sexual reproductive rights,' 'gay positive,' 'equity,' and 'anti-discrimination.'

"People's responses are always interesting. Some people go on at great length, others hem and haw a lot, and then there are those who are really quick and to the point. It's less about getting the right answer and more about getting a sense of the person's own development in this area, their analysis of the issues. Have they thought about these issues at all? Are they open and interested or do they seem uncomfortable and simply want to get on to the next question."

PPT's job postings make it clear that a commitment to being sex, gay, and youth positive is essential to working for the agency. Hazelle and the staff took care to develop a statement for the postings that would encourage a greater diversity of people to apply. It states: "Demonstrated commitment to equity goals and principles, sexual and reproductive rights and to being youth positive, gay positive and sex positive."

The pressure from funders has helped to make the organization today very different from what it was in 1998. Now, it is a given that staff must have a commitment to anti-discrimination if they want to work at PPT. They also have a deeper understanding of what is intended by the notion of "healthy sexuality" and how it is connected to their daily work and PPT's core values. Managers and the board have an understanding of what it means to be an equity-seeking, inclusive, and accessible organization.

Create a Staff Equity Committee with a Clear Mandate and Appropriate Supports

The Staff Equity Committee was created to provide leadership on equity issues in the agency. It meets once a month and takes on specific tasks, such as reviewing materials produced by PPT to ensure they are inclusive or revising the vision statement on equity. The committee also facilitates discussions with the entire staff once a year. As with all good anti-racism work, these discussions can be complex and are often turbulent as people work through conflicting ideas, attitudes, and learning needs. There are times when the executive director needs to step in to support and guide the committee as the inevitable tempests occur. Hazelle recalls, "In October 2003, the committee sponsored an anti-racism workshop for all staff. We invited in an external facilitator for the day, and at the end of the day, the group exploded! During the day, people found ways to make the conversation comfortable for White people, but did not pay the same kind of attention to the people of colour in the room. By the end of the afternoon the people of colour were so upset; people were in tears, others were really angry. I thought, 'Oh my God! How am I ever going to pull the staff together again?

"I decided to have a follow-up session in February. This time I asked people to work in two separate groups: 'White skinned' people (a designation the people in the group chose for themselves) in one and people of colour in the other. People were so upset with me when I suggested this. They thought I was separating people from each other, that it would make things worse between the two groups. I insisted that we do this because it was clear that people in the two groups had different needs. Each group had its own facilitator, and I removed myself from the process till the end of the day. As a Black executive director, I didn't want the 'White skinned' employees to be anxious about what they said in front of me, and I didn't want to join the people of colour caucus and give that group more weight because I was on it.

"When I joined them at the end of the day, there was an amazing openness—we almost had a big group hug! It was clear that the people of colour just needed to be heard without having to take care of 'White-skinned' people. And 'White-skinned' people needed a chance to say things without getting it wrong and worrying about not knowing enough about racism. By the end of the session we had a new Equity Implementation Committee that had a whole new level of energy and enthusiasm."

A Diverse Staff May Not Automatically Lead to Racially Appropriate Programs

Managers cannot assume that staff from a particular group will be more knowledgeable about anti-oppression work than others. They probably experience discrimination but they may not necessarily have the tools to analyze how these forms of discrimination operate in the organization's programs and services. "The organization must provide all staff with opportunities to discuss program planning, anti-racism and anti-oppression. We all have to learn those things. Employment equity seems to say that if you have a more diverse organization, you're done. In fact, you're just beginning; you have to ensure that there are supports and mechanisms in place to make things work more inclusively. You don't automatically become an equity-seeking organization simply because there are different bodies in the room."

Foster Leadership Skills in the Community

In programs like TEACH, which stands for Teens Educating and Confronting Homophobia, PPT recruits youth who do anti-homophobia education in the community. "We teach them presentation skills and we also teach about anti-oppression. We're enhancing their own ability to provide leadership, to work with groups in a way that is inclusive. They have the skills to bring people together to talk about the reality of their different identities and experiences. The facilitators become leaders in their own communities and use their own stories as catalysts for discussions; it's work that makes them so vulnerable but is a powerful way to talk with peers about their attitudes and ideas about sexuality and identity. In the process, PPT has become a leading provider of anti-homophobia education."

Participate in Anti-Racism Projects with Community Partners

In collaboration with Parkdale Community Health Centre, Rexdale Community Health Centre, Sistering, and Women's Health in Women's Hands, PPT has undertaken a project to examine barriers faced by Black women and women of colour when trying to access primary health care services. It is a three-year study that began in July 2004. "Although there have been a lot of studies looking at barriers to access in health care, little has been documented about the particular barriers faced by Black women and women of colour. This project provides a forum for discussing the fact that racism is real. It is a primary determinant of health. This study will go a long way to making this point clear. It raises important questions about whether the existing model of care works for these groups of women."

Hazelle's Reflections on Using Organizational Authority Well

"Executive directors have the responsibility and the opportunity to really bring about organizational change. It's important to develop the knowledge and the analysis we need to do this and to challenge ourselves in this area. While we should not expect to be experts, we need to acknowledge that we really can make a difference. As executive directors we are instructed by the board of directors and given a mandate to take the organization into the future. I can choose to be an administrator or I can be a visionary leader. I want to make sure that when I leave PPT, they remember not that I was a Black executive director, but that I helped PPT to become more reflective, think critically about the work it does, reach its mission, and challenge itself to do better.

"I've been influencing this organization for a long time. I need to find a balance between leading and not trampling on other points of view that must influence where PPT needs to go. I've found that people want you to lead them; if they feel they can trust your leadership, they will come along. It's not always easy to do, but it is deeply satisfying work."

Figure 6: PPT's **Equity Vision**

Our equity vision is to build an agency that is welcoming, safe, accessible, and inclusive.

We are committed to

- ➤ creating and implementing an accessible anti-discrimination/equity policy which promotes our vision and which includes procedures for handling issues of discrimination

- ➤ promoting equity principles as an integral part of our ongoing activities

- ➤ developing and maintaining ongoing relationships with diverse populations and communities

- ➤ encouraging and creating real opportunities for staff, service-user and volunteer participation at all levels

- ➤ creating and implementing hiring and recruitment practices that are inclusive

- ➤ ensuring that all PPT print, visual, and other promotional materials reflect diversity and inclusivity and present positive images

- ➤ promoting and conducting ongoing anti-discrimination/equity training, and

- ➤ taking a leadership role in promoting equity within our agency and within the community

Approved by the Board August 21, 1998
Reviewed 2001/2002

RAINER SOEGTROP: Leadership in Times of Resistance

Rainer Soegtrop

Rainer Soegtrop is currently the vice-president of Shared Services, a division of the Toronto Community Housing Corporation (TCHC). TCHC is the second largest social housing provider in North America, providing services to over 164,000 tenants in 57,500 households. Residents of TCHC communities include seniors, families, singles, refugees, recent immigrants to Canada, and people with special needs.

Organizational Context

When we first met Rainer, he was the director of operations for the Metropolitan Toronto Housing Company Limited (MTHCL), a municipal social housing provider that served 26,000 tenants, 75 per cent of whom were seniors, in 20,700 units, and employed 450 staff. Reporting to Rainer were twelve property managers who were the largest and most influential group of middle managers at MTHCL. They had the most direct contact with tenants and superintendents in the buildings. Each building operated by MTHCL had a superintendent and custodians who were responsible for maintaining the building and grounds; each of these superintendents reported to a property manager.

In addition, there were social workers who worked with tenants to ensure that they had access to the social services they needed and that seniors, in particular, had the supports they required to continue living in the apartments. As part of the change process, these positions were changed to community health promoters, and the emphasis shifted from doing casework with individuals to a community development approach that involved tenants and the broader community.

The tenant population had been changing over the last fifteen years and had become increasingly diverse in terms of race, ethnicity, first language, and country of origin. All MTHCL senior managers and the majority of staff were White, with racialized employees in the organization being highly represented among recent hires and front-line positions. In 1991, a new general manager came into the organization and held broad consultations with tenants of the company as part of a strategic planning process. Many tenants at the consultations spoke about their experience of racism with other tenants and with some MTHCL staff. It was clear something needed to be done, and the general manager charged Rainer with the responsibility for leading the effort to deal with racism at MTHCL.

The anti-racism initiative was one of a number of change initiatives undertaken by the MTHCL. In addition to anti-racism, the strategic directions identified the need for improved fiscal management, downsizing, tenant participation and community development, organizational decentralization, long-term care, and anti-ableism.

Factors Supporting Anti-Racism

The tenants of MTHCL reflected the population and immigration trends of the City of Toronto. At least 40 per cent of tenants were racialized people, many of whom had first languages other than English. Tenants also included single-parent families, people with disabilities, and a high proportion of women. The new general manager understood that racism among tenants and staff was a serious problem for the company and was willing to dedicate resources to addressing it. Anti-Racism made good business sense. As Rainer explains, "It sensitizes people to those issues, it changes them, makes them better at delivering services and operating in a diverse work environment and community. Tenants were constantly transferring out of our bachelor units and this was costly. How could we create an environment that would entice people to live in less desirable accommodations? Well, what if we created supportive communities, places that don't just welcome different cooking smells, but are really good about anti-racism work?"

People newly hired to promote a community development approach to social housing understood the importance of anti-racism work for creating healthy communities and building a work environment free of discrimination. They were strong allies and promoters of the anti-racism initiatives.

Factors Working against Anti-Racism

In the early 1990s, managers and front-line staff in the buildings were predominantly male, and the majority of social workers or community health promoters were female. Most other women in MTHCL were in lower paid clerical positions. As with many organizations in Toronto, there has been a history of hiring people known to those already in the organization, with the result that the majority of property managers were Anglo-Saxon and male.

Staff of MTHCL had been aware of the racism among tenants prior to the arrival of the new general manager, but as Rainer describes it, "We'd been refusing to do anything about the race problems in the company partly because we were a landlord and therefore we were neutral ... the whole thing was masked by ageism, by assuming that seniors [the majority of tenants] can't learn to change their behaviour so there's no point trying to do anything."

With regard to racism among staff, Rainer comments, "There was this system that reinforced White, particularly Scottish and Irish, values and culture; it wasn't a welcoming organization to different backgrounds."

Additional Factors at Work

MTHCL had a good reputation in Toronto as an innovative and progressive institutional provider and manager of social housing. "Social housing management by definition involves a richer cross-section of social and community issues and protagonists than almost any other municipal program." Despite this emphasis on community and social service, most employees wanted to focus on the physical maintenance of buildings. However, many of the seniors who were tenants relied on the building staff for human contact and support, and there was quite a bit of interaction between staff and tenants. When the demographics changed from seniors to families and singles, and from predominantly White people to a more racially diverse population, staff were even more reluctant to become involved in the social problems of tenants and especially to deal with racism in the community. There was a split between a "social work" versus a "property management" approach to social housing. The organization had a "fairly traditional, hierarchical, command-based culture" that kept it relatively isolated from its communities, placing its primary focus on buildings rather than people.

How Social Identities Affect Organizational Authority

Rainer's decision to actively promote anti-racism work at MTHCL is powerful because he is a White male senior manager who chooses to use his organizational authority to push this area of change. As a European immigrant to Canada, he understands some of the challenges of settlement, but as a White male senior manager, he is not himself the target of most forms of discrimination. In this regard, his experience differs quite dramatically from what Hazelle Palmer has experienced as outlined in her story above.

While many staff with less organizational power have resisted the agenda of anti-racism, they have not accused Rainer of having an agenda from which he would personally benefit. Since a number of middle managers report directly to him, or are in less senior positions, they have not publicly challenged his decisions regarding anti-racism. Rainer uses both his social identities and his organizational authority to either persuade or require employees of MTHCL to take action on racism.

What made Rainer decide to take such a strong leadership role in promoting anti-racism organizational change? He describes it as an intersection between personal growth and development and the organization's push to deal with racism. Organizationally, the general manager was making it clear that Rainer's job included dealing with racism, and he needed to act. At a more personal level, he describes a moment in an anti-racism educational session in which he arrived at an important personal insight. He says, "I recognized the way I should be handling this intellectually or emotionally is to admit that I'm a racist." He describes that moment as a liberating event. Why liberating?

Personal reflection on his background as a North European led Rainer to see himself as a product of that culture and how it has shaped him. He describes an awkward exchange with an African-descent colleague about an Italian employee, during which Rainer commented, "Africa starts south of Rome," an expression he had heard as a child in Europe. When he recognized the effect this had on his colleague, Rainer had to grapple with his behaviour. "How did that come out of my mouth? Why do these things pop out, where do they come from and how do I learn from them?" He apologized to his colleague and reflected on the roots of these ideas.

The more he thought about the environment in which he had been raised, the more it made sense that he would have learned racist ideas. "Reading books about Little Black Sambo when I was five and six probably had some effect on me. Almost fifty years of having my world view coloured by a colonial structure in which notions of progress were White and Western, believing I was entitled to certain things, was bound to have an impact. I realized that of course I was racist, and what I really need to think about is trying not to be one, and when I'm challenged on my racism to try and learn from it. It was totally freeing."

This is not a typical response for most people who are trying to come to grips with how they've learned racism. Rainer found the notion of "co-responsibility" useful for coming to terms with White privilege and racism. This concept of co-responsibility comes from Willy Brandt, a German who fought Hitler, joined the resistance, and was later the chancellor of Germany (1969–74). Speaking about the Holocaust, Brandt says, "Even though I had left Germany very early, even though I'd never been a supporter of Hitler—to put it mildly—I can't exclude myself from a certain responsibility. Or co-responsibility. ... I identify with my people. I mean with the people from whom those who had committed such terrible things

had emerged." Despite his own fierce opposition to Hitler and the Nazis, Brandt shares responsibility with all Germans for having allowed Hitler to come to power and not doing what they could to stop the Nazis once they were the government.

As we listened to Rainer explain this notion of co-responsibility, we talked about its applications to racism and colonialism. For example, the descendants of settlers in Canada may not have directly carried out British and French policies against Aboriginal people, yet they are co-responsible for previous and current impacts of colonialism. Similarly, individual white people may not be responsible for the systemic racism in their organizations, but they are co-responsible for how those systems result in unearned benefits for White people.

Rainer Soegtrop

Some Risks Connected to Promoting Anti-Racism Organizational Change

Though Rainer's social identities did not make him vulnerable to attack, and he had considerable organizational power as the director of operations, there were still risks to pushing an organizational change agenda that was unwelcome to some board members and to a number of staff and tenants. People opposed to anti-racism initiatives were creative in the ways in which they sought to undermine Rainer and other anti-racism advocates and the change agenda they came to represent.

A few managers went to the general manager and complained about the "radical people" Rainer was bringing in to do community development and anti-racism work. Some managers attempted to persuade the new general manager that Rainer was advising her badly and that the change agenda would backfire. People uncomfortable with the language of anti-racism and who preferred more familiar terms such as cultural sensitivity and multiculturalism demanded that the general manager review the definitions of racism being introduced by the anti-racism initiative. In particular, they resented the focus on power and White privilege that were now part of the content of anti-racism discussions.

In addition, these changes were taking place when MTHCL was under threat financially and had to downsize. In the midst of this crisis, Rainer was working with others in the organization to create a new community services unit that employed community development workers, and he was changing the job descriptions of property managers to include community development and anti-racism. "I was shaking a system that traditionally felt quite secure. I was forcing managers to apply for new jobs whereas the tradition would have been to just appoint them to new positions." Some fairly senior managers and the managers' association tried to challenge the company's right to make people compete for the new jobs.

How did Rainer work with other anti-racism advocates to anticipate resistance and develop tactics to build broad support for anti-racism despite these attacks? In the following section are the strategies he suggests for anti-racism change agents at all levels of the organization, and for senior managers in particular.

Acting Strategically

Begin with an Analysis of Power in the Organization

Rainer points out that "many elements and factors interact in the change process. The company actually changes itself through a complex, uneven, and messy process in response to policies, senior management requirements, challenges from tenants, training and learning programs, and numerous other processes during which jobs, issues, events, individuals, priorities, and corporate culture are changed." Because it can be so complex, the best place to start is with analysis.

"Organizations are complex social systems and administrative systems and political systems," he continues. "There needs to be a strategic analysis of power in the organization, the positioning of change and elements of resistance. You also need an evaluation of belief systems, values, communication systems and networks."

Anti-racism change work is transformative—it aims to change the organization at its core. To succeed, it requires a thorough understanding of how power operates in the organization: the values that are considered essential, how decisions are made and how they are carried out, the ways in which people learn about what is important and what is peripheral, and how people are formally and informally rewarded or punished. Power is at the root of all these systems. A systemic analysis of racism and other forms of discrimination reduces the tendency to blame individual people for organizational inequities and demonstrates how regular organizational systems reinforce power inequities. Furthermore, it shifts the focus from "Are you saying I'm a racist?" to "How are the systems of our organization reproducing inequity?"

Stick to Anti-Racism

When reflecting on the process at MTHCL, Rainer recalls, "We did need to get to other forms of oppression, and we did get to them a couple of years later, but the deepest change piece was race. That was the thing that most people were threatened by. If you try to do a broad menu of race and anti-oppression change at the same time, it just doesn't get off the ground." Furthermore, attempting to address all forms of discrimination all at once rarely succeeds. People often become overwhelmed by the change agenda and little progress is made. At times, raising other areas of discrimination is a tactic of opponents to anti-racism that is used to diffuse the focus on racism. When anti-racism organizational change is done well, it lays the groundwork for successful anti-oppression work.

Use a Community Development Model

Like Hazelle, a key aspect of Rainer's strategy is linking anti-racism organizational change to community development work. Rainer sees the importance of "applying to the organization notions that created space for different ideas and supporting certain groups that had previously been unsupported. It requires advocating on certain issues, taking the necessary time, realizing that change is something that is political between groups and is mediated by policies."

Rainer emphasizes that his "model of organizational change is internal community development! Organizational development and strategic planning are bankrupt concepts with regard to change. They assume either stable environments conducive to planning for a predictable future, or organizations that can be mapped, analyzed, and psycho-analyzed by senior managers. Community development recognizes role conflict, power analysis, and the identification of issues. It uses them dynamically to effect change through advocacy, confrontation, open meetings and group problem-solving." Key assets of a community development model involve

- placing the focus on people, processes, and issues rather than on policy and organizational structure; "it looks at organizations as social systems and not just administrative functions"
- assuming that the people who live in the communities have important knowledge about what works and what doesn't work in social housing and that they should have a say in the decisions that affect them
- appreciating community agencies and groups as important resources for establishing appropriate programs and service delivery
- recognizing individual and social forms of discrimination and inequity as factors that undermine communities; therefore, anti-racism is an essential part of community development work

Focus on Implementation when Writing an Anti-Racism Policy

Most organizations have a policy to address discrimination and harassment in the organization and to outline procedures for staff and clients to follow should they want to file a human rights complaint. Similar policies were in place at MTHCL, and of course, the Ontario Human Rights Code defines organizational and individual responsibilities in this area. However, "the practice and culture of MTHCL was unchanged and relatively unaffected" by these policies. "Our intention was not to create a policy that people would refer to when they got into trouble, but to create an organization that would reflect the content of the policy ... it would be a place where what we described in the policy would actually happen."

"The traditional approach," Rainer explains, "would have been to create a race relations office, hire a minority person to run it and watch this office fight with the rest of the organization for eternity. This is the 'paschal lamb' approach of creating an Office, feeling better about the problem, and then ritually purging the organization of the equity officer from time to time because there is no change or the change is too radical. ... If you want to have a policy sit on a shelf, hire an equity officer. People also then see that responsibility for anti-racism located in just one office and not in their own."

Making Implementation Everyone's Work

According to Rainer, "policy staff are useful for developing and writing policies but operating staff have to make them their own and implement them. Without action and the right programs to implement the policies, there is no change." For policies to bring about real change, an organization needs to involve community agencies and board members as well as a cross-section of staff in their development. This builds connections across the organization and a shared understanding of the intent of the policies.

It is equally important to ensure meaningful representation and engagement of people of colour in the process of writing the policy; to use language that is strong and clear—if the policy is ambiguous, it leaves lots of room for dilution and reinterpretation; and to make sure the policy builds in directions that point clearly to an action plan and that implementation is made everyone's responsibility. Front-line staff need to embrace the change and put it into action in their everyday jobs and, as much as possible, implement it in their own terms. Not only is this liberating for them but it also creates a powerful commitment for change within the organization.

Rainer's strategy involved all staff who were already part of the organization and a few new people who brought with them an infusion of innovative ideas, energy, and skills. Rainer points out, "It is very important to put this responsibility in the actual job descriptions of all staff, to evaluate their performance on the new criteria, and to hire and promote staff consistent with the new criteria." Senior managers have greater responsibility for bringing about change than front-line workers, and this should be reflected in the performance management process.

"The active involvement and support from senior management is critical to the success of the change effort. Support by senior management signals to staff that the change is important and cannot be avoided. The values introduced by the change have to be consistently 'lived' by senior managers publicly and informally." They can demonstrate this by finding additional budgets to resource anti-racism action properly; be prepared to act during organizational crises that arise as part of the change process; and reinforce new behaviours and confer status on new anti-racism activities within the organization. "Ideally, they should do so passionately on key occasions."

Anticipate and Work Directly with Resistance

A key to Rainer's strategy was either to bring middle managers on board or neutralize their resistance. It was clear that the people with the power to block or to bring about the change were the managers who supervised most of the staff, assigned work, had regular contact with the tenants, and paid salaries. They were also the most resistant as they were the most threatened by this new model, since it gave front-line workers power and access to decision-making. This was a radical change for property managers who were used to having sole authority and a great deal of autonomy in these areas.

So Rainer decided to make the property managers responsible for leading anti-racism work in the company. "Until they bought the change, nothing was going to happen, so we had to get past them to the front-line people; the easiest way to get past them was to co-opt them as leaders of change." In the worst-case scenario, they would simply not block the change, and in the best case, they would provide real leadership.

All the property managers formally accepted the leadership challenge, agreed to formulate plans, and agreed to participate in anti-racism learning sessions to support their role. Most property managers needed help to understand anti-racism, and while some just mimicked what they should be doing, there were others who became genuine advocates. Offering them the position as leaders gave them a certain prestige in the organization. They made presentations to senior managers and to the board of directors, met frequently, talked through the issues and developed common work plans for implementing anti-racism. They set goals for redoing promotional materials and revised purchasing and contracting procedures to remove barriers faced by racialized business owners and contractors. They also held training sessions with all staff to discuss the relevance of the policy to their jobs, the use of translation and interpretation with tenants, and other aspects of anti-racism service delivery.

The language of anti-racism was new and not entirely comfortable for people on the board, for staff, and for the tenant communities. Rainer knew that the draft policy would get blocked if it did not include elements that people were more familiar with and would understand. Therefore, he insisted on including a clause related to multiculturalism in the new policy. It would make it more palatable while maintaining the integrity of the change process. "What resulted in the MTHCL was the creation of a continuum of debate between multiculturalism and anti-racism, a much more useful debate for promoting change than a continuum of anti-racism or nothing."

Metaphors and images also became powerful tools for carrying the messages related to anti-racism. For example, Evelyn Murialdo created the cartoon image of a huge elephant being pushed through a narrow doorway by a group of relatively small but energetic people. This was a humorous yet accurate image of the effort required to bring about anti-racism organizational change. A "wedge" became the symbol for an insertion of an idea or process into the organization that could open up a path to a more significant change or event.

Communicate the Advantages

Anti-racism creates "new markets, new competencies necessary to the survival of the organization. It is also a pragmatic, dollars-and-cents issue, not ideological or imposed by external forces, and it differentiates MTCHL as an organization. Things happened more quickly and more effectively with a focus on anti-racism than they would have with a broader, traditional approach to social housing services." The MTHCL initiative has led to better customer service, marketing, and value-added services for its diverse tenant group.

"For example, the anti-racism program led to the revelation that the 'Chinese' tenants in a particular building were in fact Vietnamese, Filipinos of Chinese ethnicity, Japanese and Koreans, as well as Chinese. By connecting these groups with the appropriate ethno-specific agencies, we were able to service their needs more effectively. This has reduced our vacancies and turnover, and provides a source for new programs, ideas, and resources."

Create Both a Learning Context and a Compliance Context

It is important, Rainer points out, to "set a 'learning context,' not a teaching or training context. Training puts the responsibility on the teachers or trainers to impart the change. If the lessons are not learned, the trainers or teachers will blame the quality of the students or the complexity of the curriculum." The term "learning," however, suggests that there is room to become more knowledgeable in the area, to make mistakes, and to try new approaches. It also suggests that, in some ways, the process is ongoing and will have a number of applications. Mistakes offer us the greatest opportunities to learn.

"Learning has to be real, concrete, based on real and current situations," says Rainer. "Some of the smallest crises are worth their weight in learning gold. Make the mistakes bigger than they really are to squeeze the organizational value out of them. It's necessary to have senior management in touch enough to jump on the small crises (seize the opportunity) and to amplify the opportunity for learning (size the opportunity)."

One example of learning that involved a senior manager took place a few years ago. The superintendents in every MTHCL building had a budget from which they would purchase up to $100 worth of replacement Christmas decorations and trees for the lobby each year. A Jewish employee suggested that a superintendent in a building with a large number of Jewish tenants should also buy a menorah. The superintendent refused to do so, saying there was no money and no policy for such expenses. In this case, the senior manager called a meeting with property managers, community health promoters, superintendents, human resources staff, and others to discuss "the crisis." This led to menorahs appearing at head office and in a number of other buildings. Diwali, Eid, and Kwanzaa were added to the calendar of company celebrations the following year. Only a few hundred dollars were at stake here, but the crisis and benefits were huge!

"The best an organization can do is to help create the conditions for individual learning—the space, permissions and supports, the necessary processes and removal of barriers." However, the organization can and should regulate the behaviour of workers and service recipients who are in contact with other service users and with staff to ensure compliance. The change outcomes need to be behaviour based and breaches of the required behaviour must have clear consequences. Identify consequences for staff, contractors, and tenants who fail to comply with the anti-racism policy. Tenants of MTHCL could be at risk of eviction, while staff could be disciplined and even fired.

"Human rights policies and complaints procedures will not work until internal advocacy and conflict are legitimized by senior management as normal organizational conditions." For example, the system needs to say its okay for a property manager to be confronted by a lower-status community development worker to discuss an inappropriate decision being made from the perspective of anti-racism work.

Rainer's Reflections on Achieving Organizational Change

"Much of the change in MTHCL started at the margins with low status, powerless but innovative workers: groups of former recreation staff turned into community development workers, and clerks took on new roles in support of the change." Some of the most effective anti-racism advocates became "Race Relations Promoters" who participated in study circles and developed their skills in the area of anti-racism. They then facilitated participatory and engaging sessions with co-workers and tenants to inform them of the organization's Race Relations Policy. These advocates were primarily recreation workers and clerical assistants who were taking on a new role in the organization, and they included a few managers and head-office staff. "For the change to be anchored, it requires front-line champions and advocacy groups that confront the change everyday in the lunchroom, the washroom, the boardroom, and in everyday interactions with tenants and the community. These groups need to be nurtured and supported."

Internal advocacy groups are critical in building trust that the company is committed to anti-racism organizational change. Too many organizations have said the right things only to halt the work when power actually begins to shift. "Advocacy must not just be allowed, it must be legitimized and encouraged. Senior management roles must include the support for advocates and the legitimacy of conflict as part of change in the organization."

A neat, orderly work world is not an indication of success, Rainer reminds us. "Adults do not experience significant learning in their lives without pain, struggle, and messiness. Should organizations composed of adults be any different? It is important to recognize publicly that [anti-racism organizational change] causes more work short term, as part of a learning-curve stage … learning to do things differently from the old way will soon reduce at least some of the existing work. It is important to give permission to stop the old work if it is no longer meaningful. Change is NEW work that replaces OLD work and does not necessarily mean MORE work. But it must mean DIFFERENT work."

From this work, Rainer says, "new organizational values and leadership will emerge. There will be power shifts to new groups and individuals welcoming the change. These will often be groups or individuals either new to the organization or those currently at the margins of its power." New and different bases of influence and power are a sign that anti-racism organizational change is taking place. MTCHL now benefits from the leadership skills of racialized people and from racialized people working the front-line positions.

A Summary of Common Characteristics of Phase 2, Getting to How Things Work*

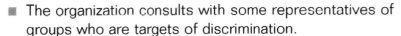

BUILDING
BLOCKS
FOR EQUITY

Decision-making

We think about who's deciding, how they are deciding, and what the results are.

- The organization consults with some representatives of groups who are targets of discrimination.
- Policies and some procedures to promote equity are in place.
- Some complaints about inequality are heard.
- An Equity Committee has been established and meets every couple of months.

What gets missed?

- There are no mechanisms for ensuring and monitoring action or follow-up on decisions that are supposed to advance equity.
- Complaints about racism and sexism are seen as a problem, occasioning more intense monitoring of that person's performance.
- Decisions about what is equitable and not equitable are still made by members of the dominant group, based on very unclear criteria (see "Bargaining for Equity").

*This tool has been adapted from the theoretical work of Jojo Geronimo and Marlene Green for the Ontario Anti-Racism Secretariat, 1993–95.

Communicating

We look for who communicates what, who's supposed to listen, where the silences are, who gets what information, whose information is valued.

- Conversations occasionally acknowledge that inequities happen.
- The organization communicates its "equity initiatives" to funders and the larger community.
- Staff are informed about workshop opportunities outside the organization, to learn about equity.
- Diversity is celebrated at different awards nights and other events in the organization.

What gets missed?

- The organization sees complaints only as problems, not as information.
- Employees are reluctant to challenge behaviours of colleagues, or to imply any criticism of what anyone else is doing (see "Who Deserves the Job?").
- Communicating is top down and out, with no mechanisms to learn from people who are the targets of inequity.
- Most employees don't know what the equity policies say or mean, and there are no real forums to discuss them (see "Who Deserves the Job?").
- Senior leaders do not communicate equity as a priority (see "Using Organizational Authority to Shift Power").
- Disagreements about equity happen in the corridors. Informally, staff align themselves in "camps" with other like-minded employees, around issues of equity (see "Who Deserves the Job?").

Expertise

We're interested in what and whose expertise is sought, valued, paid for, and used. We seek to continually widen the expertise from which the organization can benefit.

- Dominant group members become experts in equity, and rewarded for doing so with career enhancements.
- Language and cultural knowledge of specific communities are recognized.
- "Special services" are staffed by world majority people.

What gets missed?

- Expertise about equity is still seen to emanate mainly from progressive White, able-bodied, straight, middle-class people (see "Who's Afraid of the Executive Director?").
- Most racialized people's expertise is confined to "special projects or services" where they are on contract.
- Anti-oppression skills and competencies are absent from job requirements, hiring, or performance evaluation expectations (see "Using Organizational Authority to Shift Power").
- "Good leadership" includes many women who are "good team players," but still looks White.
- The organization still has difficulty recognizing "overseas" qualifications, or expertise that is not from a university, or developed within its own ranks.

Networks/ connections

We look for what and whose contacts and networks are sought, valued, paid for, and used to hire, promote, train, develop programs, and evaluate. This is the opposite of the "old boys club."

- Job postings are distributed to the ethnic press.
- A contact list of community organizations has been started.
- The "outreach programs" are consulted to find out "what communities and members think" about different issues.

What gets missed?

- Use of "new contacts" other than standard "old boy/girl" networks are still sporadic and tied to issues where the organization needs to position itself as equitable (see "Who's Afraid of the Executive Director?").
- As yet, these networks have no influence on the organization.
- The information and perspectives gathered are used inconsistently, particularly if they challenge organizational practices.

Resources

We're interested in who allocates time, energy and money to what; who benefits from the allocation of resources; who influences the allocation.

- Some money has been spent on shifting dominant group attitudes to equity.
- Managers have been trained on workplace complaint and harassment procedures to legally protect the organization from charges of discrimination.
- Consultants have been hired at various points to do an equity survey, and to consult communities or potential members on their needs.
- The board has designated equity positions.

What gets missed?

- Equity is still seen and resourced as separate from the "regular business" of the organization.
- White people have gained a language of equity and career enhancement for equity work from the resources allocated.
- Hardly any advocates who are people of colour or Aboriginal are benefiting.
- Care is taken not to create too much discomfort among White employees and managers to avoid "backlash" (see "Bargaining for Equity").
- "Outreach programs" are still job ghettos for people of colour and Aboriginal people.
- Designated board positions are viewed as "equity seats" and invariably have less influence than "regular" seats (see "Who's Afraid of the Executive Director?").
- Racialized workers still work overtime in contract employment to compensate for a lack of resources and recognition in their programs.
- Only Christian holidays receive compensation.

PHASE 3

Keeping Racial Equity on the Agenda

When an organization reaches phase three, there is a growing recognition that racial equity has to transform its core. Yet this is a most elusive task. Such organizations may have tried over several years to change themselves and the way they do their work. They have done the training, the hiring, the policy development, and the rewriting of materials. Through sheer determination, these organizations have managed to keep equity on their agenda, even in the face of competing priorities, scarce resources, and staff resistance inside as well as criticism from outside groups and allies, who now expect more. And still, real equity has not been achieved.

At this point in the equity work, different parts of the same organization may be at different stages in the change process. Change is rarely linear; often for every step forward, there are a few steps back. Leadership is inconsistent and uneven. Resistance to the change effort takes more subtle forms; opposition may be more sophisticated. There may be no agreement on strategy among the organization's equity advocates. Some may be delighted with the organization's progress, while others may argue that maintaining the pressure will yield more results. Another group may be exhausted from the effort. Still others may have given up on gradual approaches and be ready to try more radical measures.

Organizations moving towards real equity are not immune from criticism. On the contrary, an organization in phase three may be subject to more criticism than another in phase one. In fact, increased criticism can be an indicator of success. The organization has raised expectations among racialized advocates and White allies that it will actually challenge racism, and it has more real dialogue with people and groups who can push it to change. These organizations need to be recognized for the substantial work they have done and, at the same time, they require challenge and support to do more to advance equity.

We provide four situations to illustrate the challenges of this phase. "Fighting Over a Small Piece of the Pie at the Local School Board" examines the ways equity struggles can be pitted against each other. In this case the effort to challenge heterosexism has more institutional backing and could be a model for advancing racial equity. "Double Jeopardy" looks at the invisible double-standards of work for White and racialized workers doing the same job and poses questions for White people wanting to be better allies. "No Plan for Succession Planning" looks critically at token efforts to develop the next wave of younger and more racially diverse leadership and at the generational as well as racial tensions inherent in such attempts. "White Women as the 'Default' Position on Equity" examines how whiteness operates to White women's advantage in the struggle for equity. It probes the

ways in which White women who are racial equity advocates can collude in racism even as they are trying to confront it.

Our true story, from which we take the title of this book, "Dancing on Live Embers," is about transforming systems. It follows the work of Pat Case and Evelyn Murialdo, who work in a university and a public housing organization, respectively. But their strategies and wisdom are drawn from years of pushing for equity in a variety of workplaces. We summarize the challenges of phase three in the "Building Blocks for Equity."

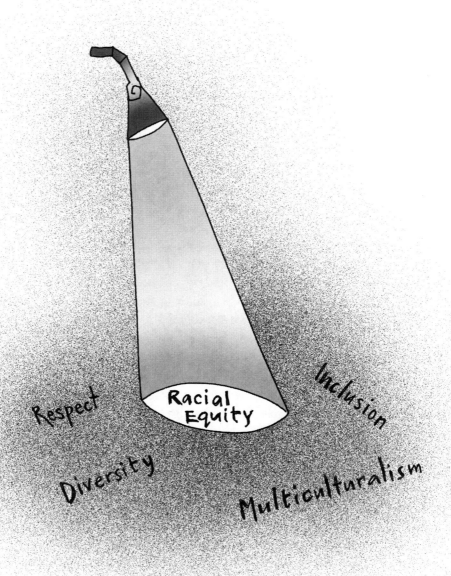

Margie Adam

Fighting Over a Small Piece of the Pie at the Local School Board

Part 1: Homophobia in the Halls

The members of the Gay and Lesbian Caucus at an inner-city high school are in an uproar. One of their group, Mary Jane, put up a poster for the Pride Day Parade in the staff lounge and someone has ripped the poster off the wall and put it in the garbage.

The Gay and Lesbian Caucus members are mostly new staff who have been hired by the board of education to work on the programs and services related to gay, lesbian, and bisexual youth in the schools. The board agreed to take over these programs and services from the small community agency, GaLeY (or Gay Lesbian Youth Agency). Members of the gay and lesbian communities in the county had run GaLeY both as board members and as staff. The agency had begun by providing counselling services to youth, but had soon realized that it needed to work with teachers in the classrooms. The agency began to develop curriculum materials on heterosexism and homophobia, as well as gay-positive resources for English, history, and world issues classes. Eventually the agency expanded its work, creating a summer camp for gay, lesbian, and bisexual youth.

It soon became clear that GaLeY could not continue to provide the breadth of services and programs that were needed; staff were struggling with the amount of work involved and greater resources were required. GaLeY's board and executive director began negotiations to have the programs transferred over to the local school board, to be incorporated into the board's Community Services Department.

As part of the negotiations between the agency and the school board, it was agreed that members of GaLeY's board would form a Gay and Lesbian Advisory Committee that would oversee the school board's efforts to incorporate programs for gay, lesbian, and bisexual youth into its work. The school board also agreed to ensure that the curriculum would challenge heterosexism. The chair of the board of trustees, the CEO of the school board, and the director of the Community Services Department would meet regularly with the Gay and Lesbian Advisory Committee to review the school board's plans to deliver the programs. A Diversity Committee, which included the director of community services, representatives from the Gay and Lesbian Advisory Committee, and staff from various departments within the board, prepared a report with recommendations for how programs for gay, lesbian, and bisexual youth would be staffed, developed, and delivered.

Meetings between the school board and the Gay and Lesbian Advisory Committee went well, and staff were soon hired to develop and deliver the programs. These staff had asked to have a Gay and Lesbian Caucus so that gay and lesbian employees could meet to provide support to one another and to brainstorm ways of integrating gay and lesbian issues into other departments within the school board. The school board agreed, and the caucus began to meet regularly in one of the meeting rooms at the board offices.

When the Pride Day poster was ripped from the wall, members of the caucus were angry but not surprised. They were aware that some of their co-workers were not pleased to have the program at the board, and they felt somewhat isolated from other board staff.

Mary Jane had found the poster in the garbage just a short while after she had put it up, and she immediately informed other members of the caucus. The caucus met that afternoon and agreed to inform the Gay and Lesbian Advisory Committee (GLAC) of the incident. The chair of (GLAC immediately contacted the CEO and the director of the Community Services Department to determine what steps would be taken to deal with this homophobic incident. Both the CEO and the director reassured the chair that they would take every step to ensure that gay and lesbian staff were provided with support to deal with the trauma of the incident. They also said they would conduct an investigation to find out who had destroyed the poster, and that they would provide all staff with training on heterosexism and homophobia as soon as possible.

Part 2: The Ingratitude of Multicultural Communities

Cecile works as an administrative assistant in the Finance Department of the same school board. She has been working for a new supervisor for the past two years and things are not going well. Cecile has consistently received glowing performance appraisals from previous supervisors, but her new supervisor, Jack, is not pleased with her job performance. Jack conducted a performance appraisal of Cecile two months ago, but Cecile has still not received a copy of it.

Over the past year, Jack has told Cecile that others have complained to him that they do not understand her Chinese accent when they call with questions about their budgets or remuneration policies. This is surprising to Cecile since no one has complained before, and she has been with the board for eight years. Cecile has also overheard Jack make demeaning comments about the food she brings for lunch.

Later that week, Jack reprimanded Cecile during a staff meeting, yelling at her in front of her co-workers for not processing a consulting firm's invoices. Many staff were surprised at Jack's treatment of Cecile and assumed that she must be particularly bad at her job to warrant such a reprimand. Some were offended that Jack would humiliate Cecile in this way, but they were afraid to say anything in case he yelled at them.

After the meeting, some of her colleagues approached Cecile to see how she was doing. Cecile was so upset she could barely speak, but she managed to communicate that the invoices did not have the GST and purchase order numbers that were necessary for processing. Her colleagues were outraged that Jack had unfairly reprimanded her and suggested that she should complain to the director of finance about Jack's behaviour. After some discussion, they agreed that Cecile would file a human rights complaint as they were not confident that the director of finance would take Cecile's complaint seriously.

The manager in human resources who received the complaint followed the procedure outlined by the school board's Human Rights Policy and Procedures and hired an external investigator to handle it. The investigator submitted a report four weeks later, in which he stated that there was evidence that supported Cecile's complaint of racism and differential treatment. The manager of human resources shared the investigator's report with the director of finance, who then discussed the report with Jack. They agreed that the investigator seemed to exaggerate the importance of "petty incidents" like laughing together about "some of the odours" in the staff lunchroom. Jack argued that the investigator did not appear to understand that Cecile was making significant mistakes and that all he was trying to do was hold her accountable so that the financial stability of the board was not jeopardized by her carelessness. Together, the human resources manager, the director of finance, and Jack decided to reject the investigator's report.

When Cecile and some of her co-workers heard that the investigator's report was rejected they were outraged. They compared this to the response of the CEO to the homophobic incident that had happened earlier. Many felt that the CEO and other senior managers of the board were unfairly focused on issues of gays and lesbians, and that they were not willing to take racism seriously. They gathered together with a few other front-line workers at the board to petition the CEO to implement an anti-racism organizational change process.

The CEO and management team were offended at the petition and the accusations that they were not dealing with racism. They pointed to the school community liaison officers who were assigned to work specifically with the Somali, Sri Lankan, and Afghan communities as an indication of their commitment to ethno-racial communities. The managers also pointed out that each of these communities had an advisory committee that met with a manager in the Community Services Department to discuss service issues. Apparently these committees always expressed their gratitude for the work the school board was doing on behalf of their children and had never mentioned any concerns about racism. The managers argued that for the past ten years the school board had poured resources into producing multicultural materials for classrooms and hosting multicultural festivals in the community. They accused Cecile and her supporters of being homophobic and resistant to change.

The management team felt unfairly attacked for their efforts to include the gay and lesbian communities, and unappreciated for all they were doing for ethno-racial communities. They shook their heads at the behaviour of "these groups" and complained about how difficult it was for managers when front-line staff refused to understand the pressures from different communities at a time when resources were so limited.

1. What inequities in power do you see in this situation? How is power being used to challenge or reinforce racism?

2. Where are the specific openings for action, to shift how power is working? At what points could you do something different as Cecile's co-workers? the human resources manager? the director of finance? the CEO? the Gay and Lesbian Caucus?

How Power Is Working

1. **Two common responses to multiple demands for equity.**

   Organizations are often forced to address systemic discrimination by a crisis of some kind—either an individual complaint of harassment or an organized protest by community advocates. Sometimes an organization begins the work because it is part of an effort to expand its services and/or become a larger company, for example, a new partnership with a smaller agency or a merger with another organization. Often the organization begins work in one area of discrimination— gender bias and language barriers— and then is pushed by another equity-seeking group to examine another type of discrimination.

   The two most common types of responses to this kind of push are "We can only do one at a time" and "Let's include everything." Yet there are risks to both these approaches. With the "one at a time" approach, risks may be that

   - the organization becomes more comfortable with one form of discrimination and may use this as an excuse not to address another (see "White Women as the 'Default' Position on Equity" in this section for an example of how a focus on gender can be used as a way to avoid dealing with race)
   - the other equity-seeking group(s), which senses this, will become impatient with the organization and resentful of the group that is the focus of the change
   - people who are the targets of more than one form of discrimination will critique an approach that only addresses one aspect of their experience
   - it may reinforce an "us and them" dynamic, which is counterproductive

   While the "let's include everything" approach lists all possible forms of discrimination (most Canadian provincial Human Rights Codes cover at least twelve "grounds" or targets of discrimination) and commits to treating everyone fairly and equitably, this approach neglects the particulars of each form of discrimination (for example, race, sexuality and sexual orientation, creed or religion), and often does not include an examination of systemic forms of discrimination.

2. **Differential treatment.**

   The school board is forced to deal with both heterosexism and racism; it cannot delay handling one or the other. Its differential treatment of gay and lesbian issues (intentionally or unintentionally) communicates to staff and communities that heterosexism is more important to confront than racism. There are four key areas that must be clearly understood and identified:

   (i) The Gay and Lesbian Advisory Committee has considerable influence and power in the organization, and it has direct contact with the chair of the board of trustees, the CEO of the school board, and the director of the Community Services Department. The Somali, Afghani, and Sri Lankan advisory committees meet with a department manager and do not have the same organizational power to advocate for racial equity. If the ethno-specific committees draw upon recently arrived people from the three communities, they may not have the economic stability, community connections, or the information they need to critically assess the work of the school board.

(ii) Managers act as though racialized people are supposed to be grateful to the organization for its efforts to provide relevant and appropriate services. These efforts are supposed to demonstrate that the organization is already inclusive. Workers and communities that raise issues of racism are seen as ungrateful troublemakers who do not appreciate the complexities of managing a large organization with limited resources. Efforts to address heterosexism are treated as an organizational priority and the Gay and Lesbian Advisory Committee actively monitors progress.

(iii) The Gay and Lesbian Advisory Committee and a Gay and Lesbian Caucus are important organizational supports to people who want to ensure heterosexism is challenged in all parts of the organization. The lack of similar supports for racialized people means that racialized workers are often isolated when racist incidents occur and that there is no formal mechanism for holding the organization accountable for its implementation of racial equity. As a result, multicultural programming and festivals can be put forward as evidence of racial equity, while systemic racism and differential access to power remain unaddressed in the organization.

(iv) The complaint from the Gay and Lesbian Advisory Committee to the CEO led to immediate commitments to provide support to gay and lesbian staff, conduct an investigation and organize training for all staff on heterosexism and homophobia. An individual complaint of racism filed under the organization's Human Rights Policy leads to an investigation that is rejected by senior managers and the respondent, with no support to the complainant and no action to address the racism identified in the investigation report.

As a result of this inequitable access to organizational power and the absence of an equally consistent and fair investigative process, staff concerned about racism are pitted against staff concerned about heterosexism. Managers deflect valid criticism of the handling of the complaint of racism, and unfairly portray the staff petitioning for anti-racism organizational change as homophobic. This intensifies tensions between the two groups, and pits the two groups against each other in a familiar "divide and rule" strategy.

TOOLS & STRATEGIES

1. **Form a coalition between equity-seeking groups that can work together and avoid competing for managerial and organizational support.**

   The Gay and Lesbian Caucus could support the petition of staff concerned about the handling of Cecile's complaint and advocate with senior managers to have a more systemic approach to addressing racism in the school board. Staff and community groups concerned about racism could applaud the school board's actions to address heterosexism and demand similar mechanisms be put in place to address racism. This coalition could then prepare a document that compares the organizational resources and supports established to address heterosexism with those allocated to challenge racism (see four key areas above) and use this to pose questions to the management team about its actions.

2. **Use visual tools to ground the discussion and summarize key points.**

   Tools, like the one shown in figure 6, can demonstrate the relationships between two seemingly separate initiatives in a concise and convincing way.

   The human resources manager could advocate for a consistent approach to handle both forms of discrimination that would benefit all workers. People who are the targets of one form of discrimination but not of the other would learn about how both discrimination and privilege work. Racialized people who are also heterosexual can learn to act as allies with gays and lesbians to challenge heterosexism. White gays and lesbians can learn to act as allies with racialized people to challenge racism. They will be more effective if they are not seen as "single-issue groups." Together, they can put pressure on managers who are predominantly White and straight to deal with both racism and heterosexism.

3. **Tackle two distinct forms of discrimination as a way to build a more complex approach to equity work.**

   The human resources manager could advocate for a consistent approach to handle both forms of discrimination that would benefit all workers. People who are the targets of one form of discrimination but not of the other would learn about how both discrimination and privilege work. Racialized people who are also heterosexual can learn to act as allies with gays and lesbians to challenge heterosexism. White gays and lesbians can learn to act as allies with racialized people to challenge racism. They will be more effective if they are not seen as "single-issue groups." Together, they can put pressure on managers who are predominantly White and straight to deal with both racism and heterosexism.

4. **Focus on the two types of discrimination that are most difficult for the organization to address.**

   How does an organization decide on the two areas of focus? Here are some key indicators that inform this decision:

■ Track which groups are most under-represented in the senior and middle management levels and which groups are over-represented in the entry or lowest paid levels of the organization.

■ Compare this information with data that identifies which people are using the programs and services provided by the organization. Are there people in the organization's catchment area who need the services provided but do not come in? Which communities might be most in need of the services the organization provides?

■ Pay attention to which areas of discrimination are avoided in staff, team, or board meetings. What topics seem to make people most uncomfortable? Who do people sit beside in all-staff meetings? What kinds of materials do people post on the bulletin boards or in their office space?

These key indicators will help you determine the two areas of equity work your organization most requires. It is possible to address two types of discrimination in a way that is manageable for staff and also supports systemic change. The systemic remedies developed to address two types of discrimination will lay the groundwork for later efforts to address other forms of discrimination more effectively.

5. **Create an effective template for organizational change.**

The structures and processes put in place to support the development of appropriate services and working conditions for gays and lesbians provide an effective template for organizational change. Similar structures could be established for racialized workers and community groups, with the same access to organizational power. Two parallel processes are often difficult to sustain and are not always the best way to manage these types of organizational change processes. A single advisory committee that addresses both racism and heterosexism could be established, provided concerted efforts are made to ensure equity in the following ways:

■ people are recruited to the committee with an understanding of how both racism and heterosexism operate in society and in organizations

■ there is equitable representation on the committee for both racialized and gay/lesbian communities (this would have to be handled carefully since there are people who are both racialized and gay or lesbian and ideally they would be on the committee)

■ the committee meetings are run in ways that ensure full and meaningful participation by both groups

■ staff education and training is only one of the ways in which the organization does its equity work; managers should ensure that organizational change work focuses on systemic barriers to equity-seeking groups in hiring, employment conditions, access to developmental opportunities, volunteer recruitment, curriculum development, service delivery, and community relations

The two equity-seeking groups would then see themselves as part of a broad organizational effort to create greater equity rather than as competitors for limited organizational resources and managerial support.

Figure 6: **Unequal Treatment of Equity Initiatives**

TYPE OF STRUCTURE OR RESOURCE ALLOCATED	SCHOOL BOARD'S ACTIONS TO ADDRESS HETEROSEXISM	SCHOOL BOARD'S ACTIONS TO ADDRESS RACISM
Advisory committees' connection to authority	The Gay and Lesbian Advisory Committee has direct access to the chair of the board of trustees, the CEO and the director of the Community Services Department.	The Somali, Afghani, and Sri Lankan advisory committees each meet separately with a manager in the Community Services Department.
Supports for staff experiencing discrimination	The school board supports the establishment of a Gay and Lesbian Caucus for staff and provides a meeting space for the group.	Staff experiencing racism have no caucus and no formal group from which to receive support.
Handling complaints of discrimination	Gay and lesbian staff contact the chair of the Gay and Lesbian Advisory Committee who demands action from the CEO and chair of the board of trustees. Senior managers are aware that they will be held accountable for their actions.	Racialized staff file individual complaints under the organization's Human Rights Policy and must rely on the managers to accept the findings of any investigation. A manager's abuse of power goes unaddressed.
Integrating anti-discrimination work into all areas of the school board	In addition to training, the school board will review the curriculum for heterosexist content and will provide programs for gay and lesbian youth in their schools. Gay and lesbian staff are hired to deliver the programs.	Multicultural content is added to the curriculum. Multicultural festivals are organized and community liaison workers are hired. Systemic racism is not an organizational priority for the school board.

SITUATION 2 Double Jeopardy: Working while Black and Muslim

At a team meeting of a social service agency, Ali reports that one of the Somali Canadian clients he's been working with has asked for a White worker. The client wants to sponsor his family to Canada, and he is worried that the church he's hoping will act as the sponsor will not respond to a request from a "Black" worker. Laughing a bit, Ali said that he had already found a "White male worker" for his client and placed his hand on the shoulder of Christopher, another team member. While Christopher laughed a little at this description, others smiled but seemed uncomfortable with what they were hearing.

The manager responded quickly, "We don't do that here; this goes against our policy." He added that clients were not allowed to demand a particular race of worker be assigned to them and that the organization had made a decision not to bow to these kinds of demands.

White colleagues weighed in with their analysis. Katie expressed concern that Ali was setting up Christopher to deliver on a sponsorship agreement with the church that might be hard to get. Another colleague expressed concern that this was "giving in to racism" and that Ali's action would do nothing to challenge that racism.

At this point, Fatima, the other Somali worker, spoke in Ali's defence. "This happens all the time. We have to make sure that our clients get what they need. They have enough problems with the system. If they think that a White worker will get them something they need, I'm not going to stand in their way. That's what Ali's talking about."

Another colleague asked whether there was any other reason for the transfer, whether the client was happy working with Ali. Ali responded, "Everything else is fine with this client. He called me to explain that it wasn't personal; he is desperate to get his family over here, and he doesn't think the church will listen to a Black Muslim worker."

Some of the White team members looked sceptical, and one said, "Why would your client think that the church wouldn't listen to you?" At that point, Fatima responded again, "The same thing has happened to me. I called a church to ask about sponsoring the family of a client, and when the pastor heard my name again, he asked me where I was from. Then he told me they don't sponsor people anymore." White colleagues continued to question her conclusion that this was about race. One White colleague said, "It would have been interesting if you had asked one of us to call and check it out. Then we'd know if it was that or something else"

Fatima replied patiently, "I did that. I asked one of my White colleagues at a partner organization to call the same church, after I had this conversation. And guess what? The client's sister will be arriving in Canada next month."

There was silence. Fatima continued, "In fact, I get it from my clients, too. I don't cover my head and I wear pants, and they think I'm too young; I have one Somali woman client who couldn't believe that I could get what she needed. I said to her, 'Let me prove to you I can do an even better job than a White person.'" Fatima laughed, "I mean, at least as good a job as a White person. Anyway, I did the job, and now the client calls me. In fact, she's calling me at three in the morning."

Tanya, one of Fatima's White colleagues says, "But I don't get it. If they're sponsoring a Somali family, why wouldn't the pastor listen to a Somali worker?"

Fatima continued, "They think that as a Somali Muslim worker, I am not objective, that I can't do a fair assessment of whether the client and her family 'deserve' to be sponsored, because 'I'm one of them.' They probably think a White worker would be more objective and professional, and could be trusted to make a fair assessment of who should be allowed to come into Canada."

Ali added, "That's why I transferred my client to Christopher. The important thing is to serve the client. They need our help."

Tanya turned to Fatima, "Aren't you upset about how the pastor treated you?"

Fatima responded, "I'm pissed off. But I can't say anything until the family arrives. Then I'm going to the church to demand an apology."

---

1. What inequities in power do you see in this situation? How is power being used to challenge or reinforce racism?

2. Where are the specific openings for action, to shift how power is working? At what points could you do something different as Christopher? As Tanya? As Ali? As Fatima?

How Power Is Working

1. **Racialized workers experience racism in employment.**

   Having been hired as "Somali workers," Fatima and Ali are viewed as employees who have been hired primarily for their language skills and cultural knowledge and as "employment equity" hires who would probably not otherwise have qualified to work at the agency as health promoters.

   In addition, they are seen by the agency and by co-workers as providing service exclusively to the Somali community, and perhaps not as qualified to serve other clients. White, English-speaking colleagues are not similarly assigned a particular ethno-specific or other socially identifiable community. It is acceptable to label Fatima and Ali as Somali workers, but White people become very uncomfortable when Ali identifies Christopher as a "White male" colleague.

2. **Racialized workers experience racism as they try to do their jobs and interact with other agencies.**

   As they attempt to advocate on behalf of their clients with other agencies (the church in this case), racialized workers are themselves the targets of racism, as well as the clients with whom they work. Workers in other agencies and institutions (judges, landlords, immigration officers, welfare workers, housing workers, doctors, teachers, guidance counsellors) assume that the racialized workers are clients rather than employees. Racism shapes broadly held ideas about what service providers look like as opposed to service recipients.

   Not only do racialized workers have to manage their own experience of racism but they also have to find ways to protect their clients from the impacts of this racism—for example, by transferring the client to a White worker or asking a White worker to intervene on the client's behalf. The racialized worker must then make a case to the White worker as to why she/he is being asked to intervene, and then become dependent on the good will of the White worker to agree to make the intervention.

3. **Clients who are also the targets of racism sometimes reject racialized workers.**

   Somali clients reject a Somali worker because they have seen that a White worker has easier access to resources and can advocate for them more effectively. In addition, expectations of clients from the same ethno-racial community may be high, and the single worker assigned to the community may be unable to cope with the workload or to influence the agency to reallocate the necessary resources. The worker runs the risk of being blamed for this by the community.

4. **White colleagues don't experience racism, and they can remain unaware of how it operates in the lives of their racialized colleagues who are "doing the same job."**

This means that Fatima and Ali have to constantly be judging who will believe what is happening to them and on whom they can afford to call on for help. They must expend huge amounts of energy anticipating and managing the responses of their White co-workers and being careful "not to offend." Racialized workers may decide not to talk about how racism affects them at work and simply appear to have the same experiences on the job so that they "fit in."

5. **White colleagues believe they can decide whether or not racism is happening, even though they do not experience it.**

When racialized workers raise a situation of discrimination (such as one based on race and religion), the burden is placed on them to prove the existence of discrimination, even as they report on situations that are painful to them. It is sometimes easier for White colleagues to raise questions about the competency of a racialized worker rather than come to terms with the racism of other White people.

The comfort levels of White workers with talking about racism define the terms of the conversation. Racialized workers learn quickly that they must behave in ways that are acceptable to their White colleagues during these conversations. If they become angry, upset, or speak forcefully about their experiences of racism, they can be accused of "silencing" White people, "blaming all White people," or being inappropriately aggressive.

6. **Racialized workers are often unfairly assessed and held to be responsible for what are, in fact, the impacts of racism on them and their clients.**

The manager held Ali accountable for not following the organization's policy and for reinforcing racism rather than challenging it. The manager did not hold himself or other (White) team members accountable for failing to challenge the racism on the part of the churches or other institutions.

Supervision and performance appraisal practices that do not anticipate inequities may only uncover that racialized workers are rejected by clients, that clients have requested that their cases be transferred to White workers, or that they are less successful in their advocacy efforts with other agencies. Supervisors may wrongly conclude that the racialized workers are less competent than their White colleagues.

TOOLS & STRATEGIES

1. Connect racism to other forms of oppression which affect White workers and their clients.

Earlier in the discussion, Tanya had bemoaned the fact that when she accompanies her clients to the welfare offices, the welfare workers are more willing to believe her and approve the clients' benefits than if the clients go to the office on their own. The manager or team member could use this example to help Tanya see how the pastor in the church was acting in a similar way to the welfare worker.

In situations like this one, it is essential to pose questions that challenge people to re-examine their assumptions. For example, the conversation began to expose the images people seem to carry about what service *providers* look like and what service *recipients* look like. It may be useful to ask the group which of the following characteristics the pastor seems to have associated with a service provider and which he assigned to clients or service recipients:

- objective
- Canadian
- honest
- Christian
- Muslim
- speaks English as a Second Language
- is from one of the First Nations

Depending on the context in which you work, you might want to add others. It is important to recognize that White people can experience other forms of discrimination, just as racialized people can also benefit from privilege if they are heterosexual or able-bodied.

2. Give people the opportunity to absorb exactly what is happening.

After Fatima had shared a particularly difficult part of her experience, the racialized facilitator asked the White people in the room how Fatima's account was sitting with them. One of her White colleagues acknowledged that this was the first time she had taken in what racialized colleagues had to contend with on the job.

Watch for moments when White people, consciously or not, incite racialized people to take care of them and intervene when it happens.

3. Examine the ways in which racism affects racialized workers, and therefore the team, and develop a team approach to addressing racism.

Conversations about how racism and other forms of oppression operate in the workplace need to be a normal part of doing the work and building a team. For example, a routine question at each staff or team meeting might be "How has inequity surfaced in your job this week? What should the team/department/union be doing about it?"

In the situation under discussion here, White team members could step forward and work with racialized colleagues to hold the churches accountable for how they are treating racialized workers. The manager could use both his organizational authority and his White male identity to ensure that racialized workers are hired, introduced to the team, assigned work, and assessed in ways that challenge inequity. He could use every opportunity to reinforce the fact that they bring to the agency skills, knowledge, and competencies that are different, relevant, and essential to the work done by the organization.

The team could develop strategies for dealing with racism in their own organization, making it clear that it is part of the job and not something that racialized workers must deal with on their own.

SITUATION 3 No Plan for Succession Planning

Sheila, the campaign manager of a union, has decided not to renew the contract of a young co-ordinator who has been running a campaign on Workers' Rights Are Human Rights for the past ten months. Sheila actually thinks the co-ordinator did a great job, but she is sick and tired of improvising patchwork solutions to a problem she says is much broader. In the next five years, half of her staff will be eligible to retire and most, including herself, will exercise this option.

The work of Njala, the young co-ordinator, is to be reassigned to existing staff reps. Several people are puzzled and upset about Sheila's decision. The three senior staff reps resent this addition to their workload, and they say the loss of this talented person will also be felt by young members who have become activists during her ten months of work. They say it's the first time they've seen young racialized workers involved and excited about the union.

Njala is surprised to hear these words of support from these staff reps, two of whom gave her none over the past ten months. Only Clarissa, a union rep for five years and the closest to Njala's age, takes time informally to explain how things work, how decisions get made, and what to watch out for. But Clarissa doesn't speak up when the other union staff are present.

Njala feels she was hung out to dry on a number of occasions. She cites as problems a complete lack of orientation, no support or budget for her work, no communication among union staff or local presidents about her work, and a climate at staff meetings that she refers to as toxic. She refers to the last meeting as an example. At that meeting she identified the need for a leadership program for young Aboriginal people and people of colour. She argued that now was the time to provide tangible support to get them more involved in the union. A leadership program would strengthen their skills. It would also provide a comfortable forum for them to talk about the racism they face at both the workplace and in the union, and would consolidate a support network to develop practical strategies. She put forward a proposal with a budget, a timeframe, and a request for a senior officer to open and close the program to communicate the union's commitment to the program and to these young people.

At that meeting, several people listened and two people were on their cell phones; the discussion was cut short when one of the reps said, "I know I'm not being politically correct here, but what about the White kids? You can't organize a conference just for the coloured kids." Njala reminded the rep of the union's Anti-Racism Strategy passed at the last convention and of the fact that the executive board had talked about the need for a Succession Planning Strategy. The rep rolled his eyes and said, "We're always passing high-sounding policy, and then there's the reality on the ground. I'm not criticizing you, kid; you haven't been here long enough to know that."

It's then that Sheila looked at her watch, and suggested that perhaps she and Njala could discuss it after the meeting and come back to the next meeting with something "more worked out." Njala felt betrayed, isolated, and patronized and found it difficult to have a constructive conversation with Sheila after the meeting. She calls the chair of the Young Workers Committee to talk through the situation.

Sheila feels unsupported and angry. She calls the director of regional operations and says she's fed up "trying to implement the union's policy all by herself. She's decided not to renew Njala's contract because she can't support her in the work, and she can't protect her from the racism of the reps. She wants the director to come in and read the riot act to the reps and to give her some support in developing a practical plan to build youth leadership in the union.

1. What inequities in power do you see in this situation? How is power being used to challenge or reinforce racism?

2. Where are the specific openings for action, to shift how power is working? At what points could you do something different as Sheila the campaign manager? as Clarissa? as one of the other staff reps? as Njala? as the director of regional services? as the chair of the Young Workers Committee?

How Power Is Working

1. **The absence of supportive systems puts individuals (young, Aboriginal, racialized, gay/lesbian/bi/transgender, women) at risk.**

   The organization recognizes its need for young staff to organize young workers. However, there are no systems in place to support Njala's work. She was only given an informal orientation through Clarissa. She has been given no budget for her work and no feedback on her performance that would encourage or support her to do better. The organization has not communicated her purpose to union staff and local presidents—the very people who need to be taking responsibility for creating conditions for success. In the absence of these basic supports, Njala risks failure, isolation, an informal performance appraisal damaging to her reputation, and loss of her job. Indeed, she is losing her job because these supports are not in place.

2. **White people are deciding the needs of racialized workers.**

   A mostly White staff is deciding at the meeting—either as active or passive participants—that racialized workers should not have their own conference. The rep who protests the idea is not asked to explain his objection or to propose anything else. His comment sits there uncontested, except by Njala who reminds him of union policy. He patronizes her by saying that policy has nothing to do with "reality on the ground." Other staff's silence colludes with this view and the resulting decision.

3. **Older people are deciding the needs of young workers.**

   The staff and leadership of this union, like many other organizations, are older and many are close to retiring. There is a Young Workers' Committee, but its role is unclear here. By the reps' own admission, there are few young people to participate in developing strategy that would attract young people to the union, and so older people are the ones making decisions that affect young workers. This deprives young people of the active protection of a union in their workplaces, and starves the union of the vitality it needs to stay relevant and effective. Despite the acknowledged need to do succession planning, there appears to be no plan to develop young activists and their leadership. Njala's work, despite the absence of support, shows that young people can be interested and attracted to the union.

4. **Racist and disrespectful behaviour in the meeting are unchallenged by the manager and staff.**

   At the meeting, Njala is taking her job seriously. She is presenting a proposal with a budget, time frame, and plan. While she is presenting, two reps are on their cell phones. One of the reps cuts discussion of Njala's proposal short with a remark that focuses on the rights of White youth, ignoring the needs of young racialized workers. When Njala challenges him, he patronizes her. Nobody else says anything. The manager tries to avoid the existing conflict by moving on, and actively colludes with the inference that Njala doesn't know what she's doing by promising to help Njala bring back "something more worked out" to the next meeting. The message is clear. Njala is the problem; racism will not be challenged, nor will the White male privilege of the older reps.

5. **Njala is carrying the union's equity agenda alone.**

The union has a Racial Equity Strategy, but it is not a working document. Indeed, the most vocal people in the field are saying the strategy has nothing to do with them. The staff don't see a role for themselves in the Racial Equity Strategy, and the union doesn't seem to be demanding that they do so. By default, the burden falls to those who care the most about it—in this case, the person with the least organizational authority and the most to risk, Njala. The union benefits by Njala's work through the increased involvement of young diverse activists, but is not acknowledging Njala's contribution.

6. **Njala loses employment because the leaders or managers don't take responsibility for challenging racism and advancing the organization's stated policy.**

Sheila cites her frustration at "patchwork solutions to broad problems" as her reason for not renewing Njala's contract. She says she's "fed up trying to implement the union's policy all by herself." But aside from hiring Njala, it's not clear what actions she's taken to implement policy. Indeed, the absence of clear ownership and leadership in the union to implement both the Racial Equity Strategy and succession planning has put Njala at risk. Sheila is not using her organizational authority to challenge the racism or create conditions for success for Njala who reports to her. She is waiting for someone else to "read the riot act to the reps."

TOOLS & STRATEGIES

Each of the players in this situation can choose to act in ways that advance racial equity.

1. **Sheila the manager can**
   - initiate more constructive steps to resolve the conflict
   - renew Njala's contract and get written confirmation from the director of regional operations that the Racial Equity Strategy is union policy and that succession planning is important
   - secure confirmation of a budget
   - hire a second young person (Aboriginal or racialized) to work with Njala, and build support by doing some work with her staff
   - take the Racial Equity Strategy passed at the convention and the stated intention to

do succession planning as her direction

- ask the research, education, or equity departments to do a practical working session on the strategy and on their roles in succession planning with the reps over the next few meetings; the session would focus on how, in their daily work, the reps could involve more young Aboriginal and racialized workers in the union and how they could mentor young activists
- communicate clearly, in writing and through individual meetings with local presidents and staff, that Njala's work is critical for the union, as well as stress the benefits to locals and indicate her willingness to assist and support the work

In taking these steps, Sheila can help Njala present her proposal in a clearer context.

2. **The director of regional operations has a lot to contribute to the situation, and his assistance should be sought out. He can, for example,**

- give immediate written confirmation of union policy and its intent to develop a succession plan
- help Sheila secure her budget, and ask what other assistance she needs to move things along
- use his organizational authority and start working with other operations under her jurisdiction to implement policy and initiate conversations with other directors to identify systems that need changing

3. **Staff reps who are allies can**

- use their internal authority to set things in motion
- apologize to Njala for their silence at the meeting and say they would like to work with her on preparing the next round
- approach Sheila to say that the meeting was upsetting, that they were sorry that they didn't speak up, that they will support Sheila to get something moving and to maintain Njala in her job, and that they will be working with Njala
- to heighten their campaign, talk with their colleagues about the value of the work Njala is doing for the union and circulate a petition to keep Njala in her job, actively recruiting the signatures of other staff reps and members

4. **Njala and the Young Workers Committee can ask Sheila to reconsider her decision.**

Although it isn't clear from this situation how active or influential the Young Workers Committee is, such committees are usually composed of members who elect their leaders and have reason to expect that the union will carry out the mandate from the convention. This committee is the voice for young workers in the union. Njala has nothing to lose at this point in summoning whatever collective support she can muster. There is every indication that she is doing a good job, so performance does not appear to be the issue. The committee can mobilize support among other youth for the work Njala is doing.

White Women as the "Default" Position on Equity*

A union women's conference was in the final plenary after two days of intensive workshops. The workshops had been facilitated by pairs of women who were members of the Women's Committee and staff of different unions. Each workshop had produced recommendations to the Women's Committee for advancing an equity agenda. Many of the recommendations acknowledged that diverse women faced many different kinds of discrimination, and that building a union meant advancing equity in all its forms. The recommendations had been summarized and presented to the plenary. There was great excitement about the collective energy, the firm presence of equity throughout, and how much the women had accomplished in so short a time.

The Women's Committee sat at the front of the room, consisting of representatives sent from different unions. Nine of ten women were White, with one woman designated as the "woman of colour seat" on the committee. No one knew better than she how long the road had been to "get equity on the agenda of the women's committee" and her union.

Indeed, the two designers of the conference were White women. They had spent considerable time revising materials and activities to ensure that the goals specified "equity" and "diverse women"; that the "union music" came from different sources; that energizers, case studies, and other activities consciously portrayed a variety of women through the names, situations, contexts. They had specified different organizing experiences which imagined women mobilizing in communities as well as in the union, and they had built in moments to probe obstacles to the participation of diverse women in their unions and in the Women's Committee. But they were aware that as two straight, middle-aged White women, no matter how conscious they were, they would miss things.

At one point in the facilitator training, one of the White participants had asked, "What if one of the participants in our workshop asks why we're spending all this time on equity? What if they feel left out? I'm not saying I feel that, but some of the participants might."

Indeed, in one of the workshops, a group of three White women had protested that "given the economic and political climate facing women workers," they felt that this focus on equity was a bit of a red herring. "Unions should be working towards more political leverage," which, apparently, was a different problem from equity.

In the plenary, after the presentation of the recommendations, a White

---

* We owe this helpful expression of "White default position" to Keith Regehr, a White colleague and committed anti-racism educator.

activist stood up and began to talk nervously. "I don't mean any offence," she began. "This is hard to say. But I'm worried that all this focus on equity is divisive. Last night we had all these caucuses—for Aboriginal women, youth, women of colour, women in non-traditional jobs. These caucuses leave some of us out, and do nothing but emphasize our differences and not what we have in common as women." There was brief applause from a few women. Then silence.

1. What inequities in power do you see in this situation? How is power being used to challenge or reinforce racism?

2. Where are the specific openings for action, to shift how power is working? At what points could you do something different as the chair of the Women's Committee and of the plenary? as a facilitator? as a White woman in the plenary? as an Aboriginal woman or as a woman of colour in the plenary?

How Is Power Working?

1. The "default to White."

Despite the fact that only 18 to 20 per cent of the world's people are "White" and 48 per cent of the world is male, "White" and "male" are the "norms" in Western cultures and everyone else must be mentioned specially. This is "default to White." What do we mean by "default"? Let's take our computers as an example.

Computers in Canada are set to the default of American English. English is imagined from an American perspective. It takes active intervention to prevent spell-check warnings that words ending in "-our," like "labour," are not misspelled. The weight of how the computer works is behind it. You either participate or you actively intervene with the machine to change it. You must do this repeatedly because each time you turn it on, the machine "defaults" to American English and insists that the correct spelling is "labor."

In a similar way, a default position is a norm with organizational momentum behind it, which requires continual intervention in order not to accept the default. This is exactly the way the "default to White male" works. For example, when we imagine generic roles such as managers, workers, lawyers, teachers, and leaders, we assume a White male unless we say "the Asian manager" or "this Nigerian worker" or "that new woman Tamil union president." If we fail to alert the listener to this fact, that person will often experience (and sometimes express) surprise that a teacher, lawyer, or leader is not White—"I didn't know she was Tamil"—but rarely specifying why this information is so important.

We do not analyze this in order to label unsuspecting men and White people "sexist" or "racist." We are calling attention to the pervasiveness of a powerful norm—a White male default—which all of us have internalized in our own ways.

2. White women as the default position on equity.

For many feminist men, "equity" means advancing the rights of women, meaning White women unless otherwise specified. Indeed, employment programs that designate four groups—Aboriginal people, women, racial minorities, people with disabilities—have statistically largely benefited White, able-bodied women. After an election, the selection of the new political leadership will invariably pay attention to "representation" and "equity," usually by emphasizing the presence of women—White women—in the cabinet, executive, top leadership. As one of our colleagues who works in government has said, "White women are the answer to 'diversity.' That's how 'diversity' initiatives have been implemented. I think it's because White men are more comfortable with White women than they are with Aboriginal people or with people of colour—men or women."

White women become spokespeople on "equity," even when they are straight and able-bodied. This is not to discourage White women from championing equity. It is to say that all of us need to be aware of the limitations of the bodies we're in. Even when

White women work consciously with their White privilege, their role as the overall experts on equity sends a message that White people can learn about racism from other White people and don't need to work with people of colour. In this scenario, the two White facilitators, despite their best efforts, are colluding in this message.

3. **But for White women, "equity" means people of colour.**

   White women are not only the "answer to equity" for White men but also for White women. This is because White people tend to equate "equity" with gender. When racialized women raise the issue of "equity" within the women's movement, they force White women into recognizing that gender is only one of many equity issues. When this happens, White women treat "equity" as a problem that they attach to racialized women and men.

   In this situation, the White women raising questions about "equity" want to advance women's influence in the union movement. They believe a focus on "equity" will distract from building that influence. But for them, "women in the union" are, by default, only White women. In this way, White women challenge the "maleness" of the "default to White male," but not its Whiteness.[2]

TOOLS & STRATEGIES

In the plenary, following the White woman's remark and the ensuing silence, several women rise and respond directly to this speaker about why it is time to build equity into everything the union movement does. A speaker who has attended the Women of Colour Caucus suggests that at the next conference there be a caucus for "White allies." Learning to be a good ally is the work of those who benefit most from the norms of being White, male, straight, and able-bodied.

Women who raise concerns about "the divisiveness of equity" are treated respectfully and are responded to without rhetoric. Given the White conference leadership, and the limited attention given to racism by the Women's Committee, what has produced these results? Here are some of the ways the organizers, facilitators, and participants tried to interfere with the "White women default" and some of the limitations of what they did.

1. **Name the irony of challenging inequalities for only some women.**

   In the plenary, several women stand and respond to the woman expressing concerns about "equity" producing "divisiveness." They name the irony of women challenging inequality produced by sexism but who hesitate to challenge the inequalities produced by racism, heterosexism, and classism.

2. **Specify "an equity agenda for diverse union women" in the conference objectives and repeat "diverse women" throughout the conference.**

   In the absence of such language, the default to White women kicks in. In this context, it is important to ensure that the word "diverse" is not used as a way to reduce White women's discomfort with racism. It's also important to take opportunities to focus specifically on the racial identities of women.

3. **Organize the event with racialized women from the beginning.**

Because the Women's Committee is mainly White, organizers decided to seek input into the conference design from the human rights staff officer and the Equity Committee. However, the women consulted did not have much to suggest as they had been excluded from the initial planning and they were now being asked to put their name to an event they had not shaped. The Women's Committee learned that the next conference should be jointly sponsored with the Equity Committee to ensure diverse perspectives and knowledge from the beginning.

4. **Ensure that racialized union women have access to training and opportunity to facilitate.**

The conference also reveals that it is mostly White women who are trained as facilitators in the union. These are also the women asked to facilitate at the conference. Part of the ongoing equity work for the Women's Committee is to insist that racialized women have access to facilitator training and other leadership developmental opportunities in the union.

5. **Publicize the event through diverse networks to ensure the participation of racialized women.**

One of the problems of the conference is that the Women's Committee has no connections to racialized women, except through their one member of colour. Racialized women activists and White allies had to work very hard to establish new networks and convince racialized union women that this conference would be relevant to them. Their efforts have resulted in the largest participation of women of colour ever at a women's conference. Fully half of the participants are attending this as their first conference and many of them have had little involvement in the union to date. But more racialized women could have participated if organizing had been done differently.

6. **Acknowledge the pitfalls of a mostly White women's leadership.**

A White women's leadership directly reinforces the "default to White women," no matter how inclusive that White leadership tries to be. This is further reinforced because the two facilitator trainers are White women. Their presence gives a message that undermines the equity work: you can learn about racism from White people and you don't have to take direction from Aboriginal women and women of colour.

Selection processes in unions favour White people. One indicator of increased equity is when locals select more women of colour, Aboriginal women, and women with disabilities as their representatives to the Women's Committee, not just to the Human Rights Committee.

7. **Demonstrate that efforts to probe difference are a genuine basis for unity.**

The conference design requires participants to examine the specific obstacles in unions facing young women, lesbians, Aboriginal women, and women of colour as part of the main agenda, and not just in caucuses. For example, when women talk about where they go for support to fight inequities, women of colour say they go to their families and community organizations, White women go to their families and union. This leads to a discussion of barriers in the union that make women of colour feel unwelcome and that limit their desire to spend all their volunteer labour in their unions. Some White women have acknowledged for the first time that their racialized sisters have had a different and less welcoming experience of the union than they have had. This discussion also leads White women to examine the ways in which they, too, feel marginalized in the union. In this way, White and racialized women can identify genuine—not just assumed—common ground, as well as the different challenges they face. In the next steps, White women need to do what they can to reduce the barriers to racialized women within their own circles of influence.

8. **Critique the default to White women when choosing and writing materials.**

Conference facilitators discovered that the names, situations, leadership, issues faced, and responses to challenges they were using were imagined as being applicable to White, straight, able-bodied women. These had to be reconceived and rewritten for the conference. For example, materials on organizing originally said that "women became persons in 1921" and that "women in Quebec were the last women in Canada to gain the vote in 1940." In fact, men and women of Asian descent did not gain the vote until 1949 because they were not eligible to become British subjects. Aboriginal women and men could not vote until 1960 when the *Indian Act* was changed.

9. **Link analysis of global inequity with discussions of local inequity.**

In the workshops, the facilitators explore the unequal impact of funding squeezes and of downsized social and health services on women in Canada and the world. Statistics highlight the unequal effect of corporate globalization on racialized women, in particular. Any union and women's movement trying to understand globalization must include the knowledge of racialized women.

The materials also include statistics to show the range of leadership in equity and globalization struggles coming from the South. In the North, some of the most visionary leadership for global justice is coming from Aboriginal people, people of colour, and young racialized people. Any local movements for social justice must recognize this leadership.

10. **Anticipate that racism will be expressed in the event.**

The facilitator training anticipates that racism will come up in the workshops and has built in some practice for facilitators to address racism when it arises. However, the training insufficiently explored the racism that continues to play out among the union women who are facilitators. Many White women are afraid of saying the wrong thing or making a mistake. Others are not convinced that racism is an appropriate focus for this women's conference and pose carefully worded questions to challenge the focus. This leaves the burden of identifying and challenging racism, once again, to women of colour.

Short facilitator training sessions inadequately prepare people to introduce new content, deal with their own racism, and handle other people dealing with racism. But they're often the only opening we get, and we must use them. In addition to fighting for more time in facilitator training, we need to be insisting on time after the event to analyze what we've learned and to develop strategies for ongoing learning and action.

KEEPING OURSELVES IN THE PICTURE

The process of writing this situation is a story in itself, and we want to tell it as ourselves—as Tina and Barb. The truth is that the conference was facilitated by Barb and a White colleague; Tina was not involved in any aspect of that work. Barb wrote up the story, the first draft of the analysis, and the tools and strategies. Then, in a conversation about that draft, Tina identified major gaps in Barb's analysis of racism. In Barb's initial version, she identified Whiteness as the default position but missed the fact that in this situation, the most important default was to White women. Barb's analysis focused on how the White facilitators had managed to integrate anti-racism content into the design of the conference. Tina's analysis demonstrated how racism was a factor in the whole scenario, from the selection of the two White facilitators through to the planning and delivery of the conference. The Whiteness of the leadership, the facilitators, and the event reinforced the default to White women, even as the conference attempted to put racial equity on the union's agenda.

It was not until Tina revealed "the default to White women" to Barb, which she did not see before, that it was possible for Barb to examine her own active participation in maintaining White privilege at the conference. This led to further conversations about the influence these actions had on a number of levels. First, two White women facilitating discussions about racism reinforced the notion that others could learn about it from White people. Second, it meant that access to employment within the union remained with White women, who already had that access. This has both short- and long-term consequences on the employment of racialized women. Third, in this scenario, even as racism is placed on the agenda, real racial equity is compromised. Thus, the union can appear to be doing something about racism even as it denies opportunities for racialized women to lead and shape the direction of the union's work.

Barb had great difficulty with the fact that she did not, and in fact could not, come up with this analysis herself. While she took direction from Tina on the analysis, she initially resisted examining the implications of that analysis for her own actions. Over time, it became clear that the situation mirrored what was happening between us. The increasing frankness between us led to greater insights about White privilege and racism, which we then applied here. (See more about this in section four, "Between Us.")

A TRUE STORY Dancing On Live Embers: Transforming the Systems

Many of us enter organizations at a young age, some from the moment of our birth. We are born in hospitals, issued birth certificates, go to daycare and school, and work most of our lives for small organizations or large corporations. We tend to accept that the way organizations operate is "simply the way things are." Despite widespread unhappiness with the way we are treated, either as service users or as employees, many of us resign ourselves to the fact that organizations operate in ways that are stressful, inequitable, and often oppressive.

Choosing to become anti-racism change agents while employees of an organization is an act of courage. Challenging inequities in organizations is hard and often risky work. It requires stamina, persistence, imagination, humour, and community support. It also calls for faith that people can create places that offer each other more meaningful work in a productive and rewarding environment. It often helps to have stories from people who have successfully effected change in their organizations. We have asked Patrick Case and Evelyn Murialdo to share some of their experiences and strategies for transforming systems in a variety of organizations. They are wily strategists and light-footed tricksters who have much to teach.

PATRICK CASE: An Unbroken Chain of Activism

Pat Case is a man of African descent and a dedicated community activist connected to numerous community organizations. He is the proud father of two extraordinary children, and the home he has created with his partner, Susan Colleran, is an important sanctuary where he cooks gourmet meals and creates his own mini film festivals. Pat currently works as the director of human rights and equity at the University of Guelph. He is also the chair of the Canadian Race Relations Foundation's board of directors. In these and many other organizations, he has achieved anti-racism, employment equity, and human rights goals.

Pat was born in Coventry, England, one of the youngest children in a family of twelve. The Case family was one of only two African-descent families in the army camp, and Pat learned early about racism. He says, "I was remembering just earlier today that I got a stone thrown at me when I was about four years old, and it hit me right in the head. These were kids from a secondary school who would come by the house every day and taunt me with racial slurs."

Pat's mother Honora (more usually called Sister Nora) was often an example to her children of how to counter racism. As a Black working-class woman, she was subjected to a great deal of discrimination, but she always found ways to fight back. Pat relates one of her acts of resistance: "My mother was a convinced and confirmed Labour voter in England. But the Tories were the ones who had the money, and who had the cars. My mother had to use a wheelchair and could not easily get to the polling stations. The Tories would call around and say, 'Mrs. Case, we're sending the car around to pick you up to go to vote again.' My mother would simply say, 'Oh yes! Thank you very much!' They'd pick her up and she'd vote Labour every single time. She'd come home laughing and say, 'Take me for a fool!'"

Pat also learned about different ways of resisting racism from his father, Edward Archibald, who had helped to organize one of the first unions among postal workers in Guyana. He was also sending money to Marcus Garvey in support of the Universal Negro Improvement Association. His father had volunteered for the British army in 1939 because he had heard about Hitler's hatred of Blacks and Jews. This history of activism in his family is a precious legacy. "One of the things that most Black people fight in themselves is a sense of rootlessness and a lack of personal history. Where do I come from? What's my history? Knowing that my father was in some measure a progressive person is important for me. It's incredibly important to me. It gives me credibility with myself. It's important to my children. I envy people in the world who can go to a church registry in their parish and trace their ancestry back over five hundred years. That's a privilege! You have a context for yourself and your history. It's so important as human beings to have that."

This sense of rootlessness was particularly poignant for a young Black boy growing up in England. Coventry was a cruel place for Pat and his siblings. While he is clear that there were some white English families who were very kind to the family, especially when they were going through financial hardships, their kindness tempered what was otherwise a brutal childhood. "Just up the road from us there was a working-man's club that had a sign No Blacks, No Pakis, No Dogs. Every day in the *Coventry Evening Standard*, the local newspaper, there were rental ads that read No Blacks, No Pakis." Throughout his school years and as he started to look for work, Pat was the target of racial taunts and assaults. This was a time when many Caribbean and South Asian immigrants had arrived in England, and there was a great deal of racist violence, which the police and most government officials did little to prevent. In an effort to escape unemployment and the constant onslaught of racism, he decided to join an older brother in Toronto, and soon discovered that racism was alive and well in Canada. He has been fighting for human rights for over thirty years in his adopted country.

The Power of Stories and Community Connections

Pat knows how important stories and community connections are to people working for change. In his early twenties, he wandered into the Third World Books and Crafts store on Gerrard Street in Toronto. For the first time he was exposed to books that were by African-descent people writing about what was happening in their lives. He began to read Marcus Garvey, George Padmore, and Malcolm X. The owner of the store, Lenny Johnson, offered to lend Pat the book he was reading in the store. It was Bobby Seal's *Seize the Time*. Pat went back often to borrow a number of books and to have conversations with Lenny. Lenny was full of stories about the Communist Party of Canada. He told Pat about the time Paul Robeson came to Toronto to perform and couldn't get a room in a hotel and was hosted by a comrade who lived in a white stucco house on Palmerston Ave., just north of Harbord, a house Pat had passed by often. Soon Pat and a number of anti-racism activists (Marlene Green, Derry Meade, Lester Green, Beth Allen, and Delroy Reed a.k.a. Debo) began to meet every Saturday afternoon to discuss the books they were reading and "the movement."

Through these readings and conversations and other formative connections, Pat became interested in the Communist Party and soon joined the Young Communist League. There, he found more stories and a sense of belonging: "I could sit next to an old comrade and listen to stories about union organizing in the thirties, about trains taking Ukrainian immigrants out to the west coast of this country to work in logging camps that were basically concentration camps in British Columbia. ...These people are the history of left labour struggles in this country. Their history goes back to the Winnipeg general strike and beyond ... there was a sense of history, and a deep and abiding sense of connectedness to something that was worldwide that I really needed."

In 1978, while still a member of the Communist Party, Pat ran for election to the then Toronto Board of Education. He wanted to become a school trustee because he was concerned about the practice of academic streaming in the schools. The various reports published about Toronto schools in the 1970s confirmed something Pat had always known: that schools tended to stream mostly children of colour, especially African-descent children, and working-class Italian and Portuguese children into special education and "less demanding" academic programs.

The reports from the Toronto Board included the 1974 *Multiculturalism Report*. While the report dealt with ethnicity and not with race, a Race Relations Working Group was established because of the deficiencies it had identified. Senior school administrators had written the report, as well as board trustees, teachers, union members, and parents. This was the first time such a participatory and democratic process was used by the Toronto Board of Education, and it became the basis of the participatory democratic model it used until 1995 when the amalgamation of the various school boards took place.

Despite such successes, Pat quickly found that the Board was a complex organization in which it was very difficult to bring about substantive change. For example, he and other members of the Race Relations Committee wanted publishers to ensure that the content of the books they provided to the Board reflected the experiences, knowledge, and contributions of the diverse communities in Toronto. The most the Board was willing to do at the time was to write letters to the publishers, and these had little effect. Pat comments about that period, "Frankly, I didn't have the skills at the time to move it any further than that. Now, it would be an easy matter for me to think about how I might get the Board to not buy these books anymore. The Board had huge economic power and moral leadership. If we had stopped buying books from publishers that didn't change their content, it would have resonated across this province and across the country."

Building Anti-Racism and Employment Equity at the Board of Education

Pat left the Board in the 1980s to attend law school, and in 1991, after graduating, returned as an equity adviser of the Equal Opportunity Office. Law school was one way of honing his strategies and ensuring he would be able to influence more change within the Board. He was returning as an employee with a particular goal: he wanted to change the way in which the Board understood and handled race-related complaints. Under the existing procedures, the Board dealt with the complaints as individual and isolated incidents. Little was done to address the prejudiced ideas underlying the racist behaviour, and even less to grapple with the systemic causes of racism. Racism was being perpetuated through the built-in biases of the curriculum, guidance practices, assessment and placement theories and practices, human resources policies and procedures, and every other aspect of the school system.

After securing agreement from the senior administrators that a section of the procedures for handling race-based complaints needed to be changed, Pat revised not only the procedures but also the entire policy for handling racial incidents. He renamed the document the "Policy and Procedures on Racial Mistreatment in Schools and Workplaces." He did this to make the point that racism did not occur in isolated "incidents" as the original document suggested but was part of an ongoing process, "an unbroken chain of experiences." He remembers that "I came back to the senior administration with the Cadillac version, and when they questioned me on it, I reminded them about the discussion we'd had about how the systems and ideas behind the behaviour were not being addressed. They had agreed to this analysis in our previous discussions."

While the senior administrators had to accept Pat's point that changing one procedure would not address the systems contributing to racial discrimination, they were still not willing to accept the range of changes he proposed. They were particularly concerned about the revisions to the policy, which now made stronger statements regarding racism and other forms of discrimination and committed the board to specific actions. The policy defined "race as a social construct" and established a clear, progressive disciplinary path to be followed in substantiated cases. The administrators insisted on amending certain sections of the policy, such as those that identified the social construction of race and some of the statements of commitment.

In anticipation of this, Pat had written the elements he considered vital to the policy into two or three different parts of the document, and said them in slightly different ways. He could willingly agree to make the amendments asked for in one area, knowing that the document still contained the essential pieces in other sections. Pat would make the changes to the drafts within twenty-four hours and always make sure that he was the one asked to make the revisions. Keeping control over the writing process was critical to crafting a policy that addressed racism directly and effectively. Making the changes demanded by the administrators was essential in ensuring that they would take ownership of the policy within the larger organization.

As a result, some potent statements remained in the final version of the policy. For example, the definition of racial and ethno-cultural mistreatment included the recognition that it is "an expression of power, authority, or control through notions of racial and/or ethno-cultural superiority." The results of such mistreatment were defined as "people of colour, Aboriginal people and members of ethno-cultural groups hav[ing] unequal access to resources, decision-making, health, well-being, employment and other opportunities." The policy further recognized that "racial and ethno-cultural mistreatment, like other forms of discrimination, are often invisible to those who are not its target, by the seeming 'normality' of the ideas and practices which perpetuate them."

When the "Policy and Procedures on Racial Mistreatment" was presented to the board of trustees, one of the trustees put forward a motion to broaden this policy to other forms of discrimination. It became the basis of a more comprehensive Human Rights Policy that Pat wrote as part of another committee. Pat says of this time, "I really began to understand how to establish myself as an equity officer in a position of power in the organization: it included keeping control of the writing of key documents and creating space where there was none before rather than stepping on others' turf. Policies and procedures establish power because they identify who will make the decisions on these questions. I made sure that the documents were always clearly within the bounds of procedural fairness. This showed senior administrators that there was nothing to fear since the procedural safeguards were always present. The other part of the strategy was to ensure at the same time that the power to implement the procedures resided in the Equity Office. The power to make decisions, and to use discretion in these matters was granted to and resided within the Equal Opportunity Office."

Changing Human Resource Practices

Human resources practices, in particular the hiring of new teachers, were another area that required attention. It was also an area that required buy-in from Toronto Board of Education administrators, superintendents, and school principals. How did Pat persuade some of the people who were at first completely resistant to become advocates for anti-racism and employment equity? Pat gives credit to Harold Braithwaite, associate director of the Board. Harold was the only African-descent senior administrator at the Toronto Board of Education, and Pat insists he was the real champion of employment equity. "He would insist that the role of the Equal Opportunity Office was to work on employment equity, and when I resisted because I wanted to do work on curriculum related issues, Harold dragged me into it. The Board set up an Employment Systems Review Committee in 1993, and Harold put me on it. Within two meetings I was hooked!"

Superintendents and principals were resistant to employment equity for reasons similar to those put forward by most people opposed to it: "We can't find qualified candidates from the equity groups—we've tried," or "What do you suggest, that we just hire them without a fair hiring process?"

As Pat describes it, "It was a titanic struggle to get the senior administration to agree to doing employment equity the way I wanted to do it." He acknowledges that real change did not happen within the Employment Equity Committee. Instead, the most gains were made when he and his allies decided to create a pool of qualified candidates within which there was an over-representation of members of racialized groups, and to set up a fair hiring process. This meant they did not have to "take away the discretion of principals to hire, but could structure and confine that discretion so it was not so open-ended."

The first step in creating a pool of qualified candidates and setting a fair hiring practice was to use existing resources. There was a greater representation of racialized people among supply teachers than there was among permanent teachers. Pat and his allies found that the professional development of supply teachers was deficient. "They were not getting mentoring from regular teachers or principals, nor were they getting professional development opportunities to develop skills. Since supply teachers would lose pay if they attended weekday workshops, we decided to host workshops for substitute teachers on Saturdays. It soon became clear that there were a number of racial miniority elementary supply teachers who were ready to apply and qualify for permanent teaching contracts. We also set a day for teacher education students who were racial minorities and studying at the University of Toronto and York University to meet Margaret Evans, the associate director of programs at the Board, and Leon Thompson, the only Black superintendent. During the full-day workshop, they worked with teachers in small groups so that they became acquainted with résumé writing and with the interview process."

In setting up a fair hiring process, Pat used the existing one. He revised the process so that it was based on a behaviour-description interview tool learned through a consultant to the Board. There were five questions attached to each of the five areas of the interview tool. One area contained questions solely on anti-racism and equity, with anti-racism and equity content woven into questions in the four remaining areas. Every selection committee had a choice about which questions it wanted to ask; however, no interview team could select questions from the matrix without choosing questions related to equity. Pat obtained buy-in from principals and staff development personnel to integrate anti-racism and equity into the questions in each section of the tool. Pat still uses this model in his work.

Twelve elementary school principals were trained in the use of this tool and worked with Pat and other staff to develop the behaviour descriptors and range of responses to each question. "It was an incredible exercise. We said to the principals, 'We're asking you to sit down and write out what it takes to be a good teacher. One principal asked, 'What qualifies us to write questions for the whole system?' My answer was that by becoming a principal he, in many ways, guaranteed to parents that he knew what it took to be a good teacher. I also asked if there was any doubt that in bringing twelve principals together they could not come out with a consensus about what candidates should be interviewed on—he had no more questions."

Pat describes the influence this process had on a superintendent who was well respected by others. Initially, he resisted employment equity, but when he used the new behaviour-based interviewing tool, "he changed, he completely changed. He became an advocate and got his whole family of schools involved in anti-racism work. It was the tool in part, but it was also that the entire process was so scrupulously fair. People everywhere think employment equity is about hiring people who don't have qualifications. We were able to build in two hurdles for every candidate. First, they had to go through these behaviour-based interviews to get onto the 'eligible to hire list.' Then it was from this pool, and only this pool, that principals could interview people to hire again using centrally designed behaviour-based questions.

As a result of the behaviour-based interviews, there were many more people from the groups designated by employment equity (women, Aboriginal people, people of colour, and people with disabilities) in the pool. In the first year of this process, 28 per cent of new teachers hired by principals were from the designated groups. In the following year, however, senior staff vetoed Pat's training plans because it had been done the previous year. "They were to get a serious lesson in the old adage that 'Equity is a process and not an event.' In the next round, only 18 per cent of new teachers were from the designated groups. The following year saw the reintroduction of employment equity training for principals. Predictably, the percentage of teachers hired from designated groups rose to 26 per cent, significant statistics when the board was hiring 200 to 300 teachers per year."

Involving Community in Changing Curriculum

In addition, school board trustees were putting pressure on principals to be community-oriented and to ensure principals were making changes with noticeable results in curriculum. "The anti-racism agenda was a really good organizing principle. It captured people; it said, 'We're going to work, we're going to do things,' and it made it easy for the superintendents to say, 'This is what we stand for, this is where we're going to put our efforts into making change." Trustees raised these issues at both the board and in the community for two reasons: over the previous two decades, trustees had come increasingly to reflect the demographics of the

Toronto community, and even in those areas not represented by trustees from racialized groups, communities were clearly raising issues having to do with equity.

The board's Community Services Office and its school Community Relations Officers played an enormous role in raising the awareness of parents. They brought parents together to discuss their aspirations for their children and for schooling. Annual parents' conferences were held across the city, and they were an effective way of keeping the board focused on working with communities. "The Organization of Parents of Black Children and its relentless work on behalf of Black children was constantly on the mind of senior staff. During this time I remember the director of education saying that equity work and considerations was actually driving change at the board. The director, in fact played his part. Every year he established three goals for the period; equity would always be one of his goals. People, no matter how reluctant they were, got the message. Everything would be looked at through an equity lens. Since that time, reproducing that state of mind and being has become my goal for organizations that I work with and within."[3]

Start With What People Can Hear

Pat began with a focus on the curriculum rather than with the employment systems because this is what people with power could hear. It was easier to capture the attention of principals and teachers by focusing on what was being taught in the classroom, which books were being used, and how teachers approached teaching in the classroom. The Equal Opportunity Office became very involved in the training of teachers, meeting with principals and teachers face-to-face, and working through curriculum content. Among the difficult issues that would be raised in teacher/principal training sessions was the disproportionate numbers of Black children who were being "sent down to the office" by a mainly White teaching force. Wasn't this a manifestation of systemic racism and weren't progressive

teachers and principals condoning the pattern? As this work took effect, Pat became satisfied that in most instances when teachers disciplined Black children, there was some clear and justified reason for the discipline.

Over the years, the principals saw the value of anti-racism work to their schools and became more open to recommendations from the Equal Opportunity Office. By the time Pat presented a case for employment equity and the behaviour-based interviewing package, a level of trust had developed between Pat and the principals. "I suddenly realized that I knew most of the people in the room, and I had absolute faith that most of them were going to do

Ned McKeown, former Director of Education at the Toronto Board, Pat Case, and Fiona Nelson, School Trustee

Dancing on Live Embers

exactly as they were asked to do on this particular topic. And that's what happened: the buy-in was virtually unanimous."

By involving everyone in equity and anti-racism work, there is no question in anyone's mind that it is of paramount importance to the entire organization. In this way, it is clear that equity and anti-racism work is everyone's responsibility and not simply the work of those hired to provide leadership on equity issues. This is what Pat achieved as the Equal Opportunity Officer at the Toronto Board of Education, and what he continues to implement in his role as the director of the Human Rights and Equity Office at the University of Guelph.

Human Rights and Equity at the University of Guelph

Pat left the Board in 1999 and sometime later joined the University of Guelph. He made it clear to the president that when he did human rights, anti-racism, and equity work, he was doing it for the university and for him. "I told my boss that I intended to speak in his name. He visibly jumped at that, but it was important for me to be clear with him. I was trying to say, 'Don't set me up. You hired me to do a job and I'm going to do it. We've all been through enough of this nonsense of half-measures and half-agreements. So if you hire me, it's important that you know I'm going to be committed to this and I'm going to make things happen.'

"I try to put myself in a position so that those who are my supervisors never have to correct or admonish me. Having to be told what to do hands tremendous power to those who have authority over you. I'm not a very easy person to supervise and I know it. I cannot decide whether it's my ego or the desire for an independent equity establishment that gets in the way. It could be both. Maybe you have to have both. I eventually get what I want through the force of argument, moral suasion, or just plain persistence. I hate being told off and work at not placing myself in that position. Part of this, deep down, has to do with the fact that when I am being admonished, the system turns to black and white in both senses. They are right and I'm wrong and they are White and I'm Black. Very bad moments. Although there are principles that must be adhered to, there are no cookie-cutter formulas to doing equity work. Much of one's approach has to do with who you are and being true to that."

With this understanding in place, it was important that Pat worked closely with the senior administrator so that the president knew what Pat was going to be doing and so there would be no surprises. "I met with the president every three weeks and I was perfectly honest and open with him about everything I was going to do. I never held anything back from him, and I didn't ask permission; instead, we discussed everything. The first time I met with him I sat about six feet away, he said, 'Get over here!' and pointed to a seat within about three feet of him. He said, 'The way this works is you talk, I criticize, you argue back.' That's what we've done ever since. You see, I do not want to give the impression that I am not deferential. One must be deferential to some degree—after all, we are talking about one's boss here."

At the University of Guelph, the president was very involved in promoting human rights on campus. "I told him how the students would feel about the president speaking at rallies to oppose racism and sexism. I was looking to him to support the implementation of the Human Rights Policy. The policy establishes a certain standard on the campus. It is only when behaviour sinks below an acceptable level that the procedure comes into play. But it is the president who has to set the tone for the policy. The educative role, communicating the university's expectations, and continuing to do this over time was the president's job. So he spoke at hate crimes vigils on campus and won tremendous respect from the students for it. He was born in Poland immediately after the Second World War. On the day of his birth there was a pogrom in his village and many Jews were killed. The man had a history. I'm proud of the fact that I got him to talk about it publicly."

The president also made it clear that it wasn't just Pat's job to address discrimination on campus. Pat describes a discussion that took place following an incident of anti-Semitism on campus when the university executive group met to discuss a response. "We were meeting in the president's office and discussing the incident. One of the vice-presidents said, 'Well, somebody needs to write an article for the university paper about this,' and everybody turned to look at me. The president said, 'What gave you the idea that only Pat was hired to do equity work? Why don't one of you do it?' So one of the vice-presidents wrote an amazing article about citizenship and how the community has to work together to ensure that the bounds of citizenship don't get crossed."

In these and other ways, Pat worked with others to demonstrate that human rights work belongs to the entire university community. "At times we've got to deal with a human rights incident as a community interest. It's an incredibly healthy thing for people to do. You've heard of Matthew Shepherd, the gay student murdered at the University of Wyoming? It was an absolutely horrifying case, and there were vigils held on campuses everywhere on the continent, including the University of Guelph. One of the students who graduated from the drama school at the university decided he was going to put on *The Laramie Project*, the play about Matthew. He pulled together a cast of seventy-five people, including the president-designate of the university. We put on the play for four straight nights before packed houses. The president had one of the biggest parts. He played the doctor who gave press conferences about how Matthew was doing in hospital. He really cried through much of the last monologue, and he had the whole house in tears. The aftermath on the campus was unbelievable. People came up to all members of the cast as we walked through the campus and said, 'Bravo, bravo!' It was such a solid community."

Pat also extends anti-racism and human rights work beyond the university campus to the broader community. The principal of a local high school invited him to her school because White Canadian students were attacking a number of Afghani students. She told Pat that she walked one of the Afghani students to the edge of the school property and that other White students hurled racial abuse at him right in front of her. Pat and the principal discussed a number of strategies for dealing with racism at the school, and Pat decided to involve university students in the process. There's a visible minority student group on campus called the Munford Centre. It is named after Clarence Munford, a former professor at the university who is now retired. Professor Munford is a Black professor who was very popular. One of the students from this group had told Pat that they were thinking of setting up a mentoring program for students on campus who were struggling. Pat suggested that they set up a mentoring program for students at this high school instead.

Twelve university students of different races and religions (Christian, Muslim, African descent, Asian descent) were matched up with twelve students from the high school, half of whom were White, and half of whom included Afghan and other racialized students. The mentoring program involved the university students going to the homes of the youth, doing academic work with them, watching movies together and discussing them. Many of the high school students were struggling academically and wanted to go to university. The intent was to transform the way racialized students were thought of in the high school and to form a bridge between the university and the families of the high-school students.

Keeping the Embers Lit

Over the years, Pat has learned a great deal about what it takes to make change within an organization and how to actively challenge racism. He has had to persevere and not give up when things looked impossible. "I never give up on the agenda. I always come back with it in some other guise. You have to be relentless. But not dogmatically relentless. You cannot hound people, harass or badger them with these things. You've got to find different creative ways to come back to what you want to change."

One of the most effective and creative ways in which Pat promotes human rights is by connecting it clearly with democracy. "There are thousands of people in the university's workplaces who don't have any stake in equity or democracy. How can we make equity real for people? We have to make our processes democratic. I know that the extent to which we can bring about change with respect to visible racial minorities at the university has every-thing to do with the degree to which all people can be welcomed into the workplace, and how people feel about their own work. That's what's really fundamentally changed about my work. Our office is a place that everybody comes to. Everybody. My slogan is—it's from *The Cider House Rules* by John Irving—We seek to be useful. If people come to our office for help and their situation isn't covered by a human rights ground, we still find some way to be of help. Human rights work happens at all levels in all kinds of places in universities and other large institutions. It's everybody's work."

For Pat, the measure of equity in an organization is the extent to which people who are least powerful have as much say as those who are most powerful. "For example, I am get-ting tradespeople onto hiring committees to hire new tradespeople. In every organization I've worked in, among custodians and tradespeople, there are huge levels of supervision. How do we reduce that? Why do we think a custodian is going to bilk the university more than a faculty member? We've got to find a way of getting beyond that and to bring a bun-dle of rights to all employees in the organization."

EVELYN MURIALDO: We Can Never Do This Work Alone

Evelyn Murialdo has described anti-racism work as "taking the horns by the bull." All too often, because Evelyn's first language is Spanish, people assume she has mistakenly inverted a common English saying; it's not a mistake. Perhaps it is because English is only one of the languages Evelyn speaks that she is able to turn the words on their head in order to capture an important point. In this case, she knows only too well that anti-racism organizational change requires wrestling with the entire body of the organization, and that it is often dangerous work.

The daughter of a German Jewish father, Hans Loewe, and a Chilean Christian mother, Ines Lobo, Evelyn lived with discrimination from an early age. "My father's family came from Breslau, Germany, and were taken to the concentration camp at Bergen-Belsen. Hitler allowed Jews who had fought in the First World War and had received the Iron Cross (the highest decoration for service) to leave the concentration camps if they also left Germany. His family had two weeks to leave for either Shanghai or Chile. My grandfather chose Chile because the common alphabet would make it easier to function in Spanish."

Her mother was a Chilean woman and the first cellist to study at the Conservatory of Music in Santiago. Evelyn's parents, both cellists, met at the conservatory and married despite opposition from their families. "Grandma Oma [father's mother], whom I loved, had very strong opinions about the cleanliness, the laziness of the Chileans, and included among them my mother. On the other side, my mother's family would lament the day she married a Jew. Home was a bit like an oasis from the constant discrimination to which we were exposed. My mother and father created for us the most unusual, secure, solid, united, diverse home."

Evelyn attributes her passion for social justice and activism to her mother. "Mother was out of the ordinary. My father was very conservative and cautious, but my mother was very much on the Left. We didn't get bedtime stories, we got chapters from Don Quixote and the poems of Rabindranath Tagore. We would talk in great detail about the struggles of Mahatma Gandhi in India. Music was always around us and she was always interested in other peoples' lives. The people who came to our house included gays and lesbians from the world of music and ballet, poets, writers, Aboriginal people, and refugees from Haiti; they captured our imagination one way or another. From my mother I learned to think of differences as ever so important, attractive, exciting, and so essential to building unity and equality."

Since arriving in Toronto over thirty years ago, Evelyn Murialdo has been immersed in community development and social justice battles, working with a variety of community groups and agencies. Anti-racism has been an integral part of these struggles. "I went to work in Regent Park as one of my first jobs. I would come back with stories that I told my ex-husband, who wasn't an activist at all but a professor of medical genetics at the University of Toronto. He would say, 'If I were Black and living in Regent Park, I would be running around with a machine gun.' Here it was more graphic and easier to capture racism than in Chile where there was no engagement between people of different races, none at all."

Shifting Focus: Moving from Multiculturalism to Anti-Racism

Evelyn's entry into anti-racism work was not easy. As a Chilean woman in Toronto, she has experienced discrimination based on her language, ethnicity, place of origin, and gender. "I feel that most people think I have an accent in my brain because of the way I speak. People assume things about my education, my intelligence and what I can do. So this whole idea of anti-racism and focusing on race as a key determinant was very difficult at first. With multiculturalism, I felt included and I could identify with it. But with anti-racism, I felt totally left out. As a White woman I haven't experienced racism. It was so difficult to see, to understand what was inclusive of me and what was not. Coming to terms with it was a compelling exercise."

What convinced Evelyn to move from a multiculturalism framework to becoming an anti-racism activist? "I had lots of respect for the people who were leading the anti-racism work at the Toronto Board of Education when I was there in the 1980s. They were like my allies in many ways, and I couldn't easily dismiss them. But the other factor was the reasoning behind the argument; it was quite powerful and painful. How inescapable it is! How graphic it is! And then I saw the phenomenal gains that anti-racism could make for us. I came to the conclusion that if people of colour could have a decent life, then we all would win. When people are able to deal with people of colour in a manner that is healthy, then the rest will automatically follow because that is the benchmark, so to speak. Once I saw that, I came along."

After leaving the Board, Evelyn took a job with the Metropolitan Toronto Housing Corporation Limited.[4] Most employees of MTHCL had never worked with, perhaps never met, anyone quite like Evelyn Murialdo before she walked into the organization in 1991. She had been hired by the general manager who knew that racism was a particular problem among tenants and staff, and he persuaded Evelyn to take a position as the first community development co-ordinator. In this role, Evelyn established a new category of workers—community development promoters (CDP). In addition to developing the job descriptions, Evelyn trained the CDP supervisors and district managers in the basics of community development and advised them on how to be part of implementing this new approach when working with tenants in the buildings. Evelyn describes community development quite simply as "a group of people coming together to work together to improve their individual lives and the lives of others—the lives of their families, neighbours, communities, or co-workers."

Rainer Soegtrop

Cha-Cha-Cha: Chaos, Challenge, and Change

A large part of Evelyn's mandate was to directly address racism, ageism, and other forms of discrimination that seemed widespread in the company. "It was a very White, Anglo-Saxon organization. There were very few exceptions, and the exceptions obviously were found at the bottom. We found that people were quite used to telling racist jokes at lunch time and were intolerant of any other languages being spoken in the workplace. People of colour who lived in MTHCL communities were absolutely unhappy, and racism was the most common source of tenant complaints."

In such an organization, Evelyn herself was seen as an oddity, an outsider, and quickly became the target of discrimination. "I came to a meeting in my third week on the job, and two of my colleagues were already there chatting with each other. I walk in and one of them says to the other, 'Here comes the Commi.' The other person bursts into laughter; she finds it absolutely funny. Because I was from Latin America, from Chile, and because I was bringing in all these 'leftie' notions about community development, they thought I was a Communist."

There were numerous other incidents in which her colleagues discriminated against her. Evelyn saw these moments as crises that led to developing critical strategies for her and her allies. "We used every little thing as an opportunity to bring about change. I remember walking from one meeting to another with a few colleagues, and I happened to be walking with someone who also speaks Spanish. It's natural that during a break you would fall into Spanish if that's your mother tongue. We were walking in the street, we weren't at a meeting. A person who was behind us complained to my manager that I was speaking Spanish with another colleague. My manager, who was trying to be helpful, says, 'You should remember that English is the business language of the company.'

"Well, I decided I was going to take issue with that. It was important and critical to my sense of well-being and acceptance. I talked to the general manager, to my manager, to everyone. I told them I was absolutely offended that if I could not speak Spanish in this place, it meant there was no room for me. I told them I thought people were strengthened by acknowledging who they were, and if this was how it would be, it meant I was being told to go back to where I came from. I told them I was going to speak Spanish with my colleague whenever it was something that didn't involve another person.

"Then I went to speak to the person who complained, and this person said that it was not inclusive for me to behave this way. That triggered a whole session for staff about what is meant by being inclusive. We found out that lots of people that worked for the company had the same problem. For example, Filipino clerks who met at lunch time were not allowed to speak Tagalog with each other. They were told not to speak anything but English."

Evelyn discovered that these same employees, those who were being reprimanded for speaking to each other in languages other than English, were being pressed into providing translation and interpretation services to managers and co-workers struggling to serve tenants for whom English was a second or third language. The double standard did not escape Evelyn, and she brought it immediately to the attention of the general manager.

There were other crises Evelyn used for organizational learning and change. When people saw the traditions and culture of the organization being challenged, their opposition to change became more pointed, and Evelyn became even more of a target. One of the most pitched battles was fought around celebrations of the "Holiday Season" in the company. In the midst of Christmas preparations, one of the supervisors of the community development promoters said to Evelyn, "We're putting up these Christmas trees in each of our buildings. If we're going to be true to community development principles, we need to buy some menorahs for the buildings in which there are large numbers of Jewish tenants." She was referring to MTHCL buildings in the area between Bathurst St. and Lawrence Ave. and Bathurst St. and Steeles Ave. in northern Toronto. This manager, who was Christian, asked if Evelyn would buy the menorahs, and Evelyn agreed.

As the menorahs were placed in the nine buildings in the area, a human resources manager went to the general manager to complain. "The way she framed it was, 'Did you know that public funds are being spent on religious objects by employees? The entire front-line staff are up in arms about this.' The general manager called me into her office and said, 'I want to talk about how you're spending money. It's social housing money. It can't be used to buy religious objects.' Well, I asked her, 'How about the Christmas trees we have in every building?' She told me we didn't buy Christmas trees. I felt so betrayed by this manager who was Jewish and had gone to the general manager's office to complain about the menorahs, and now by the general manager, that I couldn't hold back the tears. I told the general manager, 'I'm going to leave now but I'm going to come back, and I want you and the manager who spoke to you to wait for me.'

"I went to the finance department and found one of my allies there. I explained to her what had happened. She could tell I was terribly upset and she said, 'I'll get you the receipts in no time.' She came back in five minutes with two receipts, one for $150 for Building A's Christmas tree and another for $260 for Building B for Christmas decorations, and these were just two out of over a hundred buildings. Plastic menorahs were bought at a cost of $14.99 each for nine buildings. When the general manager saw the receipts, she was mortified. I told her, 'I cannot work under these conditions.' The general manager apologized."

The organization continued to struggle in its efforts to ensure religious equity for tenants. A few months later, MTHCL gave permission for a room in one of its buildings to be used for Muslim prayers. When the people who came to pray left their shoes outside during their prayer time, someone threw all the shoes in the garbage.

Create a Chain of Internal Activists

The presence of internal allies was critical to Evelyn's work, and networking with these and other activists was essential to the anti-racism organizational change process in MTHCL. Evelyn had convinced her manager, Rainer Soegtrop (who is featured in "Rainer Soegtrop: Leadership in Times of Resistance" in phase two), and the general manager that she could not bring about the desired change alone. Her strategy for building a group of activists was to create race relations study circles for interested MTHCL employees. "We had to find people who would come on board. My instinct for survival is to find allies at all levels of the organization, but particularly on the front lines. Then I invest whatever I need to invest to have a troop of people that are really there when things start to boil. Without them you become an expert but there is no possibility of change."

These study circles included building superintendents, social workers, administrative assistants, and senior managers. They were drawn from across the organization and through the study circles given many opportunities to work and connect with one another. "We were very creative in getting these people to work together. We made race relations a new value in the company. If they learned about it, they would certainly be improving their career development within the organization."

The senior managers recognized that since race relations was such an important and valued skill, people had the right to access training and education in this area. The company asked for volunteers who would like to become more knowledgeable in this area, and forty people came forward. At first they were interested because they were concerned about their careers, but they joined the study circles on condition that they made a commitment to contribute to the promotion of the Race Relations Policy in the company. "They could get time one day a month to come and learn, plus some days to do research, and they could leave their not so enticing jobs of cleaning. They could go to conferences and take time off. In exchange they had to actively promote the Race Relations Policy to staff and tenants."

As a result, when the time came to present the Race Relations Policy to MTHCL tenants, there was a team of knowledgeable volunteers from inside the organization who did the presentations. "Managers, superintendents, custodians and administrative assistants would facilitate the meetings together, take notes and make it happen. So we had a set of allies.

Without them we would have remained stuck in the theory of anti-racism change."

The study circles led to dramatic changes in people's lives. "There was a wonderful superintendent from Newfoundland who volunteered. In the first meeting he said, 'I am here to learn about racism. I have no problem, people are people, but don't get me into this gay stuff. I don't want any twinkle toes around me.' On the last day of the study circle sessions, during the evaluation, he said, 'You know, I think I'm now ready to learn about gays and lesbians.' And then there was a White manager who became so passionate about anti-racism it was like a personal crusade! No one was going to stop her. This is a woman who used to paint her face black, put on white gloves, and do a minstrel show as part of a fundraiser for the United Way. It was a big change for her."

Some of the participants in the study circles experienced reprisals from co-workers who did not agree with the goals of the Race Relations Policy, and yet they stayed with the group, willing to deal with the consequences. Evelyn describes the risks some people took to join the study circles: "I was being paid to do this work and given permission to do it. For these people in the company, it meant taking a big risk. For example, a man who worked in finance wanted to come to the study circles even though he was scared stiff that he would not be understood when he spoke English—Cantonese was his first language. Coming to the study circle would be one more thing that would make others in finance see him as an odd ball. When he attended the circle meetings, his manager would pile work on his desk and he would have to take it home to finish it."

Give Voice to the Tenants

One of the biggest changes brought about by community development at MTHCL was the creation of democratic processes that gave tenants a say in the running of their buildings. Prior to this, staff had been rewarded primarily for maintaining clean buildings and keeping the apartments in good repair. Little was done to ensure tenants got along and built community connections among tenants, community groups, and agencies in their neighbourhoods. Staff did provide some support to tenants who wanted to connect with others in the building through the promotion of social clubs; however, these social clubs were not always welcoming to racialized tenants. In very few instances did tenants and staff come together to discuss conflicts in the building and to find solutions together. This was particularly the case with allegations of racism from tenants. These were either ignored by staff or badly handled, with the onus remaining on the racialized tenants to "fit in" with the White tenants.

Evelyn began to organize meetings between MTHCL tenants, community agencies, and staff to deal with complaints. "We had given permission to the Toronto Board of Education to use the recreation room in one of our buildings for an English as a Second Language class. It was open to tenants and the community outside, and one day I found out there was a complaint from the Board of Education. I went to the building and heard that tenants and the building staff would not open the door to members of the community who came for the English class. If they did make it into the building, they were immediately asked to take off their shoes so they wouldn't dirty the building. This was in winter, and it was seniors who were coming to the class, walking on the tile floor in their socks. The Board of

Education complaint had gone to the property manager of the building and nothing had happened.

Rainer Soegtrop

"So I got the building staff, tenants, and teachers from the board to meet. The Board put forth their concern about students not being allowed into the building, and the building staff said it was for security reasons. 'If we open the door, how do we know who is coming for the class and who is not?' Remember, it was a class for seniors. At one point they were all gathering outside the building and entering the door all at once. They had to put this big label on their shirt in order to be able to come into the building. MTHCL staff kept arguing it was for security reasons, it was to keep the building clean.

"But in those meetings, whenever you do a good community process, there are so many breakthroughs. There was a Filipino woman who stood up and said to the property manager, 'You talk about security as if someone was going to come and snatch my purse. I talk about security in a different way. Security for me is when I go in the elevator and the superintendent insults me because I press the wrong floor. You make me feel terribly insecure. It makes me want to die. Or when I go out and meet another tenant that lives on my floor, and we speak in Tagalog, and a neighbour says, 'Shut up. Speak English.' That's a real security problem. I'm not concerned about my purse being snatched.' Little jewels like that are what made this work possible. The only way to catch these stories is to engage in them slowly, trying to deal with each issue at a time."

This reframing of security and questioning of the priority of clean floors over the well-being of tenants and community members led to huge changes in the way building staff interacted with tenants. It eventually led to the establishment of tenant councils, with elected tenant representatives from each building having the authority to bring the concerns of their neighbours to the attention of MTHCL staff.

Build Allies in the Community

At critical times throughout the anti-racism organizational change process, Evelyn relied on community activists to play supportive roles in a variety of ways. She recruited people from the Urban Alliance on Race Relations and the Chinese Canadian National Council to the board of directors so that there would be support at the board level for the implementation of the Race Relations Policy. In addition, at critical points in the process, community allies from legal clinics and organizations like the Ethno-Racial Disability Coalition of Ontario made deputations to the board to ensure there was support for anti-racism actions that came before them for approval.

Anti-Racism Strategies in Women's Organizations

In addition to her work in social housing and continuation of her personal commitment, Evelyn led some important initiatives in various women's organizations, a number of which have struggled to come to terms with racism within the Canadian women's movement. Many have failed. Critical battles were fought in the 1990s, and many women have heart-breaking stories about the conflicts that erupted and the impasses that have endured. During this period, Evelyn was hired as an organizational development consultant to work with a variety of agencies serving women, in which women were divided by racism and other forms of discrimination. This section attempts to capture some of the strategies Evelyn used to assist these organizations through transformational change processes.

Each of these organizations was led by "predominantly affluent White women who were familiar with corporate decision-making processes and belonged to the same social network." They invited Evelyn in to work with their organizations because tension and conflict had arisen between White women and racialized women, as well as Aboriginal women. In each case, Evelyn's task was to identify the organizational issues, facilitate dialogue between the various factions and groups in the organization, and to facilitate a development process that would establish structure, policies, and practices that would better reflect and respond to all communities of women. In particular, she was to prepare the organizations that had always had White women in positions of leadership for the leadership of racialized women.

The challenge for Evelyn was how to reveal the racism that was so present in these organizations and in which most White women self-identified as progressive and inclusive. In some organizations, Evelyn decided the most powerful thing to do would be to quote verbatim the comments of White women and racialized women made during public discussions in her interim report to the organization. She also quoted women of colour who were in senior positions in order to document the impact of racism on the new leadership. These reports were powerful tools. "The quotes said it all. I didn't have to define racism. I didn't even have to make a case because the examples were so blatant." For example:

> *"Don't get me wrong, we want to support _____. We want to help her become more confident of her own skills so she does not have to feel threatened by our expertise."*
> (White woman about a racialized woman newly elected to a position of leadership)
> *"For so long we thought [only] a white woman could lead all women ... and when a woman of colour was elected, we immediately doubted her ability to lead all of us."*
> (Racialized woman)

> *"My vision is about strong women working together to compensate for our differences."*
> (White woman)

> *"She is bright but a bit angry..."* (White woman referring to a racialized woman leader)

> *"I think women of colour have contributed enormously to the discussion and the work*

... they have brought important issues to the table that would never have been discussed before." (White woman)

"There is no one way of defining feminism ... the word feminism has been appropriated and defined by women of the industrialized countries of the world, making it meaningless for the rest of the women." (Racialized woman)

"Why do we always try to strive for consensus? Women have considerable differences: class, race, sexual orientation and language. We need to debate, disagree, and deal with conflict." (Racialized woman)

As some of these quotes indicate, many White women found working in racially diverse organizations a challenge that "created tension and uncertainty." Some White women felt they needed to "clarify their roles as White women in the organization while the leadership of the organization was in the hands of women of colour."

Quoting people directly was an enormous risk, but Evelyn felt it was a risk she had to take. "What do you do when racism is so evident in the attitudes of progressive women? In several of the organizations I worked with, all those women didn't want to be racist, but hadn't learned what racism is. These statements were made without understanding the impact. The quotes were all statements that were made in public. I took the trouble to verify each statement with the women who made them. The meetings to discuss these reports were so painful. However, the process forced the women involved to come to terms with the fact that racism was alive and well in their organizations."

The reports also identified systemic issues in the organizations. Racialized women were a numerical minority and in order for them to be represented in various committees and decision-making bodies, they had to take on three or four times more work and responsibility than White women in the organizations. In addition, racialized women from newly established communities were needed within their own communities and were required to contribute to these communities through many hours of volunteer work. These differences were not recognized in the structure of the organizations, or in the informal ways in which their peers assessed their commitment to the organization. "All too often, racialized women were criticized by their White sisters as being 'unable to focus' or 'lacking depth.' They were also criticized when they disagreed with each other, while unanimity of thought was not expected of all the White women in the organization."

In several organizations, these reports were the beginning of significant reorganization processes. "It triggered tremendous energy in these organizations. Though numerous White women left some of the organizations, others remained. They struggled hard with the notions of racism, and with racism as a factor distinct from the other factors that affect women's lives. For example, Lucille Owens was a White woman with a disability. Although she felt that her organization was insensitive to the needs of women with disabilities, and she named it occasionally, she also knew that the battle of racism needed to be tackled. She believed that once we tackled racism, we could apply what we learned to disability."

The Benefits of Creating Alternative Structures

The benefits to the organizations that grappled with racism and created these alternative structures were manifold. One clear benefit was that many women came to realize that "the strength of the women's movement lies not in its homogeneity but in its diversity. As such there is no 'one' way of doing things or 'one' definition of feminism, or 'one' interpretation of the women's struggle." In one organization, racialized and Aboriginal women conducted a huge outreach campaign that resulted in the largest and most diverse attendance at the annual general meeting. For the first time, groups working with immigrant women, women living in poverty, refugees, Aboriginal women, young women, and older women became active in the organization. The representation of racialized women on the executive body increased from six to fourteen members, which was at least half of the board.

Another organization created the conditions for poor women and racialized women to become part of its funding base and to have opportunities to contribute to the organization in a meaningful way. Immigrant women and racialized women hosted a fundraising dinner that was so successful it became a regular part of the fundraising efforts.

It is also important to note that the anti-racism and anti-discrimination change processes led to the clarification of roles and responsibilities, the refining of policies and procedures, and resulted in more effective organizations. Women working in one of these organization were finally clear about the role of each staff person, and its volunteers had better access to information. As well, the financial operations were realigned to support the organization's mandate and financial information became more readily available to the leadership and the organization's members. For the first time in many years, the Finance Committee was able to develop a three-year financial plan.

The personnel policies, performance development process, and volunteer recruitment process of another organization were revised as a result of the change process, and for the first time, staff felt confident they would be fairly treated and fairly assessed by the organization's leaders. Conflicts between the board of directors and staff that had remained unaddressed for over two years were laid to rest as the roles and responsibilities of the board were defined anew. Staff representation in decision-making forums was established, and a grievance/complaints mechanism for staff was developed. The last statement of the final report on this organization's change process declares: "The most important accomplishment so far is that board members and staff feel a sense of belonging, feel part of, useful and important to the life of the Centre."

The experiences of these women contradict the belief held by many that anti-racism organizational processes are divisive and damaging to organizations. While there were undoubtedly periods of tremendous tension and some women left the organizations, valuable gains were made as a result of the work and commitment of the women, both racialized and White, who remained involved with the process to the end. More importantly, organizations that had been established and funded to serve all women were now able to fulfill their mandate and engage diverse communities of women.

Essential Strategies

Work with the Most Resistant People

Evelyn insists that one of the most valuable strategies learned from her years of anti-racism, anti-oppression organizational change work was the importance of involving "the people who were hardest to bring along, not to work alone or only with the converted." Often this meant proceeding slowly, in order to address the fears and concerns of the people who were initially resistant to anti-racism. The more they learned about anti-racism, the less resistant they became. At times, it even meant doing considerable work behind the scenes, knowing that some of the opponents of anti-racism would get the credit for her work. Though it took considerable time, energy, and patience, the effort was always worth it as these were sometimes the people who became the most effective allies.

Use Conflict as Starting Point

Some of the experiences described above demonstrate Evelyn's strategy of using conflict as a way of encouraging the organization to begin to think and act differently. This may appear to be a radical piece of advice, given that most organizations have a culture of avoiding conflict at all costs. However, selecting particular conflicts and making them the focus of attention and energy in the organization can create an opportunity for people to discuss the issues, examine their assumptions, clarify the facts of a situation, and develop a solution together. Evelyn refers to the process for this type of discussion as a "methodological walk." The steps are as follows:

- listen to each person's view of what happened—do not agree or disagree, but give each person an opportunity to fully express her/his point of view
- write the main points of each person's point of view on flip-chart paper and post it on the wall; avoid the temptation to edit what they are saying
- post blank sheets of flip-chart paper on the opposite side of the room and ask people to think about how they would do things differently in the future, given what they heard from everyone in the room

This process works well to build common ground and to develop solutions that most people agree to support and implement.

Develop a Little Plan of Action

Few employees enjoy organizational planning processes and many dread the task of developing work and strategic plans. Evelyn's suggestion of developing a plan of action is quite different from these types of processes. For one thing, it is a short-term plan and its goal is to ensure that "the chaos is orderly." While Evelyn believes change agents must generate a certain amount of chaos in the organization, it is important that it is done in a way that is well planned. "It's not just a tactic to stir things up but it must be orchestrated so that the organization gets the most out of it. You have to know how you will position things, and make sure you have your allies in place. It has to be calculated because often there is a great deal at stake."

The "little plan" is also a way of identifying how activists and their allies are going to implement a strategy for change. "I am ever so convinced that we have to have a sequence of events—a beginning, a middle, and an end—if we are to be successful. We can't skip any steps, we have to do A, then B, then C. We must also avoid process for the sake of process. There's nothing worse than a process which goes on forever; it has to have an end."

Keeping the Embers Lit

What would Evelyn say to activists who are struggling to stay in the battle for racial equity and social justice? "It can be lonely being an activist sometimes. What conditions do you create around yourself so that you continue to believe that another world is possible? One bit of advice I would give to people would be, 'Save all your pennies and go to the World Social Forum or any similar event.' When I was at the Forum, I stopped feeling like an odd-ball and felt like I was part of a huge worldwide community. Sometimes I feel like a rethreaded tire, I've been doing this for so long. But when I saw the huge numbers of young people at the Forum, I felt excited. There you can go to hear Eduardo Galeano, Maude Barlow, Arundathi Roy, and so many others. We can never do this work alone. There is no merit in being an expert all by yourself in an organization. We need a community to do this."

What would Evelyn say to ongoing organizational change? "The work world is not a neat and orderly manufacturing plant. Both major organizational change and adult learning are messy and painful. Change needs to be persuasive, pervasive, and successful. It must keep in mind the foundations of the organization and the most powerful structures and positions within it. There will be no change until we have changed all these aspects of the organization."

Rainer Soegtrop

World Social Forum, Brazil, 2005

Evelyn's Tool for Organizational Change

Although organizational development and strategic planning exercises are essential as descriptive tools, they often are not effective as change tools. They assume stable and/or discernible environments conducive to planning for a predictable future. This is not always the case. The following is an outline for organizational change that can be brought forward for discussion when you are preparing to launch a change process.

1. **Organizational change acknowledges the complexity of the organization.**
   ➤ Organizations are not just internal systems, ideas, or concepts. They are complex social, administrative, and political systems with complex inter-relationships.

2. **Organizational change requires a strategic power analysis in the organization as well as an evaluation of beliefs/value systems, communication systems, and networks.**
   ➤ Once this is done the organization can position the change and identify resistance elements, leverage points, allies, and so on.

3. **Organizational change acknowledges that change is a matter of dollars and cents and not ideology.**
   ➤ Change is a necessary strategy for the benefit and survival of the organization. It means that new markets, new competencies, and new practices are needed. Change is a pragmatic dollars-and-cents issue; it is not ideological nor imposed by external forces such as government, agencies, or taxpayers.

4. **Organizational change acknowledges that policies, procedures, and protocols are support instruments for change.**
   ➤ Policies are not an end in themselves, nor do they implement change.

5. **Organizational change recognizes and validates the difference between learning and training.**
   ➤ Learning is an ongoing process, and is based on current work situations. A learning context encourages and permits learners to engage with, and accept the change, it uses adult education and non-traditional learning techniques, and it gives staff the message that there is time to do the work which neutralizes the opposition. "We have to go slow in order to get there fast."
   ➤ When mistakes are made it allows senior managers to say "it's a learning process and we learn from our mistakes."

6. **Organizational change acknowledges the impact of change.**
   ➤ The process of organizational change acknowledges that change causes more work in the short term.
   ➤ It underlines the conviction that change will soon stop the existing work and stresses that change is new work that replaces old work and does not mean more work.

7. **Organizational change defines and structures change.**
   ➤ Change is about careful planning as well as "seizing" and "sizing" the opportunities. During this process, mistakes and crisis can be a source of organizational learning.
   ➤ Change needs to be rooted in the front-line staff and owned by them in order to

(continued next page)

change the way the organization does its business.

➤ More change is easier than less change.

8. **Organizational change involves everybody.**

➤ Organizational change places the responsibility for change on everybody and is reflected in all policies, procedures, job descriptions, hiring processes, performance development processes, and so on. To be successful, change needs to be focused, single minded, and profound.

9. **Organizational change encourages a lot of feedback, both negative and positive, because organizational stress is accepted as part of the change.**

10. **Organizational change legitimizes advocacy and the role of conflict in the organization.**

11. **Organizational change acknowledges the role of civil society, community scrutiny, and advocacy.**

➤ Coalitions, community members, and groups participate in committees, policy groups, and complaint investigation teams where they can influence the work of the organization.

12. **Organizational change acknowledges and defines the senior mangement commitment and leadership of the change agenda as critical and fundamental.**

➤ Active involvement and support from senior management signals to staff that change is here to stay and everybody

needs to work towards the transformation of the organization.

➤ The new values introduced by the change agenda need to be constantly "lived" by senior managers publicly and informally.

➤ Interventions by senior managers are essential during this process, and their role is to create a functional environment in which the motion of change is as stable as no change.

➤ Senior management's most important role is to reinforce and recognize new behaviour, conferring status and legitimizing new activities within the organization.

➤ Although change takes years to accomplish, it is in the interests of senior managers for it to happen quickly (it's more economical for the organization to be stable).

13. **Organizational change recognizes clearly its responsibilities and objectives.**

➤ The organization is not responsible for changing individuals. Individuals are responsible for changing themselves. The organization creates the conditions for individual learning—space, permission, support, removal of barriers—and establishes behaviour standards and consequences for staff and service users. It is not important to change minds but behaviour must change.

➤ The organization can only regulate behaviour, not attitudes or thinking. It is essential that the organization symbolically and pragmatically welcome the new organizational values that emerge.

14. Organizational change acknowledges, recognizes, and deals with resistance and opposition.

➤ The more formally educated and result-oriented staff often confuse "effectiveness" with "efficiency." They are impatient for implementation and they think everything can be done with the right execution. However, important things have to be done with patience and pacing, and must be done one at a time.

➤ The opposition will delay, focus on details, and "appear" not to resist. They will criticize change agents not on the grounds of values and commitments but for lack of co-ordination, lack of planning, and a failure to meet targets.

➤ The opposition will speak of "a takeover" and set up a "them and us" dynamic.

15. Organizational change needs clear communication.

➤ The words, messages, and images of organizational change must be clear, simple, and repeated often.

➤ Using plain language in written materials—stories, translations, interpretations—and simple graphics in images is essential.

BUILDING BLOCKS FOR EQUITY
A Summary of Common Characteristics of Phase 3, Keeping Racial Equity on the Agenda*

Decision-making

We think about who's deciding, how they are deciding, and what the results are.

- The organization has an employment equity policy and plan and is acting on it.
- Middle management includes a few racialized people, as do all levels of the organization.
- There are occasional references to equity in the strategic plan, in program evaluations, and in more job descriptions.
- A clear accommodation policy outlines procedures for removing barriers to people with different kinds of disabilities, and for racial, cultural, gender barriers as well.
- Decision-makers are consulting with more people in making decisions.
- A clear complaints procedure exists and is understood by most employees.
- Managers and workers make more effort to settle little flare-ups early, rather than letting things fester.

What gets missed?

- White, straight, able-bodied, middle-aged people still exercise more informal influence than newer employees in the same job categories (see "White Women as the 'Default' on Equity").
- Equity questions are not integrated into regular evaluation and planning; consultants hired for this work are not screened for equity expertise (see "Dancing on Live Embers").
- There are no (or very few) Aboriginal workers or managers in the organization (see "No Plan for Succession Planning").
- The complaints procedure is seldom used.
- References to equity in job descriptions are generic and do little to clarify how it is an essential part of every job (see "Double Jeopardy").

*This tool has been adapted from the theoretical work of Jojo Geronimo and Marlene Green for the Ontario Anti-Racism Secretariat, 1993–95.

Communicating

We look for who communicates what, who's supposed to listen, where the silences are, who gets what information, whose information is valued.

- A higher proportion of gay/lesbian/bi/trans people are "out" in the organization.
- Staff are more comfortable talking about how inequity affects the clients/members/people they serve.
- There are more examples of people with a range of identities asking questions when something uncomfortable happens.
- There is less fear of reprisal for identifying discrimination or problems in the organization.
- People speak their own languages with colleagues.

What gets missed?

- In group settings, when people make questionable comments or actions, they are rarely addressed, even by management.
- Workers who face discrimination doing their jobs, still deal with the impact by themselves, reluctant to risk raising it with colleagues or in the organization (see "Double Jeopardy").
- Many dominant group workers remain unaware of the work realities of colleagues who face racism and of its impact on the work the organization is trying to do (see "Double Jeopardy").

Expertise

We're interested in what and whose expertise is sought, valued, paid for, and used. We seek to continually widen the expertise from which the organization can benefit.

- "Understanding equity and anti-oppression" appears on all job postings for new hires as a job requirement.
- "Developing an equitable workplace" is beginning to be an expectation of managers, particularly new ones.
- Target group members are being consulted on a wider range of their expertise, not just on equity.
- Staff involved in joint projects with other organizations are developing expertise helpful to their own workplace.

What gets missed?

- Job descriptions for veteran staff remain outdated and make no mention of equity competencies.
- Equity competencies and their application in the workplace are not yet real factors in performance evaluation.
- Staff with language skills and equity competencies are not compensated for them (see "No Plan for Succession Planning").
- Staff working with "communities at risk" still work unrecognized overtime.
- Departments/work groups are uneven in their ability to identify and challenge inequities.
- Some White staff worry about making mistakes, or looking ignorant. This hampers their effectiveness in being a good ally and doing their share of racial equity work (see "Double Jeopardy" and "No Plan for Succession Planning").

Networks/ connections

We look for what and whose contacts and networks are sought, valued, paid for, and used to hire, promote, train, develop programs, and evaluate. This is the opposite of the "old boys club."

- Joint projects are operating with a wider range of other organizations.
- Address lists are kept current for equity contacts in media, community organizations, activists, advocacy groups, unions, and government departments.
- Some staff who experience discrimination have started to bring situations to staff meetings for joint problem-solving; this happens where there is considerable trust.
- Some White people are identifying racism and acting as better allies; in these situations, their connections with colleagues and clients/members have improved.
- The organization has real connections to equity networks through its increasingly diverse staff.

What gets missed?

- Wider connections with equity advocates are through individual staff's networks; there is no mechanism to make these links organizational rather than just individual.
- New networks and connections brought by racialized workers are used as "equity credentials" but still do not influence the organization in the way that traditional networks do.
- The organization has no way of evaluating and applying what it's learning from campaigns or joint work with other organizations (see "Dancing on Live Embers").
- Oppressions still compete with each other for the organization's attention; for example, gender has been a major focus of the organization's push on equity, but White women have benefited more than racialized women (see "White Women as the 'Default' Position on Equity" and "Fighting over a Small Piece of the Pie at the Local School Board").
- The board is still drawn from a limited range of networks in the overall constituency of the organization.

Resources

We're interested in who allocates time, energy and money to what; who benefits from the allocation of resources; who influences the allocation.

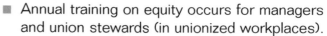

- Annual training on equity occurs for managers and union stewards (in unionized workplaces).
- Equity is appearing more and more as a routine item on many meeting agendas.
- Resources are found to update policies and procedures every few years.
- Equity appears indirectly in line items in the organization's budget—staffing, training, materials, and joint work with other less-resourced organizations.
- The organization has found outside money to take equity work further, particularly with one group of people (gay/lesbian/bi/trans; or Somali clients/members; or women in leadership, and so on).

What gets missed?

- The additional time and skill required to serve more vulnerable populations is recognized in policy but not in the budget or in how work is allocated (see "Double Jeopardy").
- While all managers are expected to take up equity issues in staff meetings, not all feel able or skilled enough to do so; results are uneven in the organization.
- Updating policies and procedures has been viewed as a technical task; consultants have done the work; few people in the organization are familiar with the latest version of policy (see "Dancing on Live Embers").
- Annual training on equity has become a bit routine; managers and stewards are prepared for emergencies but not to think and act on equity in their everyday tasks.
- Various "equity concerns" still compete for the organization's scarce resources; there is some resentment that one group gets more attention (time, staff, money) than others (see "Fighting Over a Small Piece of the Pie").

Section 3

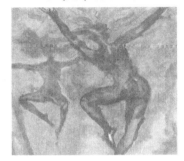

Making the Links

Making the Links: Racial Equity in Organizations and Social Movements

This section highlights people who have chosen to use in different kinds of power—organizational authority, social identity privilege, personal courage, and charisma—in the service of building equitable social movements. The two stories included here draw inspiration from equity activists in two labour organizations—the Canadian Labour Congress and the Toronto and York Region Labour Council. The Labour Council story, "Building Workers' Power through an Equity Agenda" shows how union organizers, racial equity advocates, and community residents can work together on issues critical to the community, such as school board elections, public control of water, and affordable public transit. In this story, building alliances across racial difference is critical to promoting the public interest and to increasing the capacity and influence of a workers' movement.

"Working Inside/Out," is the story of building anti-racism activism in the Canadian Labour Congress. It examines two important questions: What helps anti-racism activists have maximum impact on an organization? What are effective roles for staff and elected leadership in advancing equity?

Both these stories offer practical thinking and strategies for equity advocates regardless of their organizational location. They also emphasize that racial equity is both the basis for real coalition and a goal of social movement building.

Ethel LaValley, former Vice-President of the Ontario Federation of Labour

A National Story

Working Inside/Out: Building an Anti-Racism Activism at the Canadian Labour Congress*

The Canadian Labour Congress (CLC) is the largest central labour body in Canada and represents 2.6 million workers and their families living in communities across the county. These workers are members of 119 affiliated unions, and of provincial and territorial federations of labour, which in turn, are members of the Canadian Labour Congress. Since its founding in 1956, activists have urged the Congress to promote the links between workers' rights and anti-racism and human rights.

This story highlights some of the lessons we have been learning from anti-racism work at the Congress over the past ten years. We used two key questions to shape our writing of this story: (1) What helps volunteer anti-racism activists advance equity in an organization? and (2) How can staff and elected leadership work creatively with the pressure and the politics of their organization to advance equity?

When we look at who workers and union members are, and will be in the future, we realize that the very future of the labour movement and its organizations is at stake. The Aboriginal labour force is young and growing at twice the rate of the non-Aboriginal labour force in Canada. In Saskatchewan, one-quarter of all labour force entrants were Aboriginal in 2001. Aboriginal people will make up 35 per cent of Saskatchewan's workforce by 2045.[1] There are no current figures for how many Aboriginal workers are unionized, but racism has been a key obstacle to their entering and staying in any workplace, unionized or not. In addition, seven out of ten immigrants to Canada settle in the four largest cities of Toronto, Montreal, Vancouver, and Calgary. Soon, more than half the population of Vancouver and Toronto will be made up of people of colour and Aboriginal people. Building an anti-racism activism is critical to the health of the Canadian labour movement.

Getting Equity on the Agenda

It was labour and community activists during the 1940s, 1950s, and 1960s who lobbied successfully for human rights legislation and commissions in every province of Canada. By the end of the 1960s, these were in place across the country.

> Beginning in 1946, committees against racial discrimination, later known as Labour Committees for Human Rights, were established in Winnipeg, Toronto, Montreal, Vancouver and other centres. These committees, responsible to their local labour councils, were assigned to help protect unions and members against discrimination, and to seek legislative remedies against discrimination in areas outside the scope of collective bargaining. ... Once

---

* We draw our inspiration from the many union activists aross Canada who have contributed to racial equality work at the CLC, in particular, the CLC National Human Rights Standing Committee, the CLC National Aboriginal Working Group, and the CLC National Workers of Colour Working Group. We also draw on the past ten years of the organization-building work of Winnie Ng, David Onyalo, and Hassan Yussuff whom we interviewed over the period April to Novemebr 2004 in Toronto and Ottawa.

basic legislation was passed, they continued applying pressure to have it improved and ensure that it was administered effectively. Throughout this period, Jewish, Black and Asian organizations as well as religious and community groups joined labour in an all-out assault on racism.[2]

Then, as now, racialized workers were in the forefront of these struggles against racism; then, as now, the Canadian labour movement's record has been very uneven. Depending on the leadership, the preoccupations of activists, conditions for organizing, and how power was used, the work either moved ahead or stalled.

Canadian Unions and Social Movements

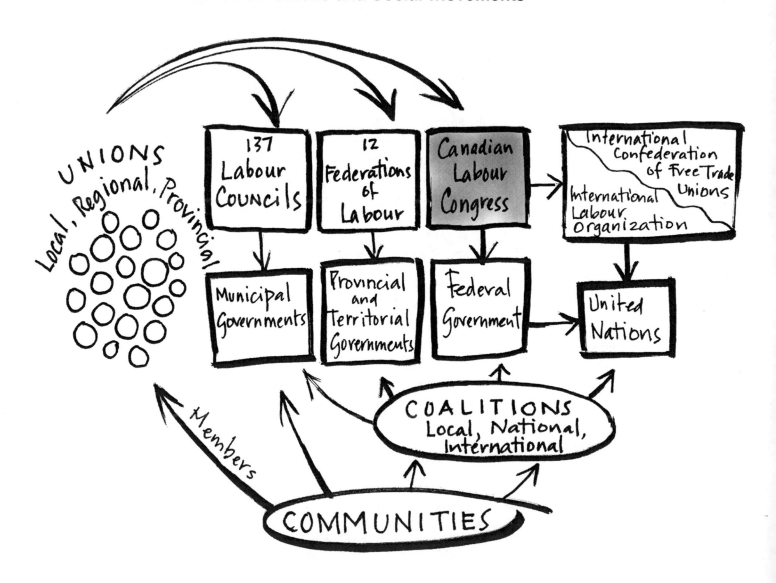

How the Canadian Labour Congress (CLC) Works

The CLC represents the concerns of working people to different levels of government. (The Quebec Federation of Labour plays a similar role in Quebec.) It lobbies for a fair unemployment insurance system, adequate pension schemes, public health care, child-care programs, and worker training. As a famous bumper sticker says: The Labour Movement: The People Who Brought You The Weekend!

Internationally, at the International Federation of Free Trade Unions and at the International Labour Organization, the Congress represents the realities and issues of Canadian workers. To the Canadian government, the CLC advocates for human rights, just immigration laws and policies, and for international trade deals that protect the environment, jobs, and the power of governments over corporations to make decisions in the best interests of its citizens. And it reminds the Canadian government of its responsibilities to challenge racism in Canada and to live up to international agreements that it has signed. These include the *Universal Declaration of Human Rights*; the *International Convention on the Elimination of all Forms of Racial Discrimination*; the *International Covenant on Economic, Social and Cultural Rights*; and the *International Covenant on Civil and Political Rights*.

To do this, CLC must have a strong connection with the lives of workers in every community. Under its structure, the CLC has twelve Provincial and Territorial Federations of Labour, and 137 Labour Councils in different Canadian cities. Every three years, some three thousand delegates from affiliated unions gather at the CLC National Constitutional Convention to set policy for the CLC and to elect its four executive officers. Between conventions, policy decisions are made by the executive council made up of forty-seven representatives from affiliate unions. Representatives of Workers of Colour, Aboriginal Workers, Workers with Disabilities, Solidarity and Pride, and Youth also sit on the executive council.

The CLC Anti-Racism and Human Rights Department has primary responsibilities for anti-racism, human rights, immigration, refugee rights, employment equity, Aboriginal rights, and workers of colour rights. On these issues, the staff of the department works closely with members of the CLC National Human Rights Standing Committee, the CLC National Aboriginal Working Group, and the CLC National Workers of Colour Working Group. The director of the department works with staff from other CLC departments and regions to integrate anti-racism and human rights into all Congress work. The director also works closely with and offers guidance to the officer directly responsible for the work of the department.

The Fight for a Representative Leadership

Hassan Yussuff, current secretary treasurer of the CLC, remembers his early work with the CLC, before designated seats on the CLC executive council. "Bob White who was the president of my union (the Canadian Auto Workers Union or CAW), called me into his office and said, 'The CLC has a Human Rights Committee. I'm not sure if it does anything useful. I want you to go in there and stir things up.' So I went to my first committee meeting, and after listening to people for a while, I asked a very innocuous question. 'What's the role of this committee?' Well, people said you're supposed to come here and give a report, and so I replied kind of rudely, 'So next time I'll fax you one; I don't have to come all the way to Ottawa to give a report.' Nobody knew quite what to do, and things continued.

"Finally I said, 'I'd like to make a motion.' This was kind of unusual at the time; nobody made motions at committees. I said, 'I move that this committee organize a human rights conference.' The chair of the committee was a very decent guy. He said, 'Fine.' Nobody spoke, so I spoke to my own motion. Then someone said, 'I think it's a great idea to have a human rights conference, but this is not the time.' I said, 'Fine, you tell me the time and the dates and I'll come back at that time and make the same motion so at least I know I'm making it in the right context.' The chair suggested a break, and I asked for a vote on the motion first. I knew that people would get talked to, and their positions would change. So the chair called for a vote, and the human rights conference was approved by one vote. That was 1990. We organized the conference; I think we had almost four hundred delegates and they had to turn away over three hundred other people."

At the 1990 CLC convention in Montreal, Dory Smith, a man of colour, ran against the slate off the floor and almost won. He had been backed by anti-racism activists from the Canadian Union for Public Employees (CUPE), the Canadian Auto Workers Union (CAW), the

David Smiley

Hassan Yussuff, Secretary-Treasurer of the Canadian Labour Congress

United Steelworkers of America (USWA), and the Public Service Alliance of Canada (PSAC). As a result, the CLC leadership realized they needed to change the structure of the CLC and established a task force that was to report to the 1992 convention. The task force report recommended that one visible minority seat be set aside, along with seats for other equity groups on the executive council. The Coalition of Black Trade Unionists organized and demanded two seats for visible minorities. The CLC agreed, and at the 1992 Convention, Hassan Yussuff and Lynn Jones were elected to occupy the two new seats. Hassan recollects, "There was expectation among our constituency that people like myself and Lynn would bring some kind of voice to their issues, and try to figure out what we should do." The CLC's decision to designate two seats was a direct result of political organizing through caucuses at convention.

What Changed at the Congress in 1994?

In 1994, the CLC convention agreed to amend its constitution to include one "visible minority" vice-president on its executive committee, and one Aboriginal vice-president on its executive council. The convention also approved a resolution calling for an Anti-Racism Task Force. This decision was the result of pressure by activists on the National Human Rights Standing Committee (NHRS) in 1993, which followed a CLC Report on Aboriginal Rights. Activists from across the country co-ordinated efforts to get their affiliates to send in the resolution, and they made sure that a staff person was attached to the process. The pressure from activists to do something wasn't new. But the leadership at the time decided to listen. They heard the demands of Aboriginal activists and activists of colour: visible representation at the staff and leadership levels and the support of CLC leadership to challenge racism.

Just prior to the 1994 decision, the CLC split the human rights co-ordinator job into two. One national representative was given the responsibility for women's issues, and David Onyalo was hired to work on human rights and anti-racism. It was also during the 1994 convention that four equity working groups were created: Workers of Colour, Aboriginal Workers, Workers with Disabilities, and Solidarity and Pride. David recalls the discussions at the National Human Rights Committee. "We agreed that different groups need their own voices. Their work can complement what the National Human Rights Committee is doing. But the work cannot move forward unless [these groups] and women who have their own national committee figure out a way to work together."

David describes the breadth of his original mandate. "I had the responsibility of working with Aboriginal workers, workers with disabilities, and workers of colour and for general human rights in my role on the National Human Rights Standing Committee. But after the convention, it became apparent very quickly that even if I could do all of those things well, if I didn't put anti-racism on the agenda of the CLC and the labour movement, I wouldn't meet the expectations of the activists. And they were right to demand it." This meant that David worked with the two groups with anti-racism responsibilities while two other staff guided the responsibilities of the Solidarity and Pride Working Group and the Disability Rights Working Group. David would also become involved with the Anti-Racism Task Force that was just about to be launched.

The Anti-Racism Task Force Begins

In 1994, the Anti-Racism Task Force was launched, and it changed everything. It has had a major impact on the analysis and strategies that the Congress uses to challenge racism, and its continuing influence is due to the determined work of elected leaders, activists, and staff. Hassan Yussuff recalls, "I think it's one of the most rewarding things I've ever been involved in. It's difficult to go and listen to people tell stories about their pain and frustration. Yet, at the same time, everyone we spoke to—and it was hundreds of people—expressed hope. They said, 'We're hopeful that the leadership will rise to the challenge and respond to the things we're saying.'"

The task force consisted of three CLC vice-presidents—Lynn Jones, Hassan Yussuff, and

Ethel LaValley—and David Onyalo, at that time the director of the Anti-Racism and Human Rights Department. Hassan Yussuff noted the trust that the officers showed in the process: "It was unusual to be leading such a controversial project without one of the four top officers overseeing it." The task force appointed additional members in the various regions and reported to the executive vice-president of the CLC. The members agreed early on that the task force "is not just about racism. It's to document the experiences of people of colour and Aboriginal people in a political context. That context is that unions are not going to survive unless they figure out that the strength of the labour movement includes Aboriginal people and people of colour." The slogan of the 1995 CLC poster signalled this message clearly: The Face of the Labour Movement Is Changing.

The task force conducted two phases of hearings with union members across Canada throughout 1995 and 1996, working closely with the Aboriginal Peoples and People of Colour Working Groups which were to be the political voice within the affiliates and ensure a visible presence within the different regions. "Members of the task force made it clear to the leadership, labour staff, and activists (including Aboriginal people and people of colour) that the task force was looking at ways of building the movement in our unions, our workplaces, and communities. This was an important political message for those who may have been uncomfortable or outright opposed to the task force."

The first phase of regional consultations was completed in time to table an interim report at the May 1996 CLC convention. With the approval of the interim report, the second phase of consultations began. Follow-up consultations were held across the country to check out the findings of the initial report in preparation of the final report. The consultations stimulated discussion among Aboriginal workers and workers of colour about how racism affected them in their workplaces, unions, and communities; about the links between racism and immigration; and about strategies for strengthening their networks within the labour movement and communities.[3] We think that the task force's decision to return to the people they consulted to confer on implementation strategies is precedent setting in the Canadian labour movement—if not Canadian society.

Consultations were also open to the general public to ensure the discussions benefited from different communities, and vice versa. This was an encouraging decision by the CLC leadership. "It was amazing that they allowed that because they could have decided to avoid any chance to show the labour movement in a bad light. But they opened it up," recalls David. He goes on to describe the process of revisiting the original interviewees: "We had never done this before—gone back to the same cities, the same people, and said, 'Okay, here's the report; does it look like your views, or the themes you put forward? If it does, how do we implement the thing?' Aboriginal people and people of colour have been to all kinds of conferences in the past, and seen tons of recommendations. We wanted to acknowledge that, 'Yes, we have recommendations, but we want to put a framework on this to really move it forward.'"

Hassan remembers criss-crossing the country again for almost a year. "It was very important in a number of ways: one, it laid out strategies. Two, it talked about things people were not even thinking about like environmental racism, racism in housing, health care, and issues beyond education and harassment policies; it looked at systemic problems that require deep responses, that are based on class as well as race. Three, it gave an internationalist perspective to racism. Given that three-quarters of the world are people of colour, how are we involving people of colour in our international work?"

Many of the racialized union members who came to the consultations became involved in the labour movement for the first time. From David's point of view, "A member from Nanaimo who travels to Victoria for this debate, is someone I would not normally ever be able to meet through the structures of a union because often there are blocks to who gets what information. But with the task force, we could contact workers through a variety of means. The first Workers of Colour Conference was held in 1998, after the final report was done, and guess who was there? All those people who had participated in the different regions."

The Importance of Leadership Buy-in

In preparing both the interim and final reports of the task force, it was essential to seek out the support of the leadership. A staff person advocating for equity from the inside is in a delicate position. She/he is lucky if external activists are pressuring the organization to act from its best principles. That's often what's needed to get decision-makers' attention. But personal commitment from the leadership is crucial for any real headway in anti-racism, and equity staff have an important role to play in nourishing that commitment.

At the CLC, the initial strategy came from activists of colour, but joint staff–leadership commitment was needed to move that strategy forward. "I worked with the officer responsible for this file, with the director of women's and human rights in the structure, and with the equity vice-presidents as the voice of the anti-racism activists," recalls David Onyalo. "We hadn't finished all the consultations before the convention in 1996. But we wanted to get the interim report passed, and before that, we had to get the buy-in of the heads of

CLC Workers of Colour and Aboriginal Workers Conference, 2002

unions. Because once the convention delegates adopted it, it would be much harder for them to say 'We've never seen that report; we don't like it' when we presented the final report."

Hassan Yussuff recalls a "heads-up" meeting with the CLC president before the meeting with executive council. "I met with him privately and said, 'This interim report is coming out and it's going to be quite controversial. But the strength of our movement is to face itself in the mirror. The voices in this report are union members who pay dues and put their life on the line every day to fight for this movement. The leadership should listen regardless of how difficult they find what this report has to say."

Both Hassan and David talk about the important role the CLC president played at that meeting. "He opened up the meeting by saying, 'You can look at all the people on the task force and give them hell. But you know what? These are our own members telling us what's wrong with us. This is not the task force speaking. This is the membership. You didn't go out there talking to these members; the task force did. So don't give them trouble because you don't like what you hear.' Well, that was incredibly helpful in setting a constructive tone for that discussion."

At the public launch of the final report in 1997, the CLC president fielded questions. Hassan remembers, "The media asked 'Why would you write a report that is so critical of your own organization?' And the president said, 'It's necessary, it's important, and we have to do it.' It's that simple."

CLC Workers of Colour and Aboriginal Workers Conference, 2002

Making Equity Everyone's Work: Post-Task Force Initiatives

People know when an "organizational priority" is really a priority because it is communicated through a variety of ways. As David points out: "The Anti-Racism and Human Rights Department was created because of the task force and because of the long years of work by activists. We knew the recommendations were being taken seriously when they gave structural recognition to anti-racism work at the Congress. In 1998, they created this department and upgraded the job to director, and they put money into project work, as much as, if not more than, any other department."

Even before the task force, the work had begun to widen human rights from a narrow legal focus, looking for ways to connect human rights to the broader social and political agenda of the CLC. "We brought in staff people to talk about immigration and refugee issues, international solidarity, fiscal and economic policy, pensions and health care," recalls David. "Then we would ask about the specific impact of these issues on Aboriginal people and people of colour. We would look at the impact of the last federal budget on people of colour. We looked for spaces to make connections between human rights and the everyday concerns of the Congress. Because remember, the Human Rights Committee has everybody. That's where we have allies from the mainstream community. So it helps to situate human rights in the broader framework of workers' social and economic rights."

A CLC Executive Council Statement of September 1995 made these links directly:

> Political conservatives have targeted employment equity, in part because it advances collective rights in the workplace and in legislation. Because it is a more recent development in our understanding of equality rights, employment equity has been easier to isolate and discredit. When we listen carefully, we hear the same arguments that have been used to discredit workers' rights in the past, now being used to discredit equality rights. Workers are familiar with arguments about how unions lower standards, how unionized workers receive special treatment, and how unions take away the individual rights of workers.

It goes on to link equality with a history of fighting for collective rights:

> Unions organized to present a common front against arbitrary employers. We know that no individual can face the power of the employer in the workplace. We also know that no individual member of an equality seeking group can tackle the systemic barriers being defended by employers.[4]

According to David, this strategic approach of linking broad issues to human rights led to the organizing of the CLC Human Rights Conference. This, in turn, pushed the theme of human rights as social, economic, and workers' rights. The conference was also a direct response to the threat of cutbacks to social programs which were initiated at the time by the federal Liberals.

In 1998, David co-ordinated two CLC staff discussions at the Canadian Autoworkers' Educational Centre at Port Elgin. TheCLC president made attendance mandatory. The purpose was to look at how everyone's work should advance an equity agenda. "We went back to some basic questions: Why are we doing this work? What is anti-racism? What are the root causes of racism? How does that fit into a working-class analysis? Why is it important to integrate anti-racism into what we do? Why is it important to work with Aboriginal people and people of colour?" A third session was held with support staff.

Hassan recalls, "Many people were supportive—most women tended to back what we were saying, with pockets of support from the men. After that session, some of the other departments started to initiate integration of equity issues into their work. But it's important to say that there was a very clear political message in terms of where the organization was going. So people who were supportive expressed their support; people who didn't support the initiative became neutral."

After the staff sessions, the officer responsible for the work organized a joint meeting (a first) between the Human Rights Committee and the Education Advisory Committee to discuss anti-racism education.

Also, after individual sessions between David and other directors, the Education Department took initiative and began integrating issues of equity into stewards, bargaining, organizing, and facilitator training courses. This was based on the work of the CLC Anti-Racism Education Working Group, which produced an "Interim Report on Anti-Racism Education" in July 2000. The Working Group was a joint initiative of the Human Rights Committee and the Education Advisory Committee, created to continue the work of the Anti-Racism Task Force and to develop an anti-racism education plan of action. In 2003, the Education Department produced *The Anti-Racism Integration Guide*, the collective work of many activists on both committees.

The Social Policy Department began integrating basic questions about the impact of social policy on people of colour and Aboriginal people into its research. For example, the director hired a woman of colour to research the effects of social devolution on newcomers and immigrants, and the department published a report entitled "Is Work Working for Workers of Colour?"[5] This has been used as the basis of government and international briefs and in arguing for more public attention to systemic racism and its effects. These efforts are a good example of how another part of the organization can support the objectives of the Anti-Racism and Human Rights Department and not let it carry anti-racism for the whole of the CLC. According to Hassan, this research is continuing: "We're doing some work on globalization, trade, and the economy, and we're specifically thinking about how women, people of colour, and Aboriginal people are affected by globalization and trade in the economy."

The research presented in "Is Work Working for Workers of Colour?" had an impact beyond the labour movement. As Hassan points out, "This research isn't new. It's just never been debated in the way we did it. Yet the media was quite shocked when the report was released. I don't know why because every study now confirms the same thing. It shows that you can't account for the disparity in income, job security, and so on by saying that people of colour don't have the education; they do. You go through all the ways you can blame inequity on the individual—they don't have the credentials, they don't meet these criteria, they don't have superior education. Yet you find that they do in fact have all of these qualities. Thus, there's only one thing left to consider—that we're a deeply racist society on the basis of how people are treated.

"We had a press conference on this study at our Workers of Colour and Aboriginal Workers Conference in 2002, and received national coverage: the CBC carried it live and we had a large article in the *Globe and Mail*. There was a real debate, umpteen people calling up, tons of people logging onto the Web site to get the study. It was a real new starting point. It showed people that the economic structure of our society is highly political—how people work, where they work, and what they make."

David Smiley

A Representative Leadership Still Needs an Activist Base

In 2002, delegates to the CLC convention elected its most representative top leadership in the history of the Congress. The four top officers consist of two men and two women, two White people and two people of colour who were re-elected at the 2005 CLC convention. Yet equity work still meets obstacles in the CLC. There are always *formal* power structures and *informal* ways that power works.° The CLC is an umbrella organization of affiliate unions that can choose to affiliate or not. The four executive officers usually come from, and require the support of, the most powerful affiliates. The leaders of those affiliates need to be able to report to their memberships that the CLC's positions and actions are helpful to their unions.

Equity activists know that leaders must constantly weigh the risks they're prepared to take. If there is a lively, noisy, anti-racism activism in an affiliate, it will have the attention of that leader who will be expected to support anti-racism work at the CLC. In the absence of that affiliate activism, it's more difficult for affiliate leaders to support equity at central labour bodies such as the CLC, federations of labour and labour councils, even when they want to. For union equity advocates, it's a double-edged sword of electing or hiring activists of colour into the movement. The movement gains their knowledge and skills on a full-time basis, but advocates lose their voices on the ground—voices that hold their leaders accountable.

Activists have been pressuring for representation, not just in who gets hired as the anti-racism director, but who gets hired, appointed, and elected across the labour movement. Immediately after the final report of the task force was released in 1998, some progress was made. People of colour were hired as the Ontario regional director and as the youth co-ordinator, but there have been set backs since then. The CLC is now considering how to develop succession plans for the replacement of many CLC staff who will be retiring before 2010, though progress on this is not yet visible.

Hassan admits that the CLC has much more work to do in hiring a more representative workforce and integrating equity into how the CLC functions. But he also mentions examples of progress. "We recruited a number of people to work with us on the labour issues campaign, just before the 2004 federal election. We made it clear to each region that we wanted to have a good representation of people of colour and Aboriginal people. It took some effort. Some places did a fairly good job; others didn't. We learned some things. Next time, we need to talk to staff ahead of time. We need to give people an opportunity to learn and grow. Maybe they don't have all the skills now, but next time round they will."

Hassan cites another interesting example of using influence to increase representation and to tighten accountability at the same time. "Through a conversation with a friend, I realized that we had no idea who our labour representatives to the Employment Insurance Appeals Tribunals were. The CLC appoints them, but we'd never looked at who they were, whether men, women, White people, people of colour, or people with disabilities. So I asked someone I knew to get me the information and the results were horrible. I went to the CLC officer responsible for this file and apologized for sticking my nose into her work. We agreed to take the census as a basis for minimum appointments for people of colour and Aboriginal people. Anyway, it's five years later and there's been a significant shift in the appointment process. Now there's a huge debate among our staff who are working on the labour councils as to how to recruit people. For people of colour to represent the labour movement on Employment Insurance Appeals, they must be going to labour council meetings. [For more on these strategies, see the story that follows.] Well, then you've got another question, Why aren't they delegates to labour council, and if they are, why aren't they coming to meetings? You have to constantly sit and think about how you can do things differently, but it doesn't make you popular with people."

Thinking Nationally and Internationally

The 2001 United Nations World Conference Against Racism (UNWCAR)

Racism is a global, not just a Canadian, issue. The 2001 United Nations World Conference Against Racism held in Durban, South Africa, represented an important opportunity to look at the connections between struggles at home and solidarity with workers in the South, a logical next step after all the analysis and organizing of the Anti-Racism Task Force. To gather a contingent of Canadian labour activists, the CLC's secretary treasurer sent a letter to all affiliates inviting them to name delegates to the conference. This resulted in a Canadian labour delegation that included eighteen people of colour. This level of organizing for an international conference had never happened before at the Congress. As well, the CLC played a leadership role in co-ordinating the discussions of all central labour bodies in the world and the Anti-Racism and Human Rights Department, for the first time, worked closely with the International Department in preparing for the conference.

At the conference, the CLC presented a statement that incorporated the internationalist analysis of racism it had been developing over the past ten years:

> The CLC and its affiliates have highlighted over the years the historical link between racism
> and the structure of global economies. The Canadian, North American and European
> economies have historically been set up to exploit the labour and resources of Aboriginal
> Peoples and People of Colour through slavery, colonialism and imperialism. The exploitation

of resources from the South and the dependency on slave and indentured labour laid the foundation for the industrial, manufacturing, military, financial and service sectors. This exploitation continues to this day. In Canada, we only have to look at who works in marginalized low-wage jobs with poor benefits and working conditions to see that this is true. ... It is critical that unions analyse the systemic racism in the structure of the economy and its role in fighting exploitation at home and abroad.

Governments can no longer ignore their contemporary and historical obligations, since the victims of historical injustices live within their borders and still suffer from the effects of these historical wrongs. Political leaders cannot abdicate their responsibility in addressing these issues. Labour should not continue to take positions on globalization outside of the context of UNWCAR. As equally important, the UNWCAR should be seen in the future as the event which finally provided an important international framework leading to concrete actions for the elimination of all forms of racism, related intolerance and xenophobia.[7]

The "Durban Statement" was the first time the CLC clearly spelt out its position at an international event on the links between anti-racism and the working class and on multiple forms of oppression. The statement was also very clear on the question of anti-Semitism, slavery as a crime against humanity, and reparations.

Drawing on the task force's experience with grassroots activism, the Anti-Racism and Human Rights Department organized a series of post-Durban regional workshops. Each one had a theme: immigration (in Toronto); environmental racism (in Halifax); youth (in Vancouver); and Aboriginal rights (in the Prairie Region). The department saw this as a way of involving activists who could not go to Durban in conversations about anti-racism work. The post-Durban national forums were also used to focus demands directed at different levels of Canadian government.

Canadian Office and Professional Employees' Union

Winnie Ng and Hassan Yussuff, UN World Conference Against Racism, Durban, 2001

9/11

Two days after the conference delegates returned home, the September 11, 2001, attacks on the World Trade Center in New York and the Pentagon in Washington, DC, occured. They shifted world attention from the racism of global economics to the politics of America's declared "war on terrorism" and the subsequent consolidation of its empire. These events have had enormous impact on the safety, security, and well-being of workers of colour in Canada. Anti-terrorism legislation, tightening of borders for immigrants and refugees, and the unsubstantiated arrests and detention of many Muslim Canadians have intensified the daily experience of racism for many workers. It has never been more urgent for unions to speak out against the racism that divides their membership and to encourage people to transform the fear of their neighbours into more constructive, more democratic political energy.

The CLC has continued the work that emerged from the Durban Conference in the context of post–9/11. David Onyalo was clear on the reasons for this commitment at the time: "Part of our job as the Canadian Labour Congress, along with some of the national affiliates, is to remind the federal government about their responsibilities here at home. When new cabinet ministers get appointed, we write saying that we're looking forward to working with them, and that there's an outstanding item—the development of a national anti-racism action plan led by the federal government. We remind them of the need to involve provincial governments in discussions of racism as a systemic issue in the workplace."

The CLC also used the occasion of the visit of the UN Special Rapporteur on Racism, in September 16, 2003, to communicate its concerns and suggestions. In its Statement to the UN Rapporteur, the Congress recommended specific actions by the federal, provincial, territorial, and municipal governments. It concluded by reaffirming the importance of labour's role in fighting racism:

> Our experience in the labour movement has taught us that combating racism is not a luxury, or a part-time job for union leadership, activists and labour staff. Society has to always remain vigilant or small gains can be eroded quickly.
>
> We have participated in this process because we believe that unions in Canada are an important part of advancing the principles of universal human rights. We have seen how an over-reliance on market forces, where aggressive right-wing governments have introduced downsizing, privatization and deregulation, has had a negative impact on our human rights legislation and institutions. It is not a coincidence that there have been massive cut backs to those institutions meant to protect Canadians facing racism and other forms of discrimination, when they are needed the most.[8]

Building a Community of Activism: An Important Congress Role

The Canadian Labour Congress plays a pivotal role in creating space for activists across unions to meet each other, find support, and strengthen their capacity to build the labour movement. This is something no one affiliate can do. This is particularly important when affiliate leaderships are preoccupied by or backing away from tough social issues that are not seen as union "bread and butter" issues. As David explains: "Some affiliates are reluctant to organize a conference on specific areas of equality rights, but they're happy that the CLC does it because it takes pressure off them from their militant membership. Other affiliates may not want to take progressive positions on other social issues because their most outspoken members are against it, but the CLC can do it on their collective behalf. It's an important role we play."

The conferences for Aboriginal workers and workers of colour have been crucial activities in this respect, and they have raised the CLC's profile in the larger labour movement. Many of the more than five hundred people who have shown up at each of the conferences had no idea what the CLC was before they attended. Now they may know more about the CLC than their own affiliate and, in fact, this can be a way of becoming more involved in their own locals.

The CLC Aboriginal/Workers of Colour Leadership forums are another example of creating space for movement building. One of these forums was sponsored in June 2000 by the Aboriginal and Workers of Colour Working Groups to provide "a place for networking, support, and self-education on economic and social issues."[9] Another was held in the fall of 2004 where agenda topics included how to strengthen networks and mentor new activists and participation in the political process, including electoral politics.

Despite these past initiatives and future directions, the costs and risks of challenging racism are great. Activists get tired, discouraged, and frustrated. Leaders who are Aboriginal, women, racialized, people with disabilities, gay, lesbian, or transgender are working in social movements that are contradictory. On the one hand, most unions and labour bodies have stated their intent to build equity. On the other, commitment to equity is patchy and can collapse quickly under pressure. Equity-seeking activists in the labour movement are caught in the middle, negotiating between a still-White male labour leadership that is not always committed to equity and community activists who expect them to make change in the labour movement. Their efforts to strengthen an equitable labour movement might be viewed by other unionists

CLC Workers of Colour and Aboriginal Workers Conference, 2002

as attacking rather than building the movement. The limits of their power are not apparent to communities, which might harshly judge any necessary compromises.

Racialized union leaders feel a commitment and loyalty to their communities, to their specific union/organization, to the labour movement, and to the struggle for a more equitable movement. This creates a tug and pull that is hard on the body and dangerous to one's health. There are few supports for equity-seeking leaders once they are hired or elected. Their actions, connections, decisions, communications are often more scrutinized and more harshly judged than those of White leaders. As one activist has said, "You don't want to be seen as vulnerable, so you just brace it and brave it through, and to me that's where the personal cost is, health wise." It is essential, then, to build community and networks that can offer racialized union leaders the support they need to carry on their work.

Hassan is clear on the importance of each person's voice to hold leadership, including himself, accountable to an equity agenda. "I think there's a space right now within the movement to move things forward in our organizations. I hear a lot of complaints from activists about how hard it is, how frustrated they are. But activists have the ability to do something in their unions because they vote for their leadership. They can make their leadership accountable if they're not right now. Can you imagine if all of us decided to set up a little network to support each other, in each of our unions and across unions? The sense of frustration that people sometimes feel would be the same, but we would have done something to make a difference, to give people an opportunity when they would not have had it. I think there are more of us who could make that difference, just by saying, 'Once a week I'll give three hours of my time to do this piece of the work.' It would make one hell of a difference."

WUT-TUN-NEE Tim Brown

David Smiley

A Local Story

Building Workers' Power through an Equity Agenda: Leadership and Alliances at the Toronto and York Region Labour Council*

> Equity is a struggle. It's not a fancy word for diversifying the movement. A lot of people have died for it.
> —Winnie Ng

> You can't even consider building power in Toronto if you don't have an equity agenda. With the reality of who is in the workforce today and who will be there tomorrow, building equity is key to building worker power.
> —John Cartwright

> I started to get excited about the labour movement because of anti-racism work. I was already involved in the union, but I started to see a world of things to change and make better.
> —Jenny Ahn

What does it take to change the face and the focus of an organization to reflect its diverse constituencies and the daily issues and concerns of those constituencies? This question haunts countless organizations across Canada that struggle with questions of legitimacy and relevance. This section examines one place where the answers to these questions are being integrated into the vision and practice of everyday operations: at the Toronto and York Region Labour Council. The Council has much to teach us about

- strategic alliances
- developing diverse leadership
- selecting battles that build capacity and have a chance of success
- useing organizational authority to build equity

The Council is making equity a central part of the ways it thinks and acts.

Building a Workers' Movement in a Diverse City

The Toronto and York Region Labour Council is one of 137 labour councils across English Canada, each of which is affiliated to the Canadian Labour Congress (CLC). Labour councils are central labour bodies working at the municipal level. They organize and advocate on issues that are vital to working people in their regions, and they carry out Canadian Labour Congress campaigns at the local levels. To do their work, they must rally the energies of

---

* For this story, we draw on and use excerpts from interviews with Jenny Ahn, CAW and executive member of the Labour Council; John Cartwright, president of the Toronto and York Region Labour Council; Hassan Yusuff, secretary treasurer of the CLC and responsible for human rights and anti-racism; and Winnie Ng, Ontario regional director of the Canadian Labour Congress. These interviews were conducted by the authors between April and November 2004 in Toronto.

both affiliate unions and community forces, as pointed out in a 2002 statement from the Council:

> Decisions made by local governments help shape the kind of cities we live in. Municipalities are responsible for a wide variety of services and programs—from public transit to social services to the water we drink. Our School Boards educate hundreds of thousands of children. All of these services are crucial to the standard of living of working families. Labour Council has a long tradition of involvement in municipal politics, including supporting candidates during elections.

Delegates from affiliated local unions participate in monthly meetings of the labour council. They elect their officers and executive board and determine the work of committees at the Labour Council.

Canadian Unions and Social Movements

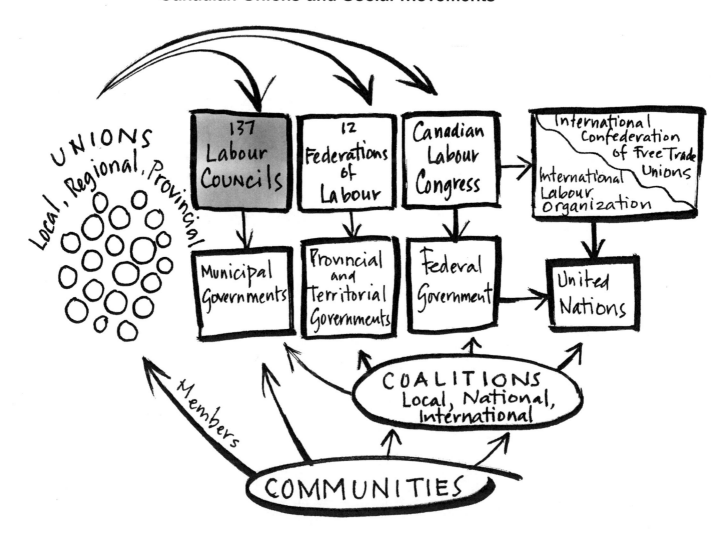

"We Walk on the Shoulders of Activists before Us, Who Opened Doors for Us"[10]

Local labour councils have always been forums for equity organizing. In the 1940s, the Labour Committee to Combat Racial Intolerance in Toronto worked with other such committees in cities across Canada to educate unionists and the general public about discrimination. "Realizing that it would be impossible to educate away discrimination, the committees began to lobby governments for anti-discrimination legislation."[11] The 1944 *Racial Discrimination Act* in Ontario was a direct result of this work. In 1951, the Ontario government passed Canada's first *Fair Employment Practices Act*, prohibiting discrimination in employment, and in 1954, it followed with the *Fair Accommodation Act*, prohibiting discrimination in service delivery.

June Veecock and Bromley Armstrong

David Smiley

Bromley Armstrong, a Black trade unionist and officer of a United Auto Workers local, was active in testing whether businesses were actually complying with the *Fair Accommodation Act*. "Testing" meant actually going to places where people of colour had been refused service, testing whether it was true, and pressing charges where they encountered unfair treatment. Bromley remembers many struggles in the ongoing fight against racism, including the trek of thirty-five union and community activists in 1954 to see the prime minister. He recalls that once in Ottawa, however, "the prime minister refused to see us and sent in his minister of immigration to see us. The Toronto and District Labour and Human Rights Committee wrote the brief that we presented."[12]

In the 1960s, activists like Lucky Rao were starting citizenship classes for workers at the Steelworkers' Hall. In the 1970s and 1980s, strikes, demonstrations, and organizing against racism in the workplace and community intensified. As Salome Lukas and Judy Vashti Persad point out:

> Following the massive construction workers' uprising of the 1960s in Toronto (in response to the death of five Italian construction workers in Hoggs' Hollow), strikes by immigrant workers at Artistic Woodwork, Keith Milrod metals, Puretex Knitting, McGregor Hosiery, Pizza Crust, ALCAN Aluminum, and Superplastics, continued to raise awareness within labour and the mainstream community and with local politicians of the "other" in the midst of the Canadian society with the issues they raised. These strikes and their outcomes benefited the labour movement as a whole, but they also started to expose racism as a particular form of workplace discrimination experienced by immigrant workers of colour.[13]

At Superplastics in 1985, forty-four out of sixty workers walked out after an unsuccessful attempt to reach a first agreement. The employer deliberately fostered racial division between White and South Asian workers through differential wages, shift allocation, and layoff rules. Winnie Ng and teachers at the Metro Labour Education Centre, a program of the Metro Labour Council, taught English classes to the striking workers.

Winnie remembers that the Labour Council was involved in setting up the first round of English in the workplace classes, in the face of overt expressions of employer contempt for English as a Second language speakers: "I was working at a Chinese community organization at the time of the Unicel strike. The workers were predominantly Chinese speakers from Vietnam and South East Asia, as well as Spanish speakers from Latin America. One Chinese worker asked the employer for a fifty-cent raise, and the employer gave him two cents 'because of his level of English.' The worker was so insulted, he contacted us to do something. That was the beginning of English in the workplace classes where we taught workers their rights and the words to speak back. This was about giving workers a voice. The success of the program encouraged workers to speak out. Some of the traditional labour leadership felt threatened and cancelled their programs. For me this was a sign that we were on the right track. It also meant we needed to work with the leaders so they could see this as democracy at work."[14]

In 1980, the Ontario Federation of Labour (OFL), one of the provincial labour bodies affiliated to the CLC, began its "Racism Hurts Everyone" campaign. The Labour Council in Toronto was an active partner, sponsoring forums on racism and co-hosting the first workers of colour conference in 1984. According to Winnie, "White supremacists who were organizing at this time, generated a sense of urgency which brought together people who had not worked together before. The Committee for Racial Equality and the Riverdale Action Committee Against Racism were mobilizing against the Ku Klux Klan." This was a time of organizing against the deportation of eight Caribbean women and for the rights of domestic workers. These events pushed the labour movement to see that they could not afford to sit idle and set the tone for the OFL campaign.

In 1983, Wei Fu, a security guard at the Ontario legislature, filed a human rights complaint against his supervisor for racial harassment in the workplace. A coalition of thirty-nine labour and community groups supported Wei Fu's complaint, including his union, the Ontario Public Service Employees Union. Winnie remembers the disappointment with the decision that the supervisor's behaviour was "morally wrong but legally right." Nonetheless, she says, "this decision strengthened human rights protection through new provisions which said that indirect harassment is against the law, a change which has benefited all workers." By the end of the 1980s the goal became more crystallized. As Winnie recalls, "We wanted access to employment and we wanted our leadership to reflect our membership. Employment equity was a way of joining the struggles of workers of colour, Aboriginal workers, women, and people with disabilities." Then, after five years of employment equity legislation and policy development in Ontario, the Conservative government repealed the law and its infrastructure in 1995. "It was an attack on equity and an attack on labour. The Days of Action, organized by a strengthened alliance of labour and community, shut down thirteen cities in Ontario. We're here for the long haul to build a community of hope. With each generation that takes on the struggle against racism and neo-liberalism, we need to build community and solidarity."[15]

A New Energy for Equity

Today, the Toronto and York Region Labour Council is the largest labour council representing the most racially diverse city in Canada. With forty-two union affiliates, it represents 190,000 union members who live and work in the Toronto and York region. "Since the first peoples named this the 'Gathering Place,' Toronto has been a city that has been built by immigrants and children of immigrants. Its population has come from 170 different countries and speaks 100 languages. Over 50% of us were born outside of Canada. Most Torontonians are now people of colour— the visible majority."[16]

As John Cartwright, the Council's president points out, "This Council has broken a lot of ground in equity struggles. In the late eighties there were four leaders of colour out of sixteen on the executive board. Many activists from the labour and social justice movements and our communities have kept the equity agenda alive. Over time things slipped a little, partly because of getting hammered time and time again by the Tories during their eight years in power (1995–2003)."

In 2001, the Council elected a new executive even more reflective of its larger community. Currently, seven of sixteen executive board members are activists of colour with positions of authority in their own unions. John Cartwright is a long-time White activist with the Carpenters' Union and the Labour Council. He has a passion for a powerful and representative workers' movement and is an advocate of hooking equity onto everything the Labour Council does.

However, by 2001, the Equity Committee, a newer version of the old Human Rights Committee, had lost its focus. John recalls, "So the first question was 'Who's out there who should be involved in this committee?' I went around and used the stature of my position to recruit people, and as president, I said, 'I would really like you to become part of this Equity Committee.' I wanted the leadership to see that they were contributing to a common peace-building power here. They would be able to see it was their member making that contribution—a member with some relationship to the union."

Once the committee had members, it had to agree on its goal. Would the committee focus on all forms of equity or focus on the particular issues of workers of colour and Aboriginal workers? How would it decide? There were members who wanted to focus on all equity-seeking groups. They looked at the leadership of the Labour Council itself, and discovered that the least represented were people of colour and

John Cartwright and Jenny Ahn, 2002

David Smiley

Aboriginal members. This was reflected in the larger picture. According to John, "If 45 per cent of the population of Toronto are folks of colour and that's not reflected in our union leadership, but our union leaderships are starting to reflect, in many cases, a balance of women and men, an involvement of gay/bi/lesbian/trans members, then the crying need is with workers of colour."

The revitalized Equity Committee called a meeting with a range of organizations who worked with communities of colour to talk about a common future. They asked Tam Goosen, an activist with ties in various communities, to help them plan and facilitate it. This helped to focus the committee's work as it began to hold regular meetings. As one activist recalls, "Our committee took a while to gel. We were all learning. But we were building consciously and saying, 'There's going to be a very strong equity agenda and it's about sharing power.'"

Connecting Equity to the "Real Business" of Affiliates

John wanted to involve the unions in the equity agenda. He describes the climate when he was first elected as Labour Council president in 2001: "I kept hearing back from affiliated unions that they felt the Labour Council was off doing things that were kind of 'out there' but it wasn't relating to their core work. They told us, 'It's got to the point of political correctness where my delegates won't go because they're afraid if they stand up and say something, and it's the wrong word, they're going to get jumped on.' So it was a really interesting challenge to think about rebuilding engagement of the key unions so that they were saying that this Labour Council is a vehicle for building power. With the changing demographics, the reality is, you can't even consider building power in Toronto if you don't have an equity agenda. But how to make those connections with affiliates?"

Winnie points out that "resistance has always been more subtle than visible. You know, the claims that all workers are the same, and 'if we just focus on the bread and butter issues, everything will fall into place.' John has been able to get more leaders to recognize that there are different strategies of organizing, and that we need to recognize where we've been divided in order to find where we're united. Divided by race; united by class." Jenny Ahn agrees. "John recognizes the demographics and he's willing to be honest. Rather than making excuses, he started to work. Delegates of colour felt very comfortable, very welcome."

Over the past decades, a key area of concern to affiliates has been organizing. Currently, only 24 per cent of Toronto's workforce has a union. This is lower than the national average because in most of the big office towers, the workers are largely unorganized. John sees the connection clearly: "If you're going to go and organize and raise the union density, where are you going to be organizing? It's new Canadians in large part, and it's workers of colour who dominate in the service and retail sectors. It's not hard to help unions make those links. "

Hassan Yussuff stresses that organizing in a city as diverse as Toronto is complicated: "One size doesn't fit all. Toronto is a series of neighbourhoods in a very large geographic area. It exists differently in different parts of the city. It will take different groups of people with different ethnic and political skills to try and make it successful."

If the equity agenda is laid out clearly it can build on, and tap into, similar struggles of the past. Winnie Ng recalls a Labour Council meeting early in 2003. The executive laid out the equity agenda and how it was connected to building the Council's power. "One of the delegates stood up and said, 'What you're talking about is exactly what we did in the sixties. We asked the Labour Council for some money to do organizing in the Italian community. They said we couldn't do this, and we couldn't do that, so we raised money ourselves and we did this thing, and the next thing you know we were able to elect school trustees and we elected city councillors. This is not new. We did it.'" In 2004, Women Working with Immigrant Women and the Labour Council produced *Through the Eyes of Workers of Colour: Linking Struggles for Social Justice*.[17] The book and accompanying video document the anti-racist struggles of the past few decades.

Beverley Johnson, 2002

David Smiley

Equity as an Urban Agenda

What do you say to labour councils and affiliates in smaller cities that are not as diverse as Toronto? Why should they see equity as a basic element of their agenda? John Cartwright has thought about this. "I spend lots of time in the North, where equity is about Aboriginal people and Anglo people. But it's interesting. In many smaller communities there is a growing population of people of colour, largely new Canadians. Sometimes you find people who've been there a few generations. But there's another piece that connects to equity; it's this question of a new urban agenda. Eighty per cent of Canadians now live in large cities. Where is the overwhelming majority of the workforce going to be? Montreal, Toronto, Vancouver. But then there's the Calgary and Edmonton corridor; there's Winnipeg, Halifax, Ottawa, Hamilton, Kitchener, Windsor. Those are big diverse cities. What we say is that if we're going to rebuild left politics and rebuild labour power, a lot of the chemistry will be happening in major cities. It's important for the Canadian Labour Congress to figure out a city's agenda, and work with affiliates to build an understanding that if they want a future, it all has to connect in some way."

It's all about relationship—building them, maintaining them, re-establishing them. As

John emphasizes, "It was my role to go out to unions, redevelop a relationship with Labour Council, and talk about a strategic plan that they would buy into. I wanted them to send us delegates for committees and the executive that weren't just interested in the Council but who had authority and a real relationship to the union."

When the Labour Council sent notices to affiliates outlining the credentials that should guide their choice of delegates to the Labour Council, the package included a covering letter from John reminding affiliates of the Council's equity agenda. It urged them to think about "emerging leaders in their memberships who were people of colour." John followed up the letter with personal conversations with most of the affiliate presidents. In those conversations, he reinforced the notion that the Labour Council wanted delegates who would actually participate and "be part of the life of this organization. I was trying to find a way to make the Labour Council more real and connected to the ongoing, day-to-day issues of an affiliated union and its members."

Connecting with Workers Where They Live: New Struggles and Alliances

Nowhere is the Labour Council's commitment to an equity agenda more apparent than through the campaigns it has undertaken since 2001. The goal has been to keep increasing the number of activists from the ranks of its 190,000 members, and to connect more directly with members, not just where they work but also where they live. Why? John explains: "Because that's what politicians respond to. They may or may not respond to ten thousand people on the lawn of the legislature. They sure respond to one hundred people who are their constituents, phoning them saying, 'I'm involved in the local church, or temple at such and such a street, and this issue is important to me. Or I'm a soccer mom, and by the way, I'm a CUPE member (Canadian Union of Public Employees) and I'm not happy about X or Y.' If we start thinking about where our members live as well as work, we have to rethink the alliances that we as the labour movement in Toronto, need to make to be successful."

If You Want Power, You Have to Engage the Base: The School Board Election

An early test of the new equity agenda came with a 2002 by-election for a public school trustee in Rexdale, a community in the northwest part of Toronto. The situation was full of possibilities for mistakes and conflict. The incumbent trustee, the president of the Conservative Riding Association, was found guilty of immigration fraud but had not been removed. John recalls, "He was selling fraudulent stuff for people to come to Toronto. The Tories wouldn't remove him because he was a Tory. Even though the law said he had to be removed, they wouldn't remove him."

To complicate matters, the incumbent was South Asian, in an area already under-represented by racialized leaders. John remembers two parts to the struggle: "First, we had to organize parents to go and challenge the board and take it to court, basically, to force them to uphold the law. Next, we had to deal with the question, Who should be representing

Rexdale? Well, actually there was somebody who had run before. He was a progressive White guy who said, 'Really Rexdale is a big, changing, diverse community, and its representatives should reflect that diversity. We've got to figure out a process for doing that.'

"We pulled together something called the Rexdale Cross Cultural Committee, which is a bunch of activists that some of our community-connected folks found who live in the area. With this group, we asked, How do we do this? The group includes some South Asian, Somalian, African, and West Indian activists. About two-thirds of them are union members, but not necessarily active in the union. We talked about living in that community, about making

CLC Workers of Colour and Aboriginal Workers Conference, 2002

David Smiley

sure the schools are open to their kids and all those issues. And for new Canadians, of course, people are willing to work eighty hours a week as long as their kids get ahead in life. Together, we went through a process of selecting a candidate. We did a lot of interviewing and a bunch of this and that. At the end of the day, the candidates that we chose—two of them—had to drop out. One had work constraints; the other was still registered with the Catholic Board of Education.

"Then the third guy was this White guy, Stan, who actually didn't even live in the area, but by the time we had gone through that process, we had worked with communities enough that they said, 'He'll be fine.' So then we had all kinds of people from the communities working on Stan's campaign, and he won. And he became the tie vote at the school board that stopped the Tory agenda from being pushed through the Toronto School Board. This then created a crisis that the Tories couldn't deal with.

"And who made the campaign a success? For Stan, it was South Asian sisters and brothers, from different organizations and unions; it was West Indian members of the Steelworkers union and CUPE (Canadian Union of Public Employees); it was African members of the CAW (Canadian Auto Workers Union). That's who was on the ground making that campaign happen. Well, that's not a hard thing to say. If you want power, you have to engage the base."

David Smiley

Patty Barrera and Grace-Edward Galabuzi, 2002

A Multi-Racial Victory: Fighting for Public Control of Water

A second important campaign by the Labour Council in 2002–03 was over the privatization of water. It was by chance that it even found out about the City of Toronto's plans to create an "arm's-length water board." When the Labour Council caught a one-line reference to this in the *Globe and Mail,* it saw the City's plan as the thin edge of the privatization wedge. The Council pulled together a coalition and again used the campaign as an opportunity to broaden its connections. The coalition included the Council of Canadians, the Canadian Environmental Law Association, the Toronto Environmental Alliance, the Metro Network for Social Justice, and the Toronto-Central Ontario Construction Trades Council, as well as the Canadian Union of Public Employees. Water Watch, as the coalition has come to be known, is part of a network of Water Watch groups across the country in communities from St. John's to Vancouver.

The Council then organized a meeting of union leaders and activists and announced the coalition's plan to go after the City's move to privatize water. Winnie recalls, "We picked that ground, because water is so much part of Canada. It's the blue gold that wars are going to be fought about." The Council asked the unions to put money into the campaign, and the affiliates agreed because they saw it as a very concrete campaign that would have support of their members.

The coalition agreed that it couldn't go after all forty-four city councillors, but would choose six or seven who were supporting the privatization move, and start organizing in their backyards. And once again, the Labour Council's equity agenda took them to the people who could make a difference. One of the councillors the Council chose to work on was influential on the City's Water Committee and had been considered a progressive candidate in her riding. The coalition worked with two groups in her constituency who began to pressure her. John recalls: "The ratepayers group, a middle-class group, couldn't understand why, after Walkerton,[18] anybody in their right mind would consider privatization. The other group had a mosque in the centre of her riding. We went to our Muslim activists, and we went to a councillor who had helped get zoning for the mosque. We asked them to start talking to people in this community. All of a sudden this councillor was getting dozens of calls. Many of the people who were calling her had helped her get elected. Soon after the calls began, she changed her mind on the issue and decided that this was not the kind of fight she wanted to be in."

In the next step of the campaign, the Labour Council and the coalition pushed the City to hold a public hearing. The Steelworkers brought in three bus loads of people from

Rexdale and other northern communities of Toronto. OPSEU and several other unions organized to get their people there. Winnie had never seen such a multi-racial crowd in the galleries of city hall. At one point, one of the councillors protested that "unions are packing this meeting," implying that "special interest" groups were taking over the City's concern for everyone. This was opening enough for one Labour Council speaker to say, "Are you saying that Steelworkers that live in X community don't have a right to determine what's going to happen? Are you telling these autoworkers that live in Y community that their concern about their family's health is less than someone else?"

The *coup de grâce*, however, was when a community leader who had successfully fought privatization of the New Orleans water services made a surprise deputation and told that city's horror story. Upon hearing this, Toronto councillors acknowledged that they had been lobbied by United Water, one of the three multinational corporations involved in the New Orleans privatization bid. The councillors voted almost unanimously to abandon the plan in the face of such opposition from a coalition of diverse communities.
Winnie recalls, "This was a multi-racial victory. If we have an agenda that involves workers of colour, and newcomers, people from all walks of life, we can put ourselves centrally into a fight for something that people feel is vital to them and their families." This struggle for public control of water illustrates some of the ways in which equity and global struggles can be linked at the local level.

According to John, the odds of a victory had not been good. "Two weeks before we won that victory, people inside were telling us, 'With all due respect, we like you but get over it. You're not going to stop this. It's the best thing for the City.' Two weeks later, the same guy was back with the final motions saying, 'Is this all right? Do we have to change this word?' Those moments are particularly delicious."

Keeping the Public in Public Transit

The public transit campaign was born shortly after Ontario's provincial election in 2003, when the new premier, Dalton McGuinty, announced he was unable to keep election promises to restore provincial funding to the Toronto Transit Commission (TTC). Traditionally, the province had paid 75 per cent of capital investment (buses, trains, subways) and 25 per cent of operating costs. These supports were cut during eight years of Conservative government and downloaded to the City of Toronto, which by then had much less money for housing and other city responsibilities. For Labour Council activists, it meant the City was hampered in bringing in resources for an equity agenda around housing, social services, day care and other issues important for working-class families and new Canadians. It also meant the already-high fares would rise further, an issue of immediate importance to diverse working-class families.

Labour Council organizers developed a plan. John recalls how they started. "So we placed ourselves in the middle of a coalition that included the Canadian Federation of Students, Rocket Riders (a reference to the name 'The Rocket,' which the TTC uses to promote its subways), the Ontario Council of Agencies Serving Immigrants (OCASI), and the Chinese Canadian National Council (CCNC), Toronto Chapter. We chose these allies particularly to send a message that this is the kind of alliance that cares about transit."

The coalition, calling itself For the Public Good, printed thousands of leaflets that included a card to send to the premier. The leaflet showed a picture of a streetcar sinking in the water of a flask in a laboratory. The title read: "It's Not Rocket Science." The Council also sponsored an advertisement campaign by placing its logo on six thousand ads appearing on buses, streetcars, and subway stations, announcing that the Labour Council cares about public transit.

The premier received between five hundred and six hundred e-mails and hundreds of cards that read "Don't break your promise on transit." John recounts the result with relish. "Just a few days after making his announcement, thinking this was all he had to announce, the premier had to announce again, that he was going to bring that money to city hall. And in the process, we were engaging our members and our activists and saying, this is a huge issue, particularly for new Canadians and people at the lower end of the income scale who just can't afford to pay more." The coalition wanted to hear their stories, and it was a diverse group of citizens who came forward to make their voices heard. For example, as John recalls, "a Filipino woman who lives in Scarborough said, 'I have to walk half an hour to get to a bus stop, and my community needs this.' A West Indian steelworker from McCowan and Ellesmere said he had to put aside two hours in the morning to get to work or he'd be late and get fired. For him and his wife and his older kid, it's three hundred a month they already pay for transit."

While the coalition has won the first round, the work is far from over. The Labour Council has produced *Labour's Transit Workbook*, a practical, nineteen-page guide that working people can use to pressure for publicly funded transit. It provides a clear rationale for publicly funded and controlled public transit, and offers a series of helpful tools: a questionnaire to help citizens talk with city councillors; a sample letter to the premier; tips for running a discussion meeting on transit issues with neighbours and union members; sample collective agreement language that unions can use to bargain with employers about public transit; tips for negotiating bulk transit discounts; and approaches to improving public transit.[19]

IT'S NOT ROCKET SCIENCE.

For the Public Good

Strengthening an Equity Infrastructure: 2004-2010

The Labour Council's *Strategic Directions for the Toronto Labour Movement 2004–2010* lays out a vision and a process for moving an equity and organizing agenda forward. The three strategic priorities are building leadership, building power in communities, and organizing unrepresented workers. This document illustrates the important connections between equity and a workers' movement:

> It is essential that we prove to newcomers that the route to improving their quality of life is through strong unions. Unions are the only way to lift income standards in any sector of the economy. But they must also be at the core of civic engagement to win better arrangements for individual communities—from the quality of their schools to decent housing. We need to dedicate more of our resources to supporting the creation and maintenance of progressive community groups.[20]

As a way of building an infrastructure for community organizing, the Labour Council has been developing databases of members and volunteer activists. This practice began during the Rexdale election campaign for a public school trustee (discussed just above) at which time the Labour Council asked its affiliate unions to break down, by postal codes, where their members lived and to contact them. John says the unions got a bit of a surprise. "The Steelworkers phoned back and said, 'There must be something wrong out there. This is just one riding and we have fifteen hundred names.' Now they have fifteen thousand members across Toronto and York region, and this is a tenth of them in one out of forty ridings. Well, it's because the light industrial plants that they represent are mostly South Asian and West Indian workers, with some Latino workers who live in that community. And so as they talked with their members, guess who was phoning who else?"

The Labour Council has encouraged affiliates to develop their membership lists by postal code as a way to build community mobilizing campaigns. By doing so, the Council has identified new leadership with a variety of expertise it can call upon—people with organizing skills, different languages, connections and networks in communities, cultural knowledge, and experience in mobilizing. Hassan Yusseff stresses the importance of locating expertise in different sectors. "If you want to organize, you have to find somebody that can speak Mandarin, Urdu, Tamil, or who is West Indian. Even if it's just to get the door open. We have to build a network of leaders with different skills, so we can support the work of affiliates and run our campaigns; so we can say, 'Oh, you've got Turkish workers in a plant who want a union, well there's a Turkish organizer with the Painters Union. Give us a call and we'll put you in touch. You've got Punjabi-speaking workers doing cleaning, well we have X and Y who would volunteer their time to help you.'"

Putting Staff in Touch with Communities

Another step in the process of strengthening the equity infrastructure involves diversifying the Council's staff and leadership. In 2003, the Labour Council executive looked at its four staff, including the president, recognized they were all White, and acknowledged that they'd been dealing with equitable staffing by means of short-term contracts—a few weeks at a time. Their first step in changing this was to put money aside to hire Daniel Yau for one year as a full-time organizer in the Chinese communities. For the Council, this was an important step forward. As a union and community organizer, with years of experience, Daniel is making the links between community and labour activism in the Chinese communities. He's played an important role in the transit campaign, by mobilizing the participation of workers more comfortable with speaking Chinese. He's the contact for the Chinese media, who can now call the Council confident they can get updates and statements in Chinese. This means that Council events and issues are getting regular coverage in newspapers read by Chinese workers, and, as Winnie points out, "there's a whole next workforce seeing that labour is playing a key role in issues that matter to working families."

Diversifying the Labour Council's staff requires a critical look at newly emerging requirements for the job. As Jenny Ahn recalls, "John and I were interviewing people to fill some positions at the Labour Council. We said that a second language is an asset because we're reaching out to unorganized workers. The largest populations are Chinese and South Asian. It's challenging to people already in positions when we change the requirements. But it's the challenge for the next ten years for all of us."

In addition to diversifying its own staff, the Labour Council is taking advantage of the organizing and equity knowledge of the staff at the Canadian Labour Congress (CLC). Winnie Ng is the Ontario regional director for the CLC. Part of her job is to help the Labour Council do its work effectively. Winnie is clear on her roles: "I'm there as a resource and support, to broaden the Labour Council's work to build workers power in the city. That means making stronger links with emerging communities. With my background as a community activist in the Chinese and immigrant women's communities, I try to act as a bridge with the Labour Council's work. We're interested in building a community where nobody needs to stand alone. So when the Labour Council develops this new vision and organizing strategy, for me it's a great union moment to build on all the work that so many people have done before us."

Winnie's credibility with communities is a huge help to the Labour Council. According to John, "Winnie has all the contacts in the Chinese community which is now the fastest-growing workforce in Toronto, and she can communicate a labour message to the diversity of that community. It's a huge piece of what we're trying to do, and now we have other leaders on our executive with roots in both their unions and communities who are getting things going there. So if I come along afterwards, as a fifty-year-old White construction guy, people say, 'That's cool because we already understand the agenda.'"

Getting Ongoing Good Advice

There are many situations where John acknowledges that good advice from people like Hassan and Winnie is critical. There are divisions to watch for in any local union, neighbourhood, and community, and within communities shaped by hundreds of years of colonialism, there are old and painful divides. "If you're not attuned and connected to the local neighbourhood or community, you need a bridge and a guide to begin to develop trust and new links."

As well, many racialized communities have been approached, used, and discarded by dominant-culture organizations before. They may not easily engage without the recommendation of a credible person. There are other pitfalls. As John explains, "On the surface, tensions can look like personality

Toronto and York Region Labour Council Conference, 2005

John Maclennan

differences. Then you've got people who are incredibly passionate about one part of the equity agenda. That's their issue and they've worked on it, and are knowledgeable about it. They get upset if it's not the centerpiece, or you're not dealing with it enough. We've been very lucky to have people like Winnie and others on our executive, to answer our questions, even if they sound like stupid questions."

Jenny Ahn is also on the Labour Council's executive and agrees that these tensions are in part due to the experience of racism over the years. "Some of our activists have been involved over years of struggle. And after all that time they may still not feel acknowledged for their work. Racism can eat you. We're trying to say, 'We're not going to get stuck in this; we're going to do something; we've got more people involved; we're going to help each other.'"

Changing How Labour Council Meetings Work

The Labour Council has also been trying new approaches to running its meetings. As John explains: "For a period of time, I personally went and recruited people to speak because we had the same eight White folks dominating the floor, time and time again." This is a common problem in mainstream Canadian organizations where an unexamined culture poses real barriers to racialized people's participation. For example, in many organizations, White people tend to speak on the "regular issues" of education and health care, and "racialized people" are expected to speak about racism but not about transit. To get more delegates of colour contributing on all issues, John phoned people at home to say there was an issue coming up and he knew they had some expertise on it and would like them to speak about it. He explains the result: "This balanced things out on the floor. People would say, 'Oh, I see. It's okay. Black, Asian, and Chinese folks have talked about stuff; it's not such a big thing for me to get up now.' Before then, it was a big issue."

The Labour Council is also experimenting with different ways of stimulating fuller discussions despite the tensions that exist between getting people to talk and getting things done. "At different times, we've put questions out and actually had people work in small group discussions, talking about what they want to do, and how they imagined they might do it," John reports. "Twice a year we might do that. But there's a tension between guided democracy like that and really getting into the issue. The same tension exists at convention. Do you actually say we've got four hundred resolutions and everybody wants to speak to their resolution, or do you ask, What is the biggest challenge to us as a movement and how do we move this forward?"

As well, the executive is still struggling to ensure that meetings are run democratically while also getting the work done. "It hasn't been as successful as I'd hoped. I wanted it to be a much more hands-on experience," John says. However, as the executive becomes more diverse in the knowledge it brings to the job, new ideas continue to emerge.

Developing New Leadership

One day, John went to a labour school in a southwestern Ontario community to give a presentation on community building and equity. "This guy came up after and said that he really enjoyed it. He was a member of a local that's not an affiliate of this Council. And he said, 'Anytime you want to get my community involved, give me a call.' He was the vice-president of the Pakistan-Canada Federation. He's also a union leader. One of the first people on our Equity Committee was the vice-president of the Canadian Hindu Association. He's a teacher. But when he's not teaching, he's doing community work. There are people like that in our movement all over the place; they are leaders in their own communities, but our unions don't know about them. These leaders don't want to play the politics game inside their locals so they don't run for positions, but meanwhile they're doing important work as real representatives of communities. It's important that our unions know these people are leaders in communities with huge strengths and assets to bring to the labour movement."

For Jenny Ahn it's a matter of "making space for new blood and new ideas. I shouldn't be a local president forever. Nobody should. As leaders, we need to be looking for new people to replace us. I've made a conscious decision to mentor and encourage people to run and be stewards and to be on the executive board of my local. When I was elected in 1996, we had all people of colour on our board. It reflected the membership. It takes energy to do the mentoring. Sometimes people of colour don't see themselves as leaders, so we need to always be thinking about who could do this and who could do that, and encouraging them."

David Smiley

CLC Workers of Colour and Aboriginal Workers Conference, 2002

The Labour Council has tried to stay focused on moving workers of colour into leadership and moving union organizations to a place where they can represent the workforce. Leaders of colour have skills, talents, and experience the whole labour movement vitally needs. However, systemic forms of racism have been at work in preventing these forms of leadership to emerge. As John says, "They want to be the same as me or anybody else, a leader who's leading all workers. And you invite them to be part of something that they can benefit from, where their families and communities can move forward."

For Winnie, this means that "White brothers and sisters have a responsibility to deal with racism, so that people of colour and Aboriginal people don't have the whole burden of it. White leaders, Aboriginal leaders, and leaders of colour can share the responsibility while playing different roles. This requires a foundation of trust to interact in a strategic way, so we figure out who, when and where we support each other, who takes the lead, and when. This is not just a question for labour leaders, but for the interaction of labour and community groups. It's the trust and respect for each other's experiences and commitment that build a workers' movement—recognizing our different spheres of influence and how we can complement each other."

Bringing New Leadership Together

The Labour Council held Workers of Colour/Aboriginal Workers Conferences in 2003, 2004, and 2005. Over three hundred delegates attended the 2003 conference at the Ontario Federation of Labour building. The Council wanted participants to be in the "house of labour," occupying all spaces and making it their own. The conference highlighted the Equity Committee's new plan of action, which is designed to encourage more workers to become active in upcoming elections and, more importantly, as a way for workers to meet one another, discuss common issues, strategize, and build community. At the conference, the Council agreed on six areas of action:

1. Strengthen Aboriginal and workers of colour participation in unions—from regular meetings to the leadership level.
2. Ensure that the Labour Council reflects the diversity of its members by encouraging the election of more Aboriginal workers and workers of colour as delegates.
3. Strengthen and help establish new connections in neighbourhoods and at the community level.
4. Work together with like-minded community organizations to advance our common goals.
5. Expand the Equity Committee.
6. Hold another conference in 2004 to move the agenda forward.[21]

At the 2004 conference, the Labour Council presented a progress report on its efforts to implement the 2003 priorities. It asked union families to support seven progressive "visible minority" candidates in the municipal elections. This was an important affirmation of leadership, not just in the labour movement but also in the community. The Council organized a Leadership Institute in November 2004 and another in November 2005 to build power at the workplace and in local neighbourhoods.[22] Jenny Ahn, president of Canadian Auto Workers Local 40 and a member of the Council's executive, clearly expressed one of the key issues: "Our next challenge is to bring in more women of colour in different capacities throughout the labour movement. The fundamental value of this movement is equality. Let's make these words a reality."[23]

Selecting Battles Strategically

The Labour Council receives daily requests to support various issues and campaigns, and it needs guidelines to make such decisions. There are legitimate requests from people on the cutting edge of an issue who feel the Labour Council is not moving fast enough; sometimes they don't see the slower work of building a foundation and an informed, involved constituency. Even with emerging clarity and focus, it's often difficult to choose where and how to target energy. Over time, the Council has developed some informal guidelines to help decide what projects to undertake and support actively. Projects and programs must:

- build broad-based worker power
- connect to the daily lives of diverse union members, so that members will say "Yes, this is important"
- get active support from leaders of union affiliates
- develop and draw on the leadership of activists of colour

Tensions in this work are to be expected. Building equitable organizations means recovering and undoing years of inequity, learning from daily mistakes, and reviewing actions that, on reflection, didn't work that well. And it means constantly making decisions about when to lead, support, or follow. An example of such an issue for the Labour Council is racial profiling. In 2002, the issue of police racial profiling became big news in Toronto. The Ontario Federation of Labour was involved, as were numerous community organizations. On its president's advice, the Council decided not to get involved but to express respect for the community coalition that was handling things.

Some of the Black activists at the Council objected. Police racial profiling was a daily issue for them, their families, and their communities. They felt the Council should be in there and active. There were real tensions about the Labour Council's role on this issue. John reflects on this time: "I didn't have the personal knowledge. And there are times that you don't know and it's better to refrain than step into a bunch of land mines. I think now, that it could have been handled differently." The issue has not gone away.

In 2004 the Toronto Police Board decided not to renew the police chief's contract. Several of his supporters at City Council and elsewhere campaigned to review the decision. Divisions on this issue were deep and shaped by race and the experience of racism. Many who were glad to see him go felt that racial profiling had flourished during his time; those who wanted him to continue as chief felt that while this was true, at least he had taken a strong stand against corruption in the force.

This time, the Labour Council was able to better grasp the different lived realities of policing experienced by its diverse members, and it found a way to act on its opposition to racial profiling that would have the support of the majority of its members, whatever side they took on the chief's tenure. The Council wrote a letter to all City councillors, reminding them of provincial government decisions over the past ten years which had encouraged racial profiling, and which had limited police accountability in Ontario, by removing such tools as civilian oversight of police. The letter took the high road. "We are deeply concerned about the long-term impact of a campaign to use the end of this Police Chief's contract as a political wedge issue. This campaign will only divide communities in our City, particularly along racial lines." The letter went on to suggest the qualities that should be sought in a new chief of police, and to urge collective work towards "the kind of city we want in future years."

David Smiley

The Labour Council felt it had found a common ground beyond the divided political positions. Recalls John, "There's no one that doesn't want a police force that's equipped to deal with young kids in the suburbs who are feeling bottled up; that it's not all right to be arresting Black kids all over the place. People understand this. So this letter was crafted very carefully to connect to the concerns of all our members. If you're an electrician, or a city water worker, or a teacher, a health care worker, or a bus driver, you can relate to that. Compared to a letter that attacks the outgoing police chief, we put ourselves in a different place. We want to build the kind of city that we can all live in."

John Maclennan

Jenny Ahn talks about the impact of years of colonialism on the relations between racialized communities. "We have to recognize that we don't all experience racism in the same way, but we don't have to reproduce the same old hierarchies of who's most oppressed. A Black brother is more likely to be pulled over by the police; an Asian sister may be segregated by language and paid less in a contracted-out sewing factory. We're building a movement here and we need to work with our differences as well as our similarities."

Celebrating the Victories

The Labour Council's work on building power through equity has produced significant results in a short time. The current executive has built on the work of many, many activists whose courage and skill have kept these issues alive over the years. The victories also came through strategic selection of battles. John describes the question that never goes away: "How do you choose the battles where you can show people a victory? And I learned this most from the Hotel Employees Restaurant Employees union (HERE). They represent people who should feel most disenfranchised—at the low end economically, with housing issues and all kinds of challenges. How do you persuade somebody in that situation that they should be part of a union, give up their time, and take the risks of being an activist? You can only do that if you can show people a victory. If you can show them they can win, they can build respect for themselves. The real union benefit is not so much dollars and cents. It's about respect. Part of the obligation of a leader is to choose fights so that you strengthen your members and your activists, and one of the best ways to do that is to get a victory that you can feel and you can taste. Then people discover that they can do this."

The Toronto and York Region Labour Council has made gains in convincing various politicians and decision-makers to pay attention to workers. It also marks its victories through increased internal capacity. Jenny gives an example from the Toronto municipal election in the fall of 2004: "We have union members that were never ever involved in municipal politics, stand up at meetings and say, 'You know this is amazing. As a teachers' union we have never talked to our members about electing mayors and councillors. This time, we put it out, and phoned our members, and it felt good.' And another teachers' union said, 'We've never talked to our teachers about anything other than Catholic education, in terms of electoral work. We had to file a grievance against the Catholic School Board so that we could put up the Labour Council lists of endorsed candidates on our bulletin boards in our schools. We won our grievance to say that's our little embassy in the school—the bulletin board. We can now put up what we want. And our members are happy we did that because they are proud to see this new mayor, and they liked the list of endorsed candidates.'"

As Winnie says, "It's a work in progress, and there's lots more to do. But in everything we do, we need to be aware of and work with that diversity of voices."

Section 4

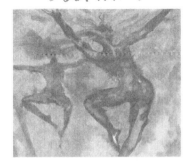

Between Us

Section 4:

Between Us

This section is for White activists struggling with their own racism, and women of colour who need to know they're not crazy.
> —Eveline Shen, Executive Director, Asian Communities for Reproductive Justice, California

What's interesting in this chapter is the back and forth between the highly personal and the analytical—it's unsettling.
> —Nora Allingham, anti-racism educator, academic, and writer on equity issues for over thirty years

Here, you take great risks in treating yourselves as racialized subjects that are not only worthy of discussion but also require this kind of examination to do anti-racism work.
> —Charles Smith, organizer, educator, policy analyst, and writer with over thirty years of experience in anti-racist activism

Ourselves as Subjects

So far we've explored practical strategies for shifting power dynamics in organizations to produce greater equity. Most people know that racial equity work rarely happens as tidily in real life as it does in the stories in section two. The reality is that anti-racism work is dreaded because it's a difficult topic for people to speak about. It's often painful, loaded with personal and social histories, and can threaten people's very sense of themselves, as well as friendships they've developed across racial lines.

In this section, we examine how racism has distorted our friendship and our capacity to work together. White privilege and racism have played out between us over and over again. It's often been fraught and difficult. It would be dishonest to simply provide tools and strategies without examining the emotional commitment that racial equity work requires of people. We draw on our experience with each other to reveal what it takes to honestly confront White privilege when it arises and to try to transform it.

What follows are a series of dialogues that arose out of deep conflicts between us, shaped by racism. We have chosen a dialogue format because these discussions are always gruelling and we didn't want to hide behind theorizing. We tape recorded many of our most difficult conversations over the past four years to keep us honest. These dialogues evolved over time and reflect our fights, our resistance, and our growth. Most recently, these conversations have shaped a new way of working together.

We also knew that we were taking a huge risk in exposing our personal struggles without taking refuge in the professional distance that writing in other parts of this book allows. We asked for, and paid particular attention to, feedback from those who read our manuscript through its many stages (see our acknowledgements). For example, one reader told us that she squirmed for two reasons: first, because she recognized herself in the exchange between us; second, because she sometimes felt as though she was eavesdropping on a private conversation. We maintained the passages where the reader's discomfort might be a source of insight, and edited more personal passages that distracted from the racism we were examining in the context of our work.

Some of our readers challenged us to dig deeper. They posed questions which provoked new thinking for us. For example, two of our readers—a woman of colour and a White woman—critiqued the initial draft as being too focused on Barb's process. They showed us how this overshadowed the impact of Barb's racism on Tina and what it took Tina to tackle it. Our colleague of colour further pointed out that Barb's learning was another benefit she derived, even while being confronted. We made significant changes based on these comments.

In contrast, a couple of readers commented that there seemed to be an unequal focus on what Barb had learned from Tina, and they were not convinced that Tina was not also learning through this process. "Where is the mutuality that is so common in such dialogues," they ask? These are *not* dialogues between two people who are *equally* learning about racism. In a racially divided world, every moment poses different experiences to both of us: the way we are treated by customs officers at the airport or by managers in an interview. White privilege can make racism invisible to Barb. Racism is always present and evident to Tina. There is no equity in the learning about racism.

Who Is the Expert?

Tina: Let's look at some of the dynamics that arose between us when we did a workshop for a group of women's shelters. It was a full-day workshop with executive directors and staff and it was their first discussion of racism in their organizations. At the end of the day I had to bring a few things to your attention.

Barb: You took me to task for "capping" you.

Tina: Yes. You kept repeating things I said that were perfectly clear. You, then, either got credit for it, or appeared to be more clear in your explanation than I was. This happened at the end of a workshop that was already really difficult. We should reconstruct that day because I think it's an important example of why "capping" is so counterproductive. Because it was a good day because … we got racism on the agenda. However, we were in an all-White room and I was the only person of colour. We had a difficult beginning because of the differential way in which the executive director of the shelter introduced us.

Barb: It was a very unequal introduction, in which she introduced me, basically, as the expert. I don't remember what the words were, but it was clear that I was the main event, and you were there as "the other."

Tina: It was as though I was being presented as your assistant. From the outset, there wasn't any question about your status and expertise. The power of what you said and did is what I'm trying to convey here. So at the end of the day, a woman came up to me to ask my advice. She had adopted a child of colour and was asking me for parenting resources and books for her child.

Barb: I remember being struck by the fact that this person had come to you and not to me, and I found myself standing beside you, "loudly" standing beside you. You were making suggestions that were quite adequate on their own as it turned out, and I started adding my own suggestions for resources, as if somehow I was an expert on this particular thing. And this, despite the fact that you are the parent of biracial children and I am not. (Pause) I couldn't stand you being in the limelight or being the expert. In this conversation, you clearly were the expert, and the woman had chosen to come to you. So there was something about envy, something about jealousy, something about needing to be the expert, which was clearly not as examined by me as it needed to be.

Tina: What is important is that the incident you're describing came at the end of the closing circle in which there were questions posed to us by the participants. My experience of you "capping" wasn't just in that moment; it was just the most blatant example.

Barb: So was I "capping" you in the circle?

Tina: It was the last straw of the whole day because, yes, you kept "capping" me in the closing circle. I would answer a question fairly completely. And then you would "add." It was the way in which you added ... I would just barely have finished talking and you'd jump in. So it was as if you knew everything that I had said, and had more to add. That was what made me livid—that little adding, which looks so innocent and like you're trying to be helpful. But the way in which it happens ... that bare pause for me to catch a breath ... it's just infuriating. (Both take deep breaths)

Barb: I don't even remember the circle. So that's how unconscious I was of even doing it.

Tina: Well, one reason that I remember it is that the executive director went home after the workshop and e-mailed a question to you, even though she had both our e-mail addresses. She e-mailed a question to you about something I had said in response to a question she had posed in the circle. I had given a fairly detailed response to what they needed to keep in mind when dealing with a complaint of racial harassment using their policy. I can't remember exactly what I said, but she followed up on it because she was interested in it. She wrote to you about it because she assumed that what I'd said was clearly known to you and that you could actually embellish it.

Barb: Which is the pattern I had established in capping, and other behaviours.

Tina: The reason I want to be so clear about the context is that your individual acts of asserting White privilege were occurring in a room in which other people's actions had already set it up. The introduction had set it up, and the fact that it was an all-White group in which you were coming in as a White anti-racism educator already marginalized me and set you in the centre. So your acting in that way just added to an already inequitable situation.

Barb: So, what you're telling me is that part of my job as a White person doing this work is to really think about that ahead of time, and to think about all the ways that, consciously or unconsciously, I contribute to a racist impact on you, which privileges me.

Tina: Yes, because even if we had done fantastic work through the day, those actions actually undercut everything that we said about racism. They just reinforced the notions that people already had about who is the expert. The result: you have people who come out of an anti-racism workshop feeling like they've learned things but practising the same old stuff with a new confidence, which is such a dangerous combination.

Barb: Oh, that's really important, because that's in fact what we're dealing with in organizations.

Tina: They now have the talk but nothing changed in the walk, and there's a righteousness in the talk now. Or there's a sense of having received the blessing in this work. That's why I was so angry. (Several pauses for both) This is what White people need to understand about *why* people of colour are often reluctant and suspicious of working with White people, especially when doing anti-racism work as well as other types of work. If they do work together, there's often conflict because of these unequal dynamics.

Barb: Okay, so this is just *one* way I participate in the unequal dynamics to my benefit and to your detriment.

The "Interpreter" Role

Tina: Another way that you and other White people establish yourselves as experts is through "interpreting" people of colour to White people. You set yourself up as a *bridge* between me and the other White people in the room. This is something racialized people experience constantly in organizations. For example, there were times in a meeting the other day, when a White manager would repeat things being said by Ahmed, a Somali-Canadian manager. Ahmed is perfectly easy to understand, and he's a brilliant man. He has the kind of analysis that just leaves me in awe. He certainly does not need any help with developing an analysis of a situation and communicating his ideas. Yet it seems to make some people uncomfortable to be around a man who is so clear about racism, and who cuts through the crap so clearly and easily. The easiest thing is to target his accent. So you have people either patting him on the back and saying, "Oh, that's very interesting," and moving right along or repeating what he said over again, "So what Ahmed is saying ..." But Ahmed had just said it.

Barb: Okay, so now you're raising another thing. It's one thing to be aware as a White person of not doing it, but how about challenging other White people when they do it, like, "I think Ahmed just said that ... and he said it better." (Laughter)

Tina: (Laughs) I know; imagine that.

Barb: There's another piece of this that's hard for me to talk about. There's a way we White people can cap and feel *good* about ourselves, telling ourselves that we're somehow helping a racialized person be clear. I can actually tell myself that I'm doing something for "them," bringing "them" into the group, on the assumption that (a) they need my help in being brought in, and (b) that other people don't understand them as well as I do. The arrogance works on several levels; the need to be front and centre is right in there and it never gets acknowledged because it's covered up by this notion that I'm helping somebody.

Tina: You're "helping" the person of colour, and the other myth is that you're trying to help the group. So if we push that analysis, you're reinforcing the perception that people of colour are problematic; that they're harder to bring into an organization, that they're harder to work with; that White people are needed to bridge; that there's some kind of mystical process to work with people of colour; it's a specialized skill.

    Plus, it leaves White people totally off the hook for the ways in which they've set up the whole meeting, the team, and the entire organization in a way that sets the person of colour on the margins. So with that whole notion of bringing the person in, your behaviour then says, "Yes it is hard to bring 'them' in and I

need to help bring them in, because they're hard to work with." The problem, then, resides in me, the person of colour, rather than putting the focus on the dominant group and saying, "Why are you requiring this person to fight their way in?" "Why are we setting this up so this person has to be 'interpreted' by a White person?"

Barb: I guess I'm just starting to realize after all these years of working, how wired into my cells this stuff is. I can recognize, at a certain intellectual level, my White superiority and arrogance. In a context of racism and White privilege, my own unexamined need for recognition makes me a dangerous ally. I do want to make a contribution, but I have also wanted acknowledgement, and I'm competitive. I have avoided looking at my own need for recognition, and of how I have benefited. While these behaviours have given me some unearned benefits in the world, they have caused pain to friends and colleagues I love, they impede our work, and they block me from working fully with the gifts I've got.

Tina: This is critical—your willingness to look at those little ways of fooling yourself so you as a White person can stay on top, climb back in the saddle. And I think, because you *are* an excellent anti-racism educator, it will carry a lot of weight to have this come from you.

Tina's Voice: "Friendly Fire: Fighting to Establish My Expertise"

There are a number of racialized people who will not do anti-racism or equity work with White people because they do not want to have to contend with the dynamics described above in the midst of work that is already so painful and demanding. A common assumption on the part of White people who employ us is that Barb is the expert, that she provides the theory, the objectivity, the skill, and professional expertise. They also presume that I'm the person who will share my personal experiences of racism. Many racialized people are similarly enthralled by a White person who speaks so clearly about racism and White privilege and often assume that I won't be as effective or have the same level of expertise as Barb. All this is established within minutes of our walking into an organization, before either one of us speaks a word or acts in any way.

Fighting to establish my competence and credibility, not just about racism and anti-racism but also about organizational change, adult education, and facilitation, becomes the first order of work. Before White people and some racialized people can work with me to address racism within the organization, I have to spend valuable time convincing them of my knowledge and expertise. It's one of the material ways that racism costs; there are also many psychological, emotional, and other human costs to this process of fighting for a legitimate level of recognition.

When my White colleague acts from her White privilege to reinforce and expand on this perception of herself as the authority on anti-racism, she does so in a context in which merit is already unquestioningly conferred upon her, whereas I have to earn it. It does damage in a number of ways:

- I am caught unawares, not expecting to be attacked by a person I rely upon to be a source of support and an ally in the work. I have to manage my hurt and anger while working to overcome the effect of her actions on other people in the room in the midst of sessions that are already oppressive.
- It's doubly difficult to establish my competence with others in the room who have witnessed this dynamic between us, since it confirms what systemic and everyday racism teach: White people are better at most kinds of work, even anti-racism work, than racialized people.
- When it takes place in the midst of an anti-racism session, it covertly reinforces the very discrimination we are *overtly* trying to address. When the very process put in place to uproot racism becomes a source of racism, it's hard to imagine how the damage will be undone.
- I also have to muster up the energy to challenge her on her behaviour after having worked to educate other White people about racism all day.

Barb's Voice: "I'm the Expert"

I have written before about why I work to fight racism. But I am still learning that some of the very ways I fight racism are themselves, manifestations of White supremacy. I have never examined publicly the extent to which White privilege shapes the very ways I fight racism.

Let's get specific. I have allowed myself to think I'm an expert on, of all things, racism which I don't myself experience. It's pretty ludicrous when you think about it. Even in challenging racism I benefit as a White person, and there are parts of this privilege I have been resistant to admitting. This is very convenient for other White people who don't want to learn from people of colour.

When Tina and I get invited to work with an organization (whether it be a union, community organization, or municipality), the employer—usually a White person—will often direct questions to me. I'm sometimes invited to view people of colour as perplexing problems that White people have to deal with. White people are more informal, more playful, less constrained and make more eye contact with me than with Tina. They are more likely to introduce me first to employees, to linger on my credentials, to follow-up with me, to prefer to make arrangements through me, to recount a story they're uneasy about with me, and to seek my advice. These observations are not about "bad White people." This is about how unconscious power and discomfort about it works. Women have made the same observations about male behaviours in relation to their male colleagues.

What It Takes to Confront a White Person's Racism

Tina: Let me talk a bit about the impact of trying to stay in relationship with you and to staying in the work with you as a woman of colour coming up against that White supremacy in many different ways. I'm not saying it's the only thing that happens between us, but I think you need to know about this if you're going to work with White people and with people of colour. You need to know that you're not the only one dealing with that White supremacist part of you—I am, too. I have to deal with you. And the consequences don't land on you, they land on me. I don't like it. It is not fun. In fact, it's excruciating, and it colours my capacity to trust the other caring, committed, and willing parts of you.

To do anti-racism work, people of colour in organizations have to become vulnerable and trust that people with decision-making power (mostly if not all White) are actually going to work on this part of themselves. It has huge consequences for the people of colour who have to let their guard down enough to actually work on changing power relations with White people.

Barb: Sometimes when I think about how entrenched this reflex of White privilege is in me it makes me despair. But what you say about staying in this conversation, I think that's an absolute requirement.

Tina's Voice: What Has It Taken?

What has it taken to confront Barb, to act to protect my knowledge and expertise, and to go through the conflict without taking the option of leaving? That option is not available to most racialized people objecting to racism in the organizations with which I've worked. And when people have left community coalitions and activist networks in which they have volunteered, their choice has cost all of us who are trying to change an unjust society. If I am to call myself an anti-racism educator, an activist for racial equity, I must have the discipline to go through the conflict, the despair, the rage, the hurt, the desire to give up, to segregate. Only then will my practice as an activist have the integrity of being grounded in lived experience.

It's been critical to remain in this process with Barb because she has a well-deserved reputation as an anti-racism educator and therefore has real credibility and influence. More importantly, she and I have made choices to stick with this process and to make it part of the book, despite the risks and challenges this poses to both of us, because we believe that this is what is required of anyone trying to do racial equity work.

Another question I need to ask is, What has it required of me? It has required

- being firm, lucid, and establishing clear expectations
- holding Barb accountable for not meeting these expectations and ensuring there were appropriate consequences
- maintaining a rigorous analysis of inequities and power differences throughout
- valuing appropriately my own knowledge, experience, expertise, and skill
- developing an accurate sense of entitlement despite the socialization that makes me question my analysis and feed my self-doubt
- critiquing my notion of a duty to educate White people and beginning to think more in terms of racialized people's collective right to redress
- recognizing that foregrounding my knowledge and analysis of racism in this book is not arrogance but an accurate and appropriate path to racial equity
- balancing this firmness with compassion, allowing for the possibility of genuine remorse, giving Barb room to make appropriate amends, and affirming later moments when she made different choices
- resisting the temptation to sever the relationship, exert power over, exact revenge, or simply dismiss Barb as unworthy of any further effort
- battling with fear of backlash from White people who would see me as attacking Barb, or promoting myself
- staying compassionate even when I feared judgements from racialized people that I being was too soft on Barb, had internalized my own oppression, had no self-worth
- staying and wrestling long enough to discover that taking my full and rightful place really does not take anything away from Barb that rightfully belongs to her
- learning about power, leadership, and expertise as capacities that can be shared to the benefit of both of us, rather than at the cost of one or the other—these capacities can multiply rather than divide

What Happens When a White Person Is Confronted on Her Racism?

Barb's Voice: Between Shame and Sullen Defiance

During the course of writing this book, I sent a section of our writing off for comment to a friend in England, another White person. Despite the fact that the key theorizing in this piece was Tina's, I told my friend, "I drafted this piece which tries to incorporate what I've been thinking about as a result of ...," it doesn't matter what. My friend responded ecstatically to me, saying how much she learned from me, and making a few encouraging suggestions. I mentioned vaguely to Tina that I had sent it off and gotten enthusiastic feedback. She smelled a rat, and asked to see the e-mails. I should have offered them and immediately proposed to fix what I had done. Instead, Tina had to confront me on the fact that I had taken credit for her analysis, which was the most essential part of the case study. She then had to analyze how my actions got me credit for something that wasn't mine. It also reinforced an already powerful tendency of people to credit me with the "real writing" in this book. Through all this, she also had to push me to do something about it.

I collapsed into a profound shame. I wrote a second letter to my friend, which Tina took considerable effort to edit. I took some of her suggestions and not others. That letter was more tactical than a genuine effort to take responsibility. In that letter, *my* pain was evident, but the letter was pretty vague about the impact on Tina. Nowhere did this letter acknowledge what Tina had given me—a sharp, critical, and caring challenge to take responsibility for my actions, work to restore my relationship with her, and be fully authentic in the work that I say I do.

Over the course of six months, Tina had to confront me again ... and again ... and again. During this time, I alternated between shame and sullen resistance. Shame, in the context of White privilege, is partially distress that one has done something that hurts someone else. But it's uglier than that. Shame says, "I should have known better; I can't believe I did that; what kind of person am I that I did that?" Shame is also regret at being caught and concern about what others will think when they find out. In this context, shame keeps the focus on the White person, distracts us from grasping the real effect our actions have on people of colour, and prevents us from making proper reparation.

In sullen resistance, I conduct a defiant, internal conversation which may sound familiar to many White people. It voices my reluctance to take responsibility and do something, and my "right" not to. It's not pretty. It goes something like, "People of colour don't always get it right; they're learning too. Why is it always my mistakes that are on display? I'm tired of always having to look at the worst parts of myself. Look at all my efforts, and do they ever get credited? I'm not going to lie down and take it."

I'm not going to eliminate shame and sullen resistance in myself just by exposing them. But exposing them to myself gives me a choice. Sometimes I have to swing between these two poles before I can reach another kind of energy that says "Do you really think Tina would go to all this trouble just to get you? Look at what Tina is giving you to do your work! Be grateful."

Differential Costs of Confronting White Privilege

Tina: I'm just realizing that in those times that you were confronted with your White priv-
        ilege and something harmful you'd done, you saw those moments as aberrations. I
        often see that happen when progressive White people are confronted with their
        racism. They say, "Okay, I screwed up this time, but generally I don't." Whereas,
        what is constantly at play is White privilege and it's actually an aberration *not* to
        act out of it.

        That's why there's such a backlash against anti-racism work. When White
        people intellectually agree that racism exists, there's often this unspoken qualifier
        right away, "But not in me … not in *my* organization … elsewhere." It's mostly
        racialized people who have to point out racism and the specific actions of White
        people that contribute to it. As a result, the White person who is confronted, along
        with other White people who hear about it, react as though this is an unjust attack
        on them. But it's really an opportunity to have the difficult conversation that is such
        an essential part of anti-racism work. It shouldn't be a five-alarm crisis. If we recog-
        nize that racism is such a normal part of the way things happen, then these kinds of
        discussions should be a matter-of-fact part of problem solving.

Barb: I think this is part of what happened in the letter to my friend. She expressed con-
        cern that as a White person who tries to fight racism, I was being subjected to criti-
        cism while other White people were not subjected to that kind of scrutiny. She
        implied that your challenge to me was an attack rather than support for me to do
        my work well.

Tina: In a way, she'd be right—I was not just supportive of you. I was confronting you
        with what you had done. I was holding you accountable for your actions. What
        struck me about her response is her silence on the fact that you had done damage
        to me. Her attention went to how you were feeling and not at all to the impact on
        me. This is a person who normally reacts deeply to hearing of injustice, and allies
        with those that are being treated unfairly. That's what made this moment particular-
        ly painful for me.

Barb: You taught me that I should have asked her why I needed to be protected from you.
        In what way were you a danger to me when I had in fact wounded you? But
        instead, I colluded with her support of me at your expense. What happens for many
        White people is that we become afraid that we will be next. We worry that our own
        actions warrant challenge and we're hoping like hell it won't happen. It's one thing
        to ally with those who are unjustly treated. It's another thing to look at the parts of
        ourselves that are also capable of that unjust treatment. That fear of having our
        racism exposed keeps the gaze of White people on the well-being of White people
        and not on the well-being of people of colour.

Tina: Reading your friend's e-mail response was terrifying. That may sound dramatic but
          it's true. I've known both of you for a long time and I have a deep respect for the
          social justice work you do. This "incident" brought home to me how caring White
          women can choose to let people of colour be dispossessed because they feel unfair-
          ly challenged or too tired to deal with racism. I gather from your friend that she's
          weary of having to constantly think through the implications of what she does and
          is willing to take the consequences. And what are the consequences? She feels real-
          ly bad, talks it through with a White friend, and that's the end of it. She's not alone.
          White people have hundreds of mundane, perfectly plausible reasons for not doing
          anything, even when it's really clear that their actions have severely impacted a
          racialized person.

          I don't have the same option not to deal with racism, and the consequences to
          me are huge. My livelihood is threatened, my health suffers, and the struggle to
          trust White people becomes even harder.

          What can I as a racialized woman do so that the impact of White people's
          racism is less dire to myself and has greater consequences for White people? I am
          grateful to Audre Lorde for her encouragement of women of colour to use our anger
          for our own health and to transform the relationships we have with White people
          and racialized men. To be clear about my anger and the ways in which racism robs,
          hurts, and erases me is a healthy and appropriate choice to make for my well-being.

The Consequences of Avoiding Racial Conflict

Barb: There *is* another consequence of White people deciding we're too tired to deal with
          racism. We rely on each other for our friendships and work, and avoid more than
          cordial relations with people of colour. It's not something many White people want
          to talk about, but somewhere we make a decision to segregate. And, it's a complete
          taboo; there's no place to have that conversation. So it is not talked about.

Tina: Well, not talked about by White people. (Laughter) That's how racial segregation
          becomes the fall-back position. And if there are friendships in a workplace between
          White people and people of colour, there's an unspoken deal that "racism will not
          now or ever be an issue between us." Things fall apart when a racialized person
          breaks the deal by raising issues of racism, whether it's in the workplace or in the
          friendship. That's when White people retreat.

Barb: Yes. This retreat comes out in a coded way in organizations. You'll hear, "We've
          seen what happens in other organizations; things go too fast; things explode; we
          think that we can do this on a more gradual basis."

Tina: In other words, do this on White people's terms. This is why the story "White
          Women as the 'Default' Position on Equity" in section two is so important. It

reveals a willingness on the part of White people to racially segregate and still convince themselves that they're anti-oppression activists; that they can have their cake and eat it, too.

Barb: So, White people can draw attention to people of colour who may choose to only work together and call that "racial segregation." Yet even White people doing anti-racism work often choose to work only with other White people! We call that "being professional." We know enough to include a racialized person in a junior role, but the equal relations are with other White people.

Tina: So, White people get to feel uncomfortable if the few racialized people in an organization sit together at meetings or at lunch, yet they don't ever notice that there are also tables that are entirely White.

Rainer Soegtrop

White People's Resistance to Learning from Racialized People

Tina: It's ironic that even when I confront you, you benefit, because I'm teaching you about how racism works. You learn a lot from me in the process. Do you remember all the times I've had to push you to acknowledge what I teach you in private and in public? It happened earlier today.

Barb: You mean when I suggested to you that I write a piece based on some work that you and I did. I wanted to write it myself as a kind of stand-alone piece. But, in fact, the content of what I wanted to write about came because you worked with me. There's a part of me that I always have to watch, that wants to be in charge of, and credited with, my own learning. And the way White privilege works is that I'm given credit and I take credit for knowing about racism.

Tina: I'm less interested in the theory of this and want to focus on exactly this moment—your resistance to learning from me, from a woman of colour, and how many times we have to revisit this conversation. Would you be willing to write about that?

Barb: That's what I'm trying to do. *And* I keep coming up against the part of me that resists wanting to. It's not that I don't learn from you. Clearly I do. What I resist is acknowledging—to myself and to others—that I'm learning from you. To say that I'm not fighting that and I'm not dealing with that would be a lie.

Tina: That's part of the reason I wanted us to write this section as a dialogue. These conversations ought to be written up the way they happen, and that will be particularly hard for you.

Barb: Well, but that's what we're saying. We're saying that what would be different about this book is the exposing of my White privilege and my resistance to exposing it. It is not what usually happens in anti-racism work. Until I am willing to show myself as a learner, nothing's going to shift.

Tina: The reluctance to learn from a woman of colour ... I still have to keep pushing you to say that clearly.

Barb: Reluctance to learn from a person of colour.

Tina: Because what you're doing in this book is you're writing as a White person who has something to say to other White people about how they learn to practise anti-racism. And, one of the most important things you have to say to them is, "What I've learned about this, I've learned from a woman of colour."

Barb: Yes.

Tina: And that to me is at the heart of anti-racism organizational change. It is to get White people to understand, at a profound level, that they can't do anti-racism work unless they are willing to learn from people of colour. For you to model that clearly, without any ambiguity, is important because the same instinct in you to cover up your learning from people of colour is a deep instinct in every White person. And having the courage to actually reveal this as someone who has all the authority and credibility of thirty years of doing anti-racism work is a huge contribution—an important piece of learning and teaching. That's what's being asked of you.

I also want to explore with you how part of this resistance to admit that you learn from people of colour is connected to a discomfort with being grateful to, or owing, a person of colour. The way it feels from here, acknowledging your learning from a person of colour is a real admission of failure. It's hard enough to say you've learned from another White person. But to have to admit to yourself and others that you've learned from a person of colour is to really hit bottom.

Barb: On the surface, I think that I acknowledge learning from people of colour all the time. But I think that the level that you're challenging me on here is a deeper one. People of colour and Aboriginal people are on the bottom of this society, the bottom that you talk about. My life's work has been advocating for people at the bottom, but in such a way that I'm still on top. It's as if to acknowledge the source of my learning would make me irrelevant and I would lose my place in the social justice communities we work in.

As I hear myself say these words, I know they're not rational. I know it's not rational to fear being irrelevant when there's so much work to do. I guess this is how internalized dominance works in me and many other White people. I have been taught that White people know better. Progressive White people don't say that out loud, but everything in this society teaches us that. Western imperialism isn't just out there. It is the internalized notion that White people know better, and if we don't, well, we should! In this frame, learning from people on the bottom, is a sign of failure, clear evidence that we couldn't come up with the answers ourselves. Coming up with answers ourselves is expected and highly rewarded. If we don't, we're not very good White people. I have been able to see this more clearly with men fighting sexism or with economically privileged progressives in anti-poverty struggles. But while I critique it out there, I find it very painful to acknowledge and grapple with it in my own insides.

Tina: White people's continued denial of what they receive from people of colour gets in the way of the larger conversations about racism. In fact, White people have benefited from racism in ways they will never be able to repay.

Barb: Yeah. It happens between us, and I think it's important to explore what that looks
        like because it's a microcosmic level of all the discussions about employment equi-
        ty, reparations for slavery, apologies for the Head Tax, and so on. I think your com-
        ment about my reluctance to accept what I owe is at the heart of it. I am deeply in
        debt to friends and colleagues—Aboriginal and people of colour—who have taught
        me. Like many progressive White people, I have worked to be the "giver," an initia-
        tor, problem-solver, an activist in a world that is unjust. When I don't grasp myself
        as a huge recipient but only as a giver and initiator, I do damage. In trying to get it
        right, trying to be recognized for getting it right, I weave and dodge the central
        issue—I can't get racism without the help of Aboriginal people and people of colour.

Tina: This was so clear in writing of "White Women as the 'Default' Position on Equity."
        You and I had to work through several levels of difficulty between us before we
        could write the final version. Your analysis of racism developed with each new chal-
        lenge I posed to you. I was challenging not just the limits of your analysis but also
        your actions.

Barb: Yes, I had great difficulty with the fact that I didn't, and in fact couldn't, come up
        with this analysis myself. We've talked about my reluctance to acknowledge my
        learning from people of colour. With you, it's been particularly difficult because we
        started out fifteen years ago with me as your mentor in the field. I am older, and at
        that time had more years of doing the work. I've struggled to shift from being your
        teacher to your apprentice, and from your apprentice to being an effective ally who
        continues to learn from you. It's actually a microcosm of my struggle to find an
        appropriate place in this work.

Tina: I think this history *has* made it harder for me to confront you. Because of our age
        difference and the fact that you were my mentor, I initially felt it was disrespectful
        to challenge you. When I stopped working with you for a while to take a job else-
        where, I began finding out how much I knew. So when we began working together
        again, it was different. I had to start challenging you. I think it's important to exam-
        ine these other factors, other than race, which have shaped our struggles together.
        But I don't want this acknowledgement of these particulars to be used as a reason
        to downplay our analysis of how White privilege has affected us. In fact, I saw the
        same dynamics at work between a younger White woman and an older woman of
        colour in a women's shelter. The young White woman resented the fact that she had
        to learn from the woman of colour. Soon after, the young White woman became the
        supervisor of the woman of colour who had trained her.

Making Different Choices

Tina: Fear is a big part of racial equity work, and it gets in the way of resolving racial conflict. You and I have different reasons for being afraid. But we've been trying to accept that we're afraid and act differently anyway.

Barb: Yes. This has been the scariest part for me—exposing how my racism works to myself and everyone else. The odd thing is that when I wrote "Between Shame and Sullen Defiance" above, it was strangely liberating. In the naming and holding it up for scrutiny, it struck me that I have choices. I don't need to act out of this stuff. I can recognize when these instincts are rising in me, name them to myself, and choose to do something different.

   Increasingly, it feels to me that this small piece of work that I'm doing with myself is connected to the work that Western culture needs to do. The resistance in me to learning from people of colour, the desire to be on top (otherwise I'll be on the bottom) is a part of what we encounter every day in the world. It's what you said earlier. My racism is not an aberration—it's a normal part of how things work, but seeing it as normal doesn't let me off the hook. I am still responsible for my racism and for transforming it.

Tina: I wonder if another part of feeling liberated is finding out that your racism could be exposed and it wouldn't cost you our friendship. I think you've felt that you had to behave impeccably, that is, never in a way that was racist, in order to have the friendship and approval of racialized people. The only times you really risked our friendship was when you wouldn't deal honestly and responsibly with my challenge to you. It wasn't necessarily the racism itself.

Barb: That makes sense to me because in my relationship with my male partner, it's not his sexism that enrages me. How could he not be sexist sometimes? It's when he covers it up and tries to look good that I feel crazy. For White women this is a potent reminder. We have experience with fathers, brothers, partners we love whose exercise of their power has an impact on us and whose refusal to take responsibility for it makes it much worse. We need to bring this experience to bear when our White privilege and racism are challenged by racialized friends and colleagues.

Tina: Usually when White women draw on their experience of sexism, it's to identify as the targets of discrimination and to abdicate positions of power they might have. What we're saying here is that it's important to stand in both locations at once: remember what "power-over" feels like from the bottom and apply that to their exercise of power from the top. It's similar to what we straight, racialized people have to do on issues of heterosexism and homophobia. It's essential learning for all of us if we're to build a real social justice movement.

   But I want to say some more about fear. As a target of racism, my fear operates at the level of survival. I have to constantly be aware of how White people are reacting to what I'm saying and doing, because usually, the person with real authority has been a White person, whether it's been teachers, managers, or CEOs. Part of surviving is knowing when I'm putting myself at risk by making a White person afraid or angry or upset. And it's not only the individual White person I'm interacting with but all the White people who will leap to the defence of the White person I'm challenging.

I also have to be aware of the other racialized people who are trying to cut deals for their own survival in the organization. They are often called upon by the White person I'm challenging, and sometimes by other White people who hear what I have done, to give their opinion as to whether my actions are justified. And since they're often at risk as well, it's in their best interests to tell White people what they want to hear. So challenging White people, or simply exposing the unfairness of a situation is dangerous. It's always risky; it's never neutral. That's one level of the work.

There's another level in relation to you as a human being, that comes out of a reluctance to cause hurt. That's part of this work, too. I had this image yesterday of a flu shot. Here we are trying to vaccinate ourselves against the built-in racist response, and we can't do it without a needle that causes pain. Why do we think we can do this work without pain? We accept a certain level of brutality in everyday life as a given. For example, daily experiences of racism are seen as an unfortunate but "normal" part of reality. It's overwhelming to think about changing it, so we move on. Somehow, accepting that brutality is the deal we make in order to keep going.

What I'm doing in this piece with you breaks all these unexamined deals. I'm saying I'm not willing to accept this brutality as a regular part of my life. And calling your attention to it feels violent to you and to me because I'm stepping out of this deal.

Barb: It's true. We've been examining the violence I've done to you, without using the word. I think that there's also a violence that I've done to myself in deciding that parts of myself—my vulnerability, uncertainty, limitations—are not worthy and therefore have to be covered up by an overconfidence and a pretense at being in control of the situation. And more and more I think that those are the parts of White people that we've "othered" on to racialized people. "Here, you carry my fear and smallness. It's not mine. I'm contracting it out." It's the spiritual version of racialized people taking care of White people's children, while White people run things.

So I do unconscious violence to myself and to people of colour in this way and then cover it up. I'm not trying to equate the impact of violence against people of colour with the internal violence I'm describing. I'm just trying to connect what happens internally to what happens externally. This deal doesn't serve me either, even though in the world I'm not hurt by it in the way you are. I'm privileged in employment, in recognition, in all kind of things that are denied to you, but in trying to be in my fullness in the world as a feeling, acting human being, it's necessary that I reclaim this part of myself and stop doing violence to it. This is very scary to talk about because it could look like just another White ploy to put the attention on me. One of the things I've been learning with you is that I am hazardous to your health without this kind of self-knowledge.

A New Moment

Barb: I want to talk about what you did this afternoon in the workshop we were giving together. I watched you help people make sense of five very different participant presentations. Then during the break, you were completely present for a participant who was distressed for a variety of reasons about what was happening in her team. You then responded to my anxiety about how to take things forward after the break. But, in fact, you were the person who guided the session for the rest of the afternoon. I was really grateful for this, because I had low energy and was having difficulty responding to all the dynamics in the room. For example, one participant in particular triggered me and it took an enormous amount of effort to stay compassionate with her. I know it did you, too, but you managed it.

And then, in the last ten minutes, you made time for a young Iraqi woman who was upset that she had not adequately confronted racism in a situation she had faced at work. And you worked six layers down from where I even dreamed of starting. You went straight to an analysis of the real question—the cost of racism. You worked with her and others to analyze how people of colour were being affected by the situation without putting her on the spot to talk before she was ready. You led all of us through an analysis of the structure and ways power was working (without using the friggin' triangle!) (Laughter) You highlighted the courage that this young woman had, in fact, shown and had erased from her own mind. And then you stayed with her fear of accepting that she had actually done something courageous. I was honoured to be with you. You were so loving with the people, and so tough with the racism. You kept your heart in and didn't lose your anger.

What was happening for you when you were doing it?

Tina: I had less fear than I usually have; I felt less vulnerable to attack at the front of the room; putting less energy into being correct in the way in which I shared time, or looked around the appropriate number of times at everyone. I was freer, and it felt like a graced moment. I felt you were less anxious, that you were genuinely partnering with me. There was a new ease.

Barb: I felt free to be "off."

Tina: You just said you were having trouble responding and you didn't get stuck in that. That's been one of your worst nightmares. You don't seem to be haunted by it in this moment.

Barb: I won't claim I didn't have qualms. But my hesitancy to be off didn't drive things. I felt off; I felt you on; I chose not to compete, and look what happened! I didn't lose anything; I gained lots, and so did everybody else. I can't remember when I last did this.

Tina: What was your worst fear about being off the other times?

Barb: The fear of being irrelevant. If you can carry it without me, what am I doing there? I'm not needed.

Tina: What made it okay today?

Barb: Well … (hesitates) … I think I'm developing more compassion for myself. Someone wise and dear to me told me recently, "You have a chance here to let go of the need for control, to learn trust by seeing your own role in this, and let the rest go." Today, I just let myself be how I was, because you were taking care of things. Did you feel abandoned by me this afternoon?

Tina: Not for a moment. When I said we partnered in a fuller way, that's what it felt like. It often takes both of us to do this work. I rest when you're at the front. It gives me time to think. I felt you had my back, which meant I could be freer. If I'm worried about friendly fire, I'm scared and distracted. I never had a moment of that today. I felt at ease again in the CEO's office, when you and I signalled each other. It takes both of us to deal with him. You go a couple of rounds with him, which gives me time to get over my rage and resentment. And then I go another couple of rounds.

Barb: This feels so simple, as we find these words, like something is getting unsnarled.

Section 5

More Tools and Strategies

Section 5

More Tools and Strategies

This section contains a selection of some of the tools we've developed with different organizations and sectors. You might think about using these in combination with the case scenarios, analyses, tools and strategies in section two.

Tool 1:   An Equity Lens for Reviewing Policies, Programs, and Materials

Tool 2:   Group Dynamics in Racial Equity Work

Tool 3:   An Organizational Checklist for Racial Equity

Tool 4:   Sample Supervision Policy that Integrates Equity

Tool 5:   Sample Human Rights and Equity Policy

David Smiley

Dancing on Live Embers

An Equity Lens for Reviewing Policies, Programs, and Materials

We developed the following questions to help ourselves and organizations bring to the surface hidden "normal" inequities in policies, procedures, programs, and materials.

1. **Does the document name and/or *anticipate existing inequities*?**
   For example, does it recognize that statutory holidays are Christian based and ensure that people with other observances have similar entitlements?

2. ***What assumptions* are being made about who and what matters?**
   For example, does the complaint procedure recognize the risks facing the complainant and the benefits to the organization of the information the complainant is bringing forward?

3. **Does the policy/document anticipate and address the *differential impact* of a practice on different groups of people?**
   For example, if "casual workers" are mostly women, racialized and Aboriginal workers, policies which exclude casual workers from entitlements will have a differential impact on these workers. A policy that anticipates differential impact would include casual workers.

4. **Does the policy/document anticipate and address *differential power/ influence* within the organization?**
   For example, a supervision policy would appraise the manager's ability to provide diverse employees with ongoing support and necessary resources to do their respective jobs, as well as the manager's responsibility to monitor an individual's performance.

5. **Does the policy or document aim explicitly to *increase equity*?**
   For example, hiring policy and practices would acknowledge that the organization needs to draw on the widest breadth of knowledge/expertise. This would be reflected in bona fide job requirements that build in equity competencies and job descriptions that utilize and assess for those.

6. **Does it *acknowledge the benefits of equity* to the organization?**
   For example, it's not just a legal obligation to have a non-discrimination/accommodation policy. The policy/document recognizes that an equitable workplace and a diverse workforce are prerequisites for effective, relevant service delivery. The organization further benefits from the resulting recognition by funders and communities.

Tool 2

Group Dynamics in Racial Equity Work

When organizations are doing racial equity work, whether it is training, policy development, or establishing an anti-racism committee, the following dynamics need to be anticipated.

White People	Racialized People
■ Often get to be the observers, the ones who listen to, and weigh evidence of racism.	■ Have to work hard at a number of levels:
	— convince White people that racism exists
■ Have to be convinced that racism and/or other forms of oppression are operating in the organization.	— provide anecdotal and other forms of evidence to make their case
	— manage the pain these discussions evoke
■ Assume that anti-racism education is an opportunity to learn about racialized people, and not about examining Whiteness.	■ Are commonly expected to share their experiences of racism as proof that it exists, but not to bring an analysis of White privilege and power to the discussion.
■ Expect that their learning should happen with as little discomfort to themselves as possible.	■ Have to be willing to hear oppressive remarks from White people in the course of educating them.
■ Often deny having White privilege and prefer to focus on ways in which they are the targets of discrimination.	■ Must behave in ways that White people consider polite, reasonable, and non-threatening.
■ May feel that acknowledging their privilege means admitting they are "bad people."	■ Are exceedingly careful in how they name racism and White privilege.
■ May need reassurance and appreciation for their efforts to learn.	■ Frequently fear reprisal and hesitate to name their experience of racism.
■ Struggle to accept they have unearned privilege when they work so hard for what they have.	■ May attempt to rescue White people when things become uncomfortable.
■ Often see racial equity as a benefit for racialized people and a cost to themselves.	■ Constantly aware of how racism benefits White people and negatively affects racialized workers' careers, status in the organization, and performance appraisals.
■ Do not have to think about racism or its impact on their career, status in the organization, and performance appraisal	■ Recognize that racism shapes their employment conditions, service delivery, and every aspect of the organization's work.
■ May see racial equity work as peripheral to the real business of the organization and their daily responsibilities.	■ Are often dismissed as "having chips on their shoulder," "playing the race card," or as "having a personal agenda."
■ Have more credibility than racialized people if they name examples of how racism is operating in the organization.	

An Organizational Checklist for Racial Equity

We developed this tool from the work we did for a municipality. The project examined how education could make a difference in moving the change effort forward. These indicators emerged out of focus groups with many employees, some of whom were involved with the change process; many were not. You can use this as a discussion tool with your own organization to identify progress and work still to do.

The Racial Equity Organizational Change Process

Organizational change for racial equity is a long-term process that requires ongoing learning and a willingness to risk and to act, often without broad support, and even in the face of resistance. The former Ontario Anti-Racism Secretariat defined anti-racism organizational change in the following way:

> A process guided by a vision and goals in which corporate values, systems, experiences and behaviours of individuals are deliberately changed to achieve access, equity and full participation for employees and customers/clients. This involves a process of identifying, challenging and reducing systemic barriers and individual acts of racism.
>
> (*Guide to Key Anti-Racism Terms and Concepts*)

A successful change process ensures that racialized and Aboriginal people are meaningfully involved as decision-makers in the process, and that evaluations measure the impact of the change efforts on racialized people. However, it is important to note that a racial equity organizational process benefits all employees, volunteers and service users in the organization.

Using This Tool

This is not an exhaustive checklist for change initiatives; readers are encouraged to adjust and add to the list in order to address the specific organizational culture, systems, policies, and practices of their agencies and institutions. Tick the square that best corresponds with where your organization is on each item.

Racial Equity Policy and Plan	No	Working on it	Yes
Has a shared definition of racism and of anti-racism work			
Acknowledges the value of racial equity to the organization			
Links racial equity to other core values of the organization			
Links racial equity and the mission and mandate of the organization			
Has approval of political management and union leadership			
Has support from and specifies roles in the implementation plan for senior managers and other leaders (board members, union presidents/stewards)			
Outlines clear actions, timeframes, people responsible for each action, indicators of progress and processes for monitoring an evaluation			
Addresses all aspects of the work done by your organization			
Is integrated into all other planning in the organization			
Is understood by all employees			
Has community support			
Requires annual reports on progress and setbacks to the decision-makers and governing bodies			

Employment systems	No	Working on it	Yes
Outreach for hiring is broad and includes a variety of strategies			
Job calls make clear the organization's desire for candidates from equity-seeking groups, including racialized and Aboriginal groups			
Job calls are specific and ask only for qualifications and experience that are necessary to do the job			
Job qualifications acknowledge the value of experience in working with racialized communities, knowledge of anti-racism work, the ability to work within racially diverse teams, and the capacity to work in languages other than English			
Staff on selection panels understand how to identify and challenge racial and cultural factors affecting selection			
The full range of expertise of racialized and Aboriginal candidates and staff is recognized, and is not limited to their connections to their communities			
Management works effectively with the union(s) on anti-racism			
Mobility exists between job categories			
Developmental assignments are used to increase equity			
Career counselling and mentoring are available to all staff			
Proportion of racialized and Aboriginal staff in leadership positions is consistent with their numbers in the communities served			
Proportion of racialized and Aboriginal staff in administrative and support positions is consistent with their numbers in communities served			
Balanced representation of racialized and Aboriginal persons sit on selection panels for hirings and promotions			
No over-representation of racialized and Aboriginal persons in temporary, contract, and part-time positions			
Few substantiated complaints from applicants in competitions and promotion processes; no comments that people got jobs because they are from an equity-seeking group and not because they are qualified			
Personnel policies and procedures acknowledge the organization's responsibility to meet the needs of people with diverse identities (care for dependents, religious observances, etc.)			

Management Practices	No	Working on it	Yes
Supervision practices are consistent and equitable, work is allocated fairly, and decisions are based on clearly communicated criteria			
Performance appraisals are conducted regularly, and managers learn how to recognize the ways in which their biases may influence the process			
Racial equity knowledge, skills, and practices are incorporated into performance objectives and appraisals for all levels of staff			
Managers demonstrate skills in fostering racial equity work, a collegial work environment, and shared decision-making			
Managers have the capacity to discuss racism, both individual and systemic, and to work with staff to identify strategies for dealing with it			
Leaders make clear statements and consistently act (e.g., allocating sufficient resources, making racial equity a standing agenda item at key meetings, ensuring racialized and Aboriginal people are among the decision-makers) to demonstrate the importance of challenging racism in the organization			

Complaints Process(es)	No	Working on it	Yes
A clear complaints process exists for all staff, in addition to the grievance procedure for unionized staff			
Both formal and informal procedures for resolving complaints are established in order to address appropriately the range of allegations of racism that can be made; management, union stewards, and others designated to address complaints are skilled in recognizing and addressing racism			
Staff are familiar with, and are confident they can use, the complaints procedures			
Race-based problems are addressed promptly; time is taken to analyze and address the roots of the problem			
Reprisals for lodging a complaint are noted and dealt with by senior people			
There are examples of effective resolutions to race-based complaints			
Performance appraisals for managers include the ability to handle allegations of racism and carry out the complaints process skillfully			
The types of complaints and the frequency with which they arise are monitored and reported to the governing body of the organization			
Complaints are seen as a source of information about systemic racism that may need to be addressed by the organization			

Communicating in the Organization	No	Working on it	Yes
All staff receive clear, relevant, and timely information about corporate discussions, decisions, and actions which affect them			
All departments routinely co-ordinate and communicate racial equity efforts			
Publications and other communications materials appropriately reflect racialized people as valued board, staff, volunteers, service users, and community members			
All materials (publicity, educational, program, etc.) are assessed for bias and revised as necessary			
Staff understand the racial and cultural factors that influence communication			
Staff are able to detect and challenge bias in their own written and oral communications and in those of others			
People are supported for speaking about racism and racial equity in the workplace			
Meetings are conducted in ways that recognize and value different ways of speaking, thinking, debating, and making decisions			
Knowledge and expertise of staff are recognized, used, and fairly compensated			
Knowledge and expertise of community representatives are recognized, used, and fairly compensated			
The organization uses an updated list of community media and information networks			
Communication can occur in languages appropriate to the service users or target audience			

Programs and Work with Communities	No	Working on it	Yes
Major policy is developed with substantial community participation			
All policy is developed to be consistent with racial equity and other equity policies			
Mechanisms for community participation are fully utilized even when community representatives challenge the organization's leaders and its staff			
Community access to facilities includes considerations of childcare, scheduling around days and times of religious significance, a range of food and dietary restrictions, translation and interpretation requirements, and physical accessibility			
A clear plan for ensuring service equity is an integral part of the racial equity policy and implementation plan, as well as all other planning initiatives of the organization			
Staff and volunteers know where to refer clients when programs cannot meet their needs			
All aspects of service delivery have been assessed for their consistency with the racial equity policy			
Programs are evaluated in terms of their impact on racialized communities, and changed as required			
Advocacy on behalf of equity is seen as part of the organization's work			
Support is given to community groups doing advocacy work			
The organization requires the vendors and contractors it does business with to abide by its racial equity policy, as well as to practice racial equity as employers and as the providers of goods and services			
The organization ensures that Aboriginal and racialized business people benefit equitably from contracts			

Education and Professional Development	No	Working on it	Yes
Education for all staff is a component of the racial equity policy and implementation plan			
Education and training is seen as one among many strategies to achieve equity			
All education and professional development offered by the organization incorporates racial equity and other areas of equity work			
All educators and staff responsible for planning the professional development of staff can integrate racial equity into their work; specific racial equity education is planned jointly with other education and professional development activities for staff and volunteers			
Racial equity education is designed to assist people to practice anti-racism in their daily work			
Education utilizes community expertise			
Racialized and Aboriginal staff, volunteers, and service users have equitable access to education and professional development opportunities			
Racialized and Aboriginal staff are equitably represented as educators and facilitators			

Monitoring and Accountability	No	Working on it	Yes
A clear structure and process exist for monitoring and evaluating progress on implementing racial equity			
The process is adequately resourced			
The structure and process are clearly communicated to staff, volunteers, and community representatives			
There are clearly identified champions for the policy who take active leadership in ensuring that the racial equity plan is regularly reviewed and acted upon			
Organizational leaders issue clear statements periodically on the importance of this effort			
Regular reports are made to organizational leaders and community representatives on progress with the implementation plan			
One or two pilot programs exist in the organization, which are adequately resourced, known to staff and community representatives, and evaluated as organizational change efforts			

Tool 9

Sample Supervision Policy that Integrates Equity

We developed this policy over three working sessions with managers at Community Resource Connections of Toronto. We congratulate them for this far-sighted policy. We hope this will inspire other organizations to take equitable supervision seriously and to adapt some of the principles here for their own use.

Supervision

Supervision is a daily, ongoing process between manager and worker, with the team, and with the organization.

The supervisor's role is to:

■ ensure equitable recruitment and hiring practices for new staff

■ clarify the job requirements and the organization's expectations (ongoing)

■ orient new staff members to the organization, and the organization to the new staff

■ develop an ongoing relationship with the employee that fosters open communication regarding the demands and activities of the job

■ anticipate and deal with the ways in which the workers' social identities influence working conditions

■ provide organizational conditions for each worker to do his/her job well

■ make decision-making transparent to team members, by clarifying when the manager is sharing information, inviting input into a decision, sharing decision-making authority

■ ensure workers most affected by decisions provide input into decisions

■ communicate organizational decisions equitably

■ foster anti-oppression/equity as core competencies for each worker

■ provide opportunities for professional growth, feedback, and direction

■ strengthen relationships among team members, by encouraging constructive conversations and a climate for learning

■ encourage different forms of leadership and joint problem-solving on the team

■ monitor and support job performance

- initiate and participate in the performance appraisal process
- draw on the experience of their own team's work to shape, with other managers, equitable organizational policy and practices
- use his/her authority (organizational and social identities) to support equity at work

In order to carry out these roles, the supervisor should meet regularly with each worker, with the team, and with other managers. The supervisor needs to ensure that the work of each member of her/his team is carried out in accordance with each program's policies, workers' job descriptions, and the vision and mission of the organization.

Managers should ensure that a worker knows when a supervision issue becomes a discipline issue. In such cases, managers should inform workers of their option to bring a support person and specify the role(s) of that support person. In situations of progressive discipline, where a worker opts to be accompanied by a support person, the manager should have another manager present.

Workers also have a role to play in ensuring effective supervision. Specifically:

- attend scheduled supervision meetings
- prepare for supervision conversations by identifying issues requiring discussion
- attend and participate in team meetings
- identify and problem-solve issues that affect not just one's own job but the broader organization

Performance Appraisal

Performance appraisal is provided in two ways, through regular ongoing supervision and through a more formal written process, which occurs after three months of a probationary period and annually after that.

The annual process is a two-way conversation between the worker and the manager. It assesses the worker's service to clients, and the worker's relationship to team, manager, and organization. It is also a chance for the worker to talk about the supports and obstacles she/he is encountering in doing the job.

The manager will draw on the following sources of information in assessing performance:

- observations of the worker on the job (e.g., interacting with clients during client appointments; work with staff in the organization and/or partner organizations; work with volunteers and community members)
- compliments or complaints about the worker's performance (note: first-hand, specific information is most reliable; investigate rumours and critically consider the sources of the information)

The organization is considering ways to formalize other sources of information about performance such as:

- asking staff to provide feedback on a worker's performance as part of the Program Evaluation process
- staff providing feedback on colleague's skills and performance before probation ends, and as input to the annual performance appraisal; a 360-degree process is already beginning with the executive director's performance appraisal and will move next to the managers and then to staff; staff will be involved in developing the tools for this

The manager should take into account the impact of inequities/discrimination on a worker's performance. For example, when workers face discrimination from clients, co-workers, or partner organizations, it affects their productivity and morale. When clients face discrimination, the worker needs to spend more time finding resources and dealing with institutions. The situation may require adaptations to workload and working conditions.

This annual conversation also provides an opportunity to set goals. The worker should set goals for his/her work and for personal and professional development. The manager should take steps to improve organizational conditions helpful to this worker's job performance. Both parties contribute to the assessment of the worker's performance and organizational conditions, using the Performance Appraisal tool developed for the position.

The annual performance appraisal form will be signed by the employee and the manager. This will be completed within 30 days prior to or 30 days immediately following the anniversary date, or other pre-determined date, of each employee. If an employee's job performance is determined to be unsatisfactory by the manager, the manager will work with the employee to establish a plan to assist the employee to achieve performance standards within a specified time period.

Final wording of the performance appraisal form is the manager's responsibility. The worker has a right to append a note to the performance appraisal form, in situations where the manager and worker disagree.

When an employee of the organization is hired for a different position within the organization, that person's seniority will continue to accrue from the initial (first position) hiring date. In the new position, the employee will receive a written, interim performance appraisal at 3 months or 60 working days of assuming the position, and a full performance appraisal at 6 months or 120 working days (both will be pro-rated for part-time positions). Subsequent appraisals will be conducted according to the anniversary date when the employee assumed this new position, or another pre-determined date.

Managers will have their annual performance appraisal with the executive director, following the process outlined above. Managers will be assessed on the ways in which they carried out their supervisory roles (outlined above.)

The board president or past president or designate will conduct an annual performance appraisal with the executive director. The board will solicit input into this appraisal by staff and managers. The president or designate and the executive director will sign the appraisal. This will be completed within 30 days prior to or 30 days immediately following the anniversary date, or other pre-determined date, of the executive director. If the executive director's job performance is determined to be unsatisfactory by the board of directors, similarly, the board will work with the executive director to establish a plan to assist him/her to achieve performance standards within a specified time period.

Tool 5

Sample Human Rights and Equity Policy

This is a sample Human Rights and Equity Policy we developed with Community Resource Connections of Toronto.

1. Policy

The Organization recognizes that the diversity of its staff, board, and communities is a source of strength and knowledge essential to delivering effective mental health services.

"Diversity" is often used to refer to differences in people's social identities. But human diversity simply exists, and is not, itself a problem. Diversity only becomes a problem when people's social identities are used to justify differential access to the economic, political, and social benefits of society. The problem is discrimination and its resulting inequities. Just as these inequities exist in our society, they exist in all organizations, including mental health institutions and our agency. Unless discrimination (racism, sexism, ableism, classism, heterosexism, ageism, and all others) is actively challenged, it reproduces itself whether we intend it to or not.

Human rights legislation was developed to redress the negative impact of discrimination in the lives of people—residents, service users, workers, and members of the community. The Human Rights Code requires this Organization to protect its employees, service users, volunteers, and contractors from systemic and individual discrimination based on the following grounds: race, ancestry, place of origin, colour, ethnic origin, citizenship, creed, sex, sexual orientation, same-sex partnership status, age, marital status, family status, disability, and record of offences.

The Organization is committed to creating an equitable organization in which everyone benefits. To do this, we will increase the power of individuals and groups in the organization who experience inequity and oppression. We will:

- ensure that our Organization's diverse constituencies and clients participate in its governance, and set policy and direction that will advance equity

- create equitable employment systems (including job descriptions, hiring, orientation, established working conditions, supervision, performance management, promotions, and professional development)

- integrate equity into all aspects of our program and service delivery

- establish effective ways to address complaints of discrimination and/or harassment
- strengthen working connections with organizations in communities that experience inequity and oppression
- advocate for equity with funders, partner organizations, and other institutions serving our communities
- build community inside the Organization by connecting staff, board, volunteers, service users, and community members to each other, and
- monitor, evaluate progress, and adapt strategies to ensure that the Organization becomes an equitable organization

2. Purpose

This policy recognizes that an equitable workplace and a diverse workforce are essential for effective, relevant service delivery. It seeks to challenge systemic and individual forms of discrimination in the Organization so that it fully benefits from the skills, knowledge, and experience of our employees, service users, and community partners.

3. Scope

This policy applies to all the Organization's board members, managers, workers, service users, volunteers, and contractors.

4. Responsibility

The board is responsible for:

- setting policy and direction that furthers the implementation of this policy
- working with the executive director to establish concrete measures of increased organizational equity
- reviewing the allocation of resources to ensure equity
- assessing and evaluating the executive director and the performance of the organization based on these measures
- recruiting and retaining a diverse board of directors with a commitment to equity

■ being accountable to the larger community for the Organization's equity work, and

■ advocating for equity with funders and the broader community

The executive director is responsible for:

■ working with the board to establish concrete measures of increased organizational equity

■ allocating adequate resources for equity work in the organization

■ working with managers to revise employment, program, and service delivery policies to integrate equity as prescribed in this policy, and

■ working with all employees to ensure effective discrimination and harassment complaints policy and procedures

The management team is responsible for:

■ ensuring equitable employment systems and daily practices

■ working with their teams to ensure equitable program and service delivery practices

■ acknowledging and addressing tensions arising from the change process

■ working with staff of the Organization and partner organizations to ensure equitable relations with communities that experience discrimination

■ ensuring sustained communication between all stakeholders in the organization, and

■ creating conditions for building community within the Organization

All staff of the Organization are responsible for:

■ learning and acting together for equity

■ bringing inequities to the attention of their teams and managers

■ refraining from discrimination and harassment of co-workers, service users, and volunteers

Definitions

Discrimination is the impact of imposing unequal burdens or denying benefits, resources, and access to individuals and groups, based on their social identities (e.g., disability, race, gender, sexuality, social class, and others). An organization's rules, policies, procedures, and practices may not be directly or intentionally discriminatory, but may have an adverse effect on workers, clients, volunteers, or partner organizations. Adverse effects may include barriers in employment, promotion, and services. It may also prevent individuals and groups from fully participating in and contributing to the organization.

Equity is both a goal and a process. Equity work recognizes and challenges unequal power and privilege in organizations and in society.

Prohibited grounds is against the law in Ontario; it is illegal to discriminate against people on the basis of sixteen grounds—age, ancestry, citizenship, colour, creed, disability, ethnic origin, family status, marital status, place of origin, race, record of offences, sex, same-sex partnership, sexual orientation, and receipt of public assistance. These protected identities of people are called "prohibited grounds."

Procedure

For the board:
- evaluate progress with carrying out its responsibilities once a year
- report on progress at the AGM

For the executive director:
- use regular budget and work planning processes to ensure appropriate allocation of resources for equity policy implementation
- report on progress to the board once a year
- make equity policy implementation a standing agenda item for management and all-staff meetings
- ensure prompt and effective application of Workplace Harassment Policy and Procedures when a complaint is filed

For the management team:

- make equity policy implementation a standing agenda item for all team meetings
- use supervision and performance appraisal processes to support staff implementation of policy
- use program planning and development processes to ensure equitable service delivery

For agency staff:

- raise equity-related issues in team meetings and supervision
- use all-staff meetings to influence the implementation of this policy

For board, management, and staff:

- recognize complaints filed under the Workplace Harassment Policy as another way to identify additional areas of work to implement this policy

Glossary

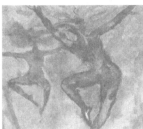

Below are some of the words you will find in this book. Racial equity language is a tricky thing; it changes as racialized people keep developing analysis and language that resists racism and renames their communities, social relations, and circumstances. Many White and racialized people feel awkward and irritated that it's so "hard to get it right." Even a word or definition which seems to have wide support may offend someone named by it. So it's always best to check it out.

These are the definitions we currently use, emerging from our ongoing work and helped by the thinking of colleagues[1]. As our collective understanding of oppression, social identities, and racial equity work continues to develop, so will our vocabulary. Therefore, these definitions will require review and updating over time.

Ableism: A pervasive system of discrimination and exclusion that oppresses people who have mental, emotional, and physical disabilities. People with disabilities experience discrimination, segregation, and isolation as a result of other people's prejudices and institutional barriers, and not because of the disability itself.

Aboriginal peoples: This is the overall term used in Canada's *Constitution Act, 1982* to refer to Native Indians, Inuit, and Métis peoples. The word recognizes the fact that Aboriginal peoples are the original inhabitants of Canada. There are many other words which Aboriginal peoples use to describe themselves. It is always best to ask how people wish to be named.

African Canadian: This is a more recent term for Canadians of African descent. "African Canadian" is preferred by some people who want to be designated by their ancestry rather than their skin colour. Still others continue to refer to themselves as Black. It's always best to ask (see *Black people* below).

Ally: An ally is a member of the dominant group who acts against oppression out of a belief that eliminating oppression will benefit the targets of oppression *and* dominant group members. In the struggle against racism, White people are allies who take leadership from activists who are people of colour and Aboriginal people.

Anti-Arab racism: The systematic ways and individual practices of racism that target and have particular impact on Arab people. In Canada, examples of anti-Arab racism include the negative stereotyping of Muslim people and the depiction of Islam as essentially violent and fundamentalist. It is reflected in the depiction of all Arabs as Muslim, and all Muslims as Arab. It can be seen in the prolonged detention without warrant or charges of Canadian residents who are Muslim and Arab in Canadian jails, and their subsequent deportation even to situations where they will be in danger. After the attacks of September 11, 2001, on the World Trade Center and the Pentagon, anti-terrorist legislation in both Canada and the United States began to particularly target Muslim and Arab men and women. Internationally, anti-Arab racism is pervasive. It has been used to build support for the American invasion of Iraq and to mask American appropriation of Iraq's resources. It shapes the unequal concern for the well-being of Palestinian and Israeli citizens and the current focus on Iranian nuclear capability while ignoring Israeli or American armaments. See also *Racism.*

Anti-Black racism: Includes systemic and individual forms of racism that target and have particular impact on Black people. The history of anti-Black racism extends back to slavery in Canada and the specific laws and practices enforcing segregation in education, employment, housing, and access to professions. Today, Black racism practices in Canada include racial profiling of young Black men by police and immigration officials; extra monitoring of Black men and women in stores; and streaming of Black youth in schools. Internationally it includes negative depictions of African and Caribbean countries and their leaders; United Nations response, or lack of it, to conflicts and invasions of African and Caribbean countries; and the depiction of (and reluctant international response to) the AIDS pandemic in African countries. See also *Racism.*

Anti-racism: "Anti-racism is an action-oriented strategy for institutional, systemic change to address racism and interlocking systems of social oppression."[2] Anti-racism mobilizes the skills and knowledge of racialized people in order to work for a redistribution of power in organizations and society. It also equips White people with knowledge and skills to acknowledge their own privilege and to work for social change.

Anti-Semitism or anti-Jewish oppression: The word Semite, literally, refers to "any of the peoples supposed to be descended from Shem, son of Noah, including especially the Jews, Arabs, Assyrians, and Phoenicians."[3] However, the term "anti-Semitism" has been used primarily to define discrimination against Jewish people. Anti-Jewish oppression is the systematic discrimination against Jews, Judaism, and the cultural, intellectual, and religious heritage of Jewish people. It has also been expressed through individual acts of physical violence and organized destruction in communities.

Asian: The term can be broken down into these groups:
- *East Asian:* Includes people who are Chinese, Fijian, Japanese, Korean, or Polynesian.
- South Asian: Includes people from India, Pakistan, Bangladesh, Sri Lanka, and Asian Africans.
- *Southeast Asian:* Includes people from Myanmar, Cambodia, Philippines, Laos, Malaysia, Thailand, and Vietnam.
- *West Asian:* Includes people who are Arab, Armenian, Egyptian, Iranian, Iraqi, Israeli, Lebanese, North African Arab, Palestinian, Syrian, and Turkish. This area has been called the "Middle East" by Europeans for whom this region was midway between themselves and "the east." "West Asian" is increasingly preferred to "Middle East."

Bias: A tendency to be for or against something without a reasonable justification. A bias influences an individual's or group's ability to evaluate a situation objectively.

Black people: People originally of Black-African heritage. Because of a long history of slavery, colonialism, and migration, Black persons now come from all parts of the world, including Canada. The term "African Canadian" is now commonly used to claim this heritage. (In England, the term "black" has been used politically, to refer to people of African and Asian origins who share an experience of racism.)

Class and classism: Class denotes the differences between those who rule the economy and those employed in or outside the margins of that economy. Indicators of class include income, wealth (sometimes inherited), formal education, networks of influence, and access to basic and other resources. In a class system, the wealth of those at the top results from exploiting the labour of those at the bottom and middle. Classism refers to the practices and beliefs that assign differential value to people according to their perceived social class. The language of most workplaces reflects and reinforces this hierarchy. For example, support staff often experience the undervaluing of their work, knowledge, and opinions through exclusion from decision-making, lower pay scales, and disrespectful behaviours.

Colonialism: A process by which a foreign power dominates and exploits an indigenous group by taking their land and resources, extracting their wealth, and using them as cheap labour. The term also refers to a specific era of European expansion into the Americas and countries of the South between the sixteenth and twentieth centuries. Colonialism was explained by racial doctrines that tried to justify these practices. These ideas about race, superiority, and inferiority are still widespread. Uncovering and challenging both the ideas and ongoing practices of colonialism is an important part of racial equity work.

Corporate globalization: Refers to the rising power of transnational companies to increase their profits by influencing and controlling governments around the globe. Of the one hundred largest economies in the world today, fifty-two are multinational corporations.[4] International trade policies are strengthening corporate economic and political control, which is felt in communities and workplaces across Canada and other countries.

Culture: Culture refers to the collective experience, beliefs, values, knowledge, economy, and ways of life of a group of individuals who share certain historical and/or present experience. Culture is not static and changes constantly. Culture gets shaped by the land and spaces people inhabit together—riding the subway, taking a ferry to work, cod fishing, tending cattle, or living in a high-rise condominium. Other aspects of individual and group culture can also be shaped by language, religion, racialization, gender, experience of migration and immigration, social class, political affiliations, family influences, age, sexual orientation, geographic origin, ethnicity, experience or absence of experience with discrimination, and the experience of fighting oppression.

Disability: Refers to physical, mental, or emotional conditions which limit and/or shape an individual's participation in work and society. Canadian law now requires employers to accommodate people with disabilities to ensure their maximum participation and contribution.

Discrimination: The unequal treatment and differential allocation of resources to individuvals who are members of particular social groups. Discrimination can occur in education, accommodation, health care, employment, and the delivery of services, goods, and facilities; it may be based on race, nationality, sex, gender identity, age, religion, political affiliation, marital or family status, physical or psychiatric disability, sexual orientation, or class. Discrimination may be direct differential treatment, or it may result from treating individuals and groups with unequal resources and advantage the same way. If a behaviour or practice has a disproportionately negative effect on a particular social group, this is discrimination.

Diversity: This word gained popularity in the 1990s as a way to refer to, but not quite mean, "equality." It suggests the range of human characteristics found in any workplace or community. It also implies "cross-cultural communication," "dealing with difference," and "creating harmonious workplaces." Diversity, as a concept, does not provide a framework to examine power and racism or to identify the elements of racial equity.

Dominant group: Refers to people whose social identity confers on them unearned power and privilege. Most of us have one or more dominant identities. In most parts of Canada, dominant identities are White, male, English-speaking, heterosexual, able-bodied, Christian, affluent and middle class, thirty to sixty-five years of age, university educated, from central Canada.

Employment equity: A program designed to identify and eliminate discriminatory policies and practices that act as barriers to fair employment. Networks, friendships, and favouritism have shaped employment practices to exclude those who would otherwise merit the job. Employment equity promotes fair hiring and personnel practices to ensure that employees are hired for only one reason, their qualifications to do their job.

Equity: Refers to the rights of individuals and groups to an equitable share of the resources and influence in society. "Equity" means equitable *access* and *outcomes*. Equity work analyses and challenges unfair systems and practices and works towards the creation of equitable outcomes.

Ethnic: The beliefs, practices, and traditions held in common by a group of people who share an identity, whether linguistic, historical, geographical, religious, or racial. While everyone belongs to an "ethnic" group, the word is often used to identify only non-dominant or less powerful cultural identities in Canada.

First Nations: Reflects the self-naming process of some Aboriginal peoples in Canada today. The word "first" recognizes the fact that Aboriginal peoples are the original inhabitants of what is now considered Canada. The word "nation" stresses the fact that Aboriginal peoples are political collectivities who had their own forms of government prior to European settlement. Many First Nations peoples are fighting to re-establish that sovereignty. The term also refers to a group of Aboriginal people who were previously called a "Band" by the Department of Indian Affairs. "First Nation" can also mean a group or several groups of Aboriginal people who have the same ethno-cultural background.

Gender identity: Characteristics linked to an individual's intrinsic sense of self as a man or as a woman, which may not be the same identity as one's biological sex.

Gender roles: The socially constructed and culturally specific behaviour, appearance, and other expectations imposed on women (femininity) and men (masculinity).

Genocide: The deliberate decisions and actions made by one nation or group of people in order to destroy and eliminate an entire other nation or group. The term has also been used to refer to the destruction of the culture of a people, as in "cultural genocide."

Harassment: Persistent, ongoing behaviour that communicates negative attitudes towards an individual or group with the intention of intimidating and humiliating. Harassment is an exercise of power. It includes name-calling, jokes, slurs, graffiti, insults, threats, discourteous treatment and gestures, verbal or physical abuse—behaviour that is known, or ought reasonably to be known, to be unwelcome. In most Canadian provinces, the Human Rights Code prohibits harassment based on any of the prohibited grounds of race, religion, sex, ethnicity, and so on.

Heterosexism: A system of practices that communicate that heterosexuals are inherently superior. It includes the assumption that everyone is or must be heterosexual. Like other forms of prejudice and discrimination, heterosexism awards privilege and rights to members of the dominant group—heterosexuals—that are not accorded to gay or lesbian people. For example, heterosexuals do not have to change the law to have their marriages recognized or to receive spousal benefits.

Immigrants: People who have arrived and settled in Canada in their lifetime. The term "landed immigrant" refers to persons with legal status who are permanent residents, rather than visitors, refugee claimants, temporary workers, or citizens. The word "immigrant" is sometimes used incorrectly to refer to Canadian-born racialized people who are assumed to be born elsewhere.

Imperialism: The policy and practice of extending a country's power, influence, and control through colonization, use of military force, and other means. "At some very basic level, imperialism means thinking about, settling on, controlling land that you do not possess, that is distant, that is lived on and owned by others."[5]

Internalized dominance: Occurs when members of the dominant group accept their group's socially superior status as normal and deserved, and when they deny the oppression experienced by target groups.

Internalized subordination: Occurs when members of an oppressed social group accept the superior status of the dominant group and their own subordinate status as deserved, natural, and inevitable.

Multiculturalism: Federal policy in Canada since 1971, multiculturalism endorses equal status for all cultures and encourages Canadians to recognize contributions made by the diversity of Canadian residents. However, the concept does not explain racism or its role in preventing equal participation in society by racialized groups.

Oppression: Exists when one social group exploits (knowingly or unconsciously) another social group to its own benefit. It results in privilege for the dominant group and disenfranchisement for the subordinated group. Oppression is achieved through force or through the control of social institutions and resources of society. After a while, it does not require the conscious thought or effort of individual members of the dominant group, and unequal treatment becomes institutionalized, systemic, and looks "normal."

People of colour: This term began in the United States as one attempt by racialized people to name themselves, not as "non-whites," "coloured," "ethnics," or "visible minorities" but as people with a positive identity. It applies to people who are not White or Aboriginal.

Poisoned environment: A poisoned (work) environment is a situation in which harassing or offensive behaviour goes unchallenged. Behaviours include jokes, posting offensive images, excluding co-workers, name-calling, or bullying. Poisoned work environments thrive where people with authority condone and do not interrupt discriminatory and harassing behaviour. They are also created by unfair personnel practices, unequal work loads, and other systemic inequities. A person does not have to be a direct target to be adversely affected by the negative environment.

Prejudice: To pre-judge, based on stereotyped ideas about a group of people. It is an attitude about the inferiority of another person or group. Prejudice is often very hard to change because in an environment of discrimination, many other people may have the same idea. It can look like "common sense" and can be a normal explanation used to justify acts of discrimination.

Privilege: Unearned power that gives dominant group members economic, social, and political advantages. It can also include rights that are denied to others and should be available to all.

Race: A social category used to classify humankind by physical features such as skin colour, hair texture, facial characteristics, or stature. There is, in fact, more genetic variation within a single "race" than there is between two different "races." Despite the fact that there is no scientific or biological basis of the term "race," ideas about racial difference continue to thrive. "Whatever race was in its origins, it is now an intrinsic part and fundamental principle of social organization and identity formation."[6]

Racial equity: By "racial equity" we mean the equitable distribution of resources and influence in ways not shaped by racism. In a racially divided society and world, racial equity is both a goal and a process. It requires racialized and White people to analyze and challenge the daily ways in which power and White privilege (re)produce racial inequities. The progress of racial equity work is measured by the degree to which racialized people benefit from actions taken and the extent to which power and influence are more equitably shared. Since racialized people(s) are the global majority (70 to 80 per cent of the world's people), racial equity is a key aspect of other struggles for global justice.

Racialization: Racial identities are not fixed categories. They are shaped by history, nationality, gender, class, and identity politics, and racial designations often differ from country to country. The term "racialization" makes explicit that this is not about inherent characteristics but about the ways in which we are socialized to differentiate groups of people on the basis of physical characteristics. It emphasizes the active process of categorizing people while at the same time rejecting "race" as a scientific category. This is emphasized in the *Report of the Commission on Systemic Racism in the Ontario Criminal Justice System*, which defines racialization "as the process by which socieities construct races as real, different and unequal in ways that matter to economic political and social life."[7]

Under this definition, White people, Aboriginal people, and people of colour are all racialized. However, in this book, we use the term "racialized" to refer to people of colour. While Aboriginal Peoples are also the targets of racism, they have distinct goals of self-government and the recognition of land claims confirmed through treaties. We recognize the limitations of this. But we want to differentiate the negative impacts of being racialized as people of colour and Aboriginal people, from the power and privilege conferred to people racialized as White. This is in keeping with the usage suggested by the Ontario Human Rights Commission in its recently published *Policy and Guidelines on Racism and Racial Discrimination*, which states: "When it is necessary to describe people collectively, the term 'racialized person' or 'racialized group' is preferred over 'racial minority,' 'visible minority,' 'person of colour,' or 'non-White,' as it expresses race as a social construct rather than as a description on perceived biological traits. Furthermore, these other terms treat 'White' as the norm to which racialized persons are to be compared and have a tendency to group all racialized persons in one category, as if they are all the same."[8]

Racism: Those aspects of Canadian society that overtly and covertly attribute value and normality to White people and Whiteness and that devalue, stereotype, and label racialized communities as "other," different, less than, or render them invisible.
- *Individual racism:* The beliefs, attitudes, and actions of individuals that support or perpetuate racism. Individual racism can be unconscious or conscious, active and passive.
- *Institutional racism:* The network of institutional structures, policies, and practices that create advantages for White people and discrimination, oppression and disadvantage for racialized people.
- *Systemic racism:* The conscious or unconscious policies, procedures, and practices that exclude, marginalize, and exploit racialized people. Systemic racism is supported by institutional power and by powerful (often unexamined) ideas which make racism look normal and justified. Systemic racism allows individuals to practise racism in organizations, unchecked by effective complaints procedures, performance appraisals, and promotions which require equity competencies.

Refugee: Persons who have to flee their country because they have a "well-founded fear of persecution based on race, religion, nationality, political opinion, or membership in a particular social group."[9] In some countries, gender is also recognized as a basis for claiming refugee status.

Religious discrimination: Consists of institutional and individual practices that exclude and discriminate against a person because of her/his religion. A common form of such discrimination in Canada is the inequitable provision for religious observance in the workplace. Supreme court cases have recently ruled that employers must accommodate employees who need to pray or take days for religious observance not recognized in the Christian-based statutory holidays such as Easter and Christmas. Religious discrimination often links to other forms of discrimination. For example, Irish Catholics were often marked by their class, ethnic origins, and language as well as their Catholicism. Racialized Muslims often experience racism mixed with religious discrimination.

"Reverse racism": When racialized communities identify racism, their challenge is often called "reverse racism." This term is often used to dismiss employment equity initiatives, and other efforts to push back against White privilege. It equates equity with "racism against White people" and serves to focus on the concerns of White people. It avoids dealing with the differential access that White people have to political, economic, and social resources.

Sexism: The systemic and individual practices that privilege men, subordinate women, and debase woman-identified values.

Sexual orientation: Refers to desire for intimate emotional and sexual relationships with people of the same sex (lesbian or gay), the other sex (heterosexual), or either sex (bisexual).

Targets: We use the term "targets" to mean members of oppressed groups who experience the impact of oppression. The targets of racism are racialized people—people of colour and Aboriginal people.

Transgender person: A transsexual person is someone who is not comfortable with, or who rejects, in whole or in part, their biologically assigned gender identity. The umbrella term is used to describe transsexuals, transvestites or cross-dressers, and intersex people.

Transsexual: Someone who has a strong and persistent feeling that they are living in the wrong sex. A male transsexual has a need to live as a woman and a female transsexual has a need to live as a man. Some, but not all, transsexuals have full-sex reassignment surgery; some have partial-sex reassignment procedures; some use hormone therapy. Transsexual people's sexual orientation can be heterosexual, homosexual, or bisexual.

Visible minority: The term was originally created by the Department of Employment and Immigration to classify individuals into groups for the purpose of employment equity programs. The term has been criticized for several reasons, including that racialized peoples are, in fact, the global majority. By the year 2017, one in five Canadians will be "visible minorities" and will form more than half the populations of Toronto and Vancouver.[10]

White: Refers to people belonging to the dominant racial group who enjoy skin privilege in North America, Europe, Australia, New Zealand, and anywhere European colonialism has created racial inequity. People who are White may also face discrimination because of their class, sexual orientation, gender, religion, and age. But this does not erase White skin privilege. We capitalize the term "White" for different reasons than we capitalize other racial designations—Aboriginal and Black. The latter identities are claimed with pride in opposition to the names imposed by dominant White society. One of the ways that racism operates is to leave the racial identity of White people unidentified. We capitalize White to interrupt the privilege of having Whiteness go unnamed.

Whiteness and White privilege: White privilege has been usefully described by Peg MacIntosh as "the invisible knapsack of unearned assets which White people can count on cashing in each day, but about which they are meant to remain oblivious."[11] These are benefits White people receive in a racist society at the expense of racialized people. Examples include the ability to be unaware of race; the assurance that police will not stop them because of their race; the expectation that they speak for themselves and not their "race"; the assumption that getting hired or promoted was due to their competence and not because of their "race."

White supremacy: A system based on assumptions of the "rightness of Whiteness," in which political, economic, and social systems result in White people having more privilege and power than racialized people. The term "White supremacy" is often associated only with apartheid or with extreme racist groups like the Ku Klux Klan. But White supremacy can be seen in any society, including Canada, where there is a racial hierarchy with Whites at the top.

World/global majority people: This term reminds us that racialized people are 70 to 80 per cent of the world's population. It's a helpful name that links racial equity work in organizations to global struggles for justice.

Notes

INTRODUCTION

1. Medard Gabel and Henry Bruner, *Global Inc.: An Atlas of the Multinational Corporation* (New York: New Press, 2003), p.vi.

2. While we recognize that all of us are "racialized," in this book we apply the term to people of colour and recognize Aboriginal people as distinct. We use the term "White" for dominant racialized people.

3. George J. Sefa Dei, Leeno Luke Karumanchery, and Nisha Karumanchery-Luik, *Playing the Race Card: Exposing White Power and Privilege* (New York: Peter Lang Publishing, 2004), p.149.

4. Adriane Paavo, in her comments on the first draft of this book.

5. See also Linda Griffiths and Maria Campbell, *The Book of Jessica: A Theatrical Transformation* (Toronto: Coach House Press, 1989) as an example of such reflection and conversation.

SECTION ONE

1. Albert J. Mills and Tony Simmons, *Reading Organization Theory: A Critical Approach to the Study of Organizational Behaviour and Structure* (Toronto: Garamond Press, 1995), p.3.

2. Ibid, p.6.

3. Ibid., p.7.

4. To mention only a few, see for example, Multicultural and Race Relations Division, Chief Administrative Officer's Department, *The Composition and Implications of Metropolitan Toronto's Ethnic, Racial and Linguistic Populations* (Toronto: Municipality of Metropolitan Toronto, March 1990); Commission on Systemic Racism in the Ontario Criminal Justice System, *Report of the Ontario Commission on Systemic Racism in the Criminal Justice System* (Toronto: Queen's Printer, 1995); Stephen Lewis, *Stephen Lewis Report on Race Relations in Ontario* (Toronto: Government of Ontario, 1992); Rosalie S. Abella, *Equality in Employment: A Royal Commission Report: Research Studies* (Ottawa: Canadian Government Publishing Centre, 1985); and Victor Satzewich, ed., *Racism and Social Inequality in Canada: Concepts, Controversies and Strategies of Resistance* (Toronto: Thompson Educational Publishing, 1998).

5. See situation 3, "Building Community Coalition and Capacity," under phase one of section two in this book.

6. Richard Bocking, "Reclaiming the Commons: Corporatism, Privatization Drive Enclosure of the Commons," *The CCPA Monitor* (October 2003). Available online from the Canadian Centre for Policy Alternatives at www.policyalternatives.ca.

7. Edward W. Said, *Culture and Imperialism* (New York: Vintage Books, 1994), p.7.

8. James M. Blaut, *The Colonizers' Model of the World: Geographical Diffusionism and Eurocentric History* (New York: Guilford Press, 1993), p.23.

9. Andrew Jackson, *The Case against More Corporate Tax Cuts* (Ottawa: Centre for Canadian Policy Alternatives, 2005). Available online from www.policyalternatives.ca.

10. Elmear O'Neill, "From Global Economies to Local Cuts: Globalization and Structural Change in Our Own Backyard," in L. Ricciutelli, June Larkin, Elmear O'Neill et al., eds., *Confronting the Cuts: A Sourcebook for Women in Ontario* (Toronto: Inanna Publications, 1998), p.3.

11. Ibid.

12. "Provincial Policies Make Working Life Tougher for Women." News Release, December 2004. Retrieved July 20, 2005, from www.policyalternatives.ca.

13. Tim Wise, "See No Evil: Perception and Reality in Black and White." *ZNet Magazine*. Retrieved August 2001 from www.zmag.org/Commentaries.

14. Ipsos-Reid survey to mark International Day for the Elimination of Racial Discrimination, *The Globe and Mail*, March 21, 2005, p.1.

15. Sid Kirchheimer, "Racism Should Be a Public Health Issue," *Medscape Medical News*, Jan. 9, 2003, p.1. Available online from www.medscape.com/viewarticle/447757.

16. Ibid.

17. Ibid.

18. See Grace-Edward Galabuzi, *Canada's Creeping Economic Apartheid: The Economic Segregation and Social Marginalisation of Racialised Groups* (Toronto: CSJ Foundation for Research and Education, 2001); *Poverty by Postal Code* (Toronto: United Way of Greater Toronto and the Canadian Council on Social Development, 2004); Michael Ornstein, *Ethno-Racial Inequality in the City of Toronto: An Analysis of the 1996 Census* (Toronto: Access and Equity Unit, Strategic and Corporate Policy Division, Chief Administrator's Office, 2000); Andrew Jackson, *Is Work Working for Workers of Colour?* (Toronto: Canadian Labour Congress, 2002).

19. Joseph Hall, "Weaving a New Canada," *The Toronto Star*, March 23, 2005, p.B1.

20. Mary Jo Hatch, *Organization Theory: Modern, Symbolic and Postmodern Perspectives* (New York: Oxford University Press, 1997), p.361.

21. Ibid., p.364.

22. Kathy Ferguson, *The Feminist Case against Bureaucracy* (Philadelphia, PA: Temple University Press, 1985), p.94.

23. See, for example, Carl James and Adrian Shadd, *Talking about Difference: Encounters in Race, Ethnicity and Language* (Toronto: Between the Lines, 2001); bell hooks, *Sisters of the Yam: Black Women and Self-Recovery* (Boston, MA: South End Press, 1993); and the organization Colours of Resistance Web site www.colours.mahost.org.

SECTION TWO/PHASE ONE

1. Our eternal gratitude to colleague Alok Mukherjee for first mapping this distinction.

2. Statistics Canada 1999, special tabulations from the 1996 Census of Canada, quoted in Hieu Van Ngo, *English as a Second Language Education: Context, Current Responses, and Recommendations for New Directions* (Calgary: Coalition for Equal Access to Education, 2001), p.4.

3. Citizenship and Immigration Canada (2001) quoted in Ngo, *English as a Second Language Education*, 8.

4. Ibid.

5. CBD Preliminary Budget 2001/02 quoted in Ngo, *English as a Second Language Education*, n.p.

6. Ngo, *English as a Second Language Education*, pp.5,6.

7. Pearl Yip, "A Case Study Analysis of the ESL Issue" (MA thesis, University of Calgary, 1997), p.43.

8. Ibid., p.37.

9. Ibid., p.6.

10. Ibid., p.37.

11. Ngo, *English as a Second Language Education*, p.24.

12. Susan Lillico, "Civic Participation Project—Calgary," an internal document prepared for the Multiculturalism Department of Heritage Canada.

13. Yip, "A Case Study Analysis of the ESL Issue," p.20.

14. Ibid., p.59.

15. Ngo, *English as a Second Language Education*, p.2.

16. Yip, "A Case Study Analysis of the ESL Issue," p.47.

17. See, for example, an exploration of union culture in D'Arcy Martin, *Thinking Union: Activism and Education in Canada's Labour Movement* (Toronto: Between the Lines, 1995); and Bev Burke, Jojo Geronimo, D'Arcy Martin, Barb Thomas, and Carol Wall, *Education for Changing Unions* (Toronto: Between the Lines, 2002), chap. 3.

18. See the final report of this project prepared by Hieu Van Ngo, *Toward Innovative Vision for Quality,*

Equitable ESL Education (Calgary: Coalition for Equal Access to Education, 2003).

19. See Andrew Duffy, "Why Canada's Schools Are Failing Newcomers," *The Toronto Star*, Sept. 25, 2004. This article is part of a year-long project entitled "Class Struggles: Public Education and the New Canadian," which was funded by the Atkinson Charitable Foundation and published in *The Toronto Star* as a week-long series in September 2004. The study is available at www. atkinsonfoundation.ca/ updates.

20. See Coalition for Equal Access to Education, *Written Submission to the Standing Policy Committee on Learning and Employment* (Calgary: CEAE, June 3, 2003).

21. Ibid., pp.50, 51.

22. Quoted in Ngo, *Toward Innovative Vision for Quality, Equitable ESL Education*, p.27.

SECTION TWO/PHASE TWO

1. Some examples are Arnold Minors, "Towards Eliminating Racism from the Ontario Human Rights Commission: A Report to the Anti-Racism Committee," an internal document prepared for the OHRC, 1992; Anti-Racism Project Team, "A Plan of Action for Anti-Racism Organizational Change in the Ontario Human Rights Commission," an internal document prepared for the OHRC, May 1993; Barb Thomas, "Putting Anti-Racism Organizational Change on the OPS Agenda: The Experience of the Ontario Human Rights Commission," submitted to the Ontario Human Rights Commission Anti-Racism Committee, Toronto, ON, August 1993; Multicultural and Race Relations Division and Doris Marshall Institute for Education and Action, "Challenging Racism at Metro: How Education and Training Can Make a Difference—Internal Discussion Paper," Toronto, ON, April 4, 1994; Hitner Starr Associates, "Race Relations Program Review," prepared for the Toronto Board of Education, December 1985.

2. See Bev Burke, Jojo Geronimo, D'Arcy Martin, Barb Thomas, and Carol Wall, *Education for Changing Unions* (Toronto: Between the Lines, 2002), p.97 for a write-up of how to do this.

3. The Ontario Public Service Employees Union developed and trained "workplace mobilizers" several months prior to bargaining as a way to circulate the bargaining survey to *all* workers, and also developed diverse mobilizing committees in each workplace to address exactly these issues.

4. See Communications, Energy and Paperworkers Union of Canada, *Bargaining Equality: Joining Hands in Solidarity* (Ottawa: CEP National, 2001), available online from www.cep.ca/human_rights/ equity_issues_e_ html; and Canadian Auto Workers Union, "Collective Agreement Equity Audit" (Toronto: CAW, n.d.), available online from www.caw.ca.whatwedo/women/ index.asp.

5. The Ontario Prevention Clearinghouse, *Community Development Resource Package* (Toronto: OPC, 1992), p.68.

6. Oriana Fallaci, "Willy Brandt," in *Interview with History* (Boston: Houghton Mifflin, 1976), pp. 218–19.

SECTION TWO/PHASE THREE

1. For example, in 1995 the rate of unemployment for racialized women equalled 15.3 per cent, and 9.4 per cent for other women. Jennifer Chard, "Women in Visible Minority," in *Women in Canada: A Gender Based Statistical Report* (Ottawa: Statistics Canada, 2000), quoted by Grace-Edward Galabuzi, *Canada's Creeping Apartheid: The Economic Segregation and Social Marginalisation of Racialised Groups* (Toronto: Centre for Social Justice, 2001), p.16.

2. We draw on the many helpful analyses by Aboriginal women and women of colour on this subject. See, for example, Angela Davis, *Women, Race and Class* (New York: Vintage, 1983) for an analysis of racism in the American White women's movement; Gloria T. Hull, Patricia Bell Scott, and Barbara Smith, *All the Women Are White, All the Blacks Are Men, but Some of Us Are Brave: Black Women's Studies* (New York: Feminist Press, 1982); and Kim Anderson, *A Recognition of Being: Reconstructing Native Womanhood* (Toronto: Sumach Press, 2001).

3. Readers who would like to learn more about the equity work being done at the Toronto District School Board during this time can refer to Tim McCaskell's *Race to Equity: History of Equity Work at the Toronto Board of Education* (Toronto: Between the Lines, 2005). See also, Tara Goldstein and David Selby, eds., *Weaving Connections: Educating for Peace, Social and Environmental Justice* (Toronto: Sumach Press, 2000).

4. For a brief description of the Metropolitan Toronto Housing Company, please see Rainer Soegtrop, "Leadership in Times of Resistance" in phase two, "Getting to How Things Work," in this section.

SECTION THREE

1. "The Impact of Saskatchewan's Growing Aboriginal Community," *The Saskatchewan Indian* (Spring 2000), p.18.

2. Dan Hill, *Human Rights in Canada: A Focus on Racism* (Toronto: Canadian Labour Congress, 1977), p.122.

3. "Fighting for Our Rights: Social and Human Rights," CLC National Anti-Racism Task Force Discussion Points (1997).

4. "The Fight for Our Lives: Equality and Union Rights," CLC Executive Council Statement, September 1995.

5. Andrew Jackson, "Is Work Working for Workers of Colour?" Research Paper No. 18 (Ottawa: Canadian Labour Congress, 2002). Available online from www.canadianlabour.ca/index.php/ Reports/ Is_Work_Working_colour.

6. See the "Building Blocks for Equity" that follow phases one, two, and three of section two.

7. *CLC Statement to the UN World Conference Against Racism*, August 27–September 7, 2001, Durban, South Africa.

8. *Canadian Labour Congress Statement to the UN Special Rapporteur on Racism*, Sept. 16, 2003. Available online from www.canadianlabour.ca/updir/ Statement-Sept16-UNSR-Racism-E.pdf.

9. Anti-Racism and Human Rights Department Report," presented at the 23rd Constitutional Convention, Vancouver, BC, June 2002.

10. Winnie Ng, interview with Glen Richards, in *Breaking Barriers, Linking Struggles,* prod. by Toronto and York Region Labour Council, 24 min., 2004, videocassette.

11. Salome Luckas and Judy Vashti Persad, *Through the Eyes of Workers of Colour: Linking Struggles for Social Justice* (Toronto: Women Working with Immigrant Women, and Toronto and York Region Labour Council, 2004).

12. Bromley Armstrong, interview with Glen Richards, *Breaking Barriers, Linking Struggles.*

13. Lukas and Persad, *Through the Eyes of Workers of Colour,* p.21.

14. Ng interview, *Breaking Barriers, Linking Struggles.*

15. Ibid.

16. Toronto and York Region Labour Council, "Organizing Strength in Toronto's Diverse Communities," Executive Board Statement, October 3, 2002.

17. Lukas and Persad, *Through the Eyes of Workers of Colour.*

18. Walkerton is a small city in Ontario where seven people died and hundreds were made sick by contaminated water in 2001. The Walkerton Inquiry found that the privatization of water testing and the lack of accountability of the arm's-length board were key factors in the tragedy.

19. The *Labour's Transit Workbook* is available from www.labourcouncil.ca/ Transit%20Workbook.pdf.

20. Toronto and York Region Labour Council, *Strategic Directions for the Toronto Labour Movement 2004-2010* (Toronto: TYRLC, n.d.). Available online from www.labourcouncil.ca/ strategic2004-2010rans.pdf.

21. Toronto and York Region Labour Council, "Update and Report on Workers of Colour/Aboriginal Workers Conference, 2004."

22. Toronto and York Region Labour Council, "Progress Since the 2003 Workers of Colour/Aboriginal Workers Conference: A Report Presented to the 2004 Workers of Colour/Aboriginal Workers Conference."

23. Jenny Ahn, interview with Glen Richards, *Breaking Barriers, Linking Struggles.*

GLOSSARY

1. These include Maurianne Adams, Lee Anne Bell, and Pat Griffin, eds., *Teaching for Diversity and Social Justice* (New York: Routledge, 1997); Bev Burke, Jojo Geronimo, D'Arcy Martin, Barb Thomas, and Carol Wall, *Education for Changing Unions* (Toronto: Between the Lines, 2002); Anti-Racism and Human Rights Department and Education and Campaigns Department, *Anti-Racism Integration Guide, Book 3*

(Ottawa: Canadian Labour Congress, 2003); Canadian Labour Congress, *LGBT Definitions* (Ottawa: Canadian Labour Congress, October 2004); Community Advisory Committee on Anti-Hate and Anti-Racism, *Hate Activity: Communities Can Respond* (Toronto: Municipality of Metropolitan Toronto, 1996); Tania Das Gupta, *Racism and Paid Work* (Toronto: Garamond Press, 1996); Grace-Edward Galabuzi, *Canada's Creeping Economic Apartheid* (Toronto: Centre for Social Justice, 2001); Frances Henry, Carol Tator, Winston Mattis, and Tim Rees, *The Colour of Democracy: Racism in Canadian Society* (Toronto: Harcourt Brace, 1995); and Tina Lopes, "Glossary of Terms," unpublished document (2003), in the possession of the author.

2. George Dei, *Anti-Racism Education: Theory and Practice* (Halifax: Fernwood, 1996), p.25.

3. R.E. Allen, ed., *The Concise Oxford English Dictionary*, 8th ed. (Oxford: Clarendon Press, 1991).

4. Medard Gabel and Henry Bruner, *Global Inc.: An Atlas of the Multinational Corporation* (New York: New Press, 2003), p.vi.

5. Edward W. Said, *Culture and Imperialism* (New York: Knopf, 1993), p.7.

6. Ibid., p.29.

7. D. Cole and M. Gittens, Co-Chairs, *Report of the Commission on Systemic Racism in the Ontario Criminal Justice System* (Toronto: Queen's Printer for Ontario, 1995).

8. Ontario Human Rights Commission, *Policy and Guidelines on Racism and Racial Discrimination* (Toronto: OHRC, 2005). Retrieved August 15, 2005, from www.ohrc.on.ca/english/publications/racism-and-racial-discrimination-policy.shtml.

9. United Nations' 1951 Geneva Convention Relating to the Status of Refugees.

10. Statistics Canada study quoted in "The Way We'll Be, Visible Majority. By 2017 More than Half of Greater Toronto Will Be Non-European. How Will This Change Our City?" *The Toronto Star*, 23 March 2005, p.A1.

11. McIntosh, quoted in George Dei, Leeno Luke Karumanchery, and Nisha Karumanchery-Luik, *Playing the Race Card: Exposing White Power and Privilege* (New York: Peter Lang Publishing, 2004), p.84.

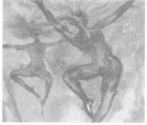

Selected Bibliography

Abella, Rosalie S. *Equality in Employment: A Royal Commission Report: Research Studies.* Ottawa: Canadian Government Publishing Centre, 1985.

Abu-Laban, Yasmeen, and Christina Gabriel. *Selling Diversity: Immigration, Multiculturalism, Employment Equity and Globalization.* Peterborough: Broadview Press, 2002.

Adams, Maurianne, Lee Anne Bell, and Pat Griffin, eds. *Teaching for Diversity and Social Change.* New York: Routledge, 1997.

Allen, Lillian. *Psychic Unrest* (Poems). Toronto: Insomniac Press, 1999.

Anderson, Kim. *A Recognition of Being: Reconstructing Native Womanhood.* Toronto: Sumach Press, 2001.

Arnold, Rick, Bev Burke, Carl James, D'Arcy Martin, and Barb Thomas. *Educating for a Change.* Toronto: Between the Lines, 1991.

Blaut, James. *The Colonizers' Model of the World: Geographical Diffusionism and Eurocentric History.* New York: Guilford Press, 1993.

Burke, Bev, Jojo Geronimo, D'Arcy Martin, Barb Thomas, and Carol Wall. *Education for Changing Unions.* Toronto: Between the Lines, 2002.

Calliste, Agnes, and George Sefa Dei. *Anti-Racist Feminism: Critical Race and Gender Studies.* Halifax: Fernwood, 2000.

Canadian Auto Workers Union. "Collective Agreement Equity Audit." Toronto: CAW, n.d. Available online from www.caw.ca.whatwedo/women/ index.asp.

Canadian Labour Congress. *Anti-Racism Integration Guide.* Ottawa, ON: CLC, 2003. Available online from www.clc-ctc.ca.

Cho, Eunice Hyunhye, Francisco Argüelles Paz y Puente, Miriam Ching Yoon Louie, and Sasha Khokha. *Bridge: Building a Race and Immigration Dialogue in the Global Economy.* Berkeley: National Network for Immigrant and Refugee Rights, 2004.

Commission on Systemic Racism in the Ontario Criminal Justice System. *Report of the Ontario Commission on Systemic Racism in the Criminal Justice System.* Toronto: Queen's Printer, 1995.

Communications, Energy and Paperworkers Union of Canada. *Bargaining Equality: Joining Hands in Solidarity.* Ottawa: CEP National, 2001. Available online from www.cep.ca/ human_rights/equity/eba_e.pdf.

Curry-Stevens, Ann. *An Educator's Guide for Changing the World: Methods, Models and Materials for Anti-Oppression and Social Justice Workshops.* Toronto: Centre for Social Justice, 2003.

—. *Expanding the Circle: People Who Care about Ending Racism, We Need Your Help.* Toronto: Centre for Social Justice, 2005.

Dancing on Live Embers

Davis, Angela. *Women, Race and Class*. New York: Vintage, 1983.

Dei, George J. Sefa, Leeno Luke Karumanchery, and Nisha Karumanchery-Luik. *Playing the Race Card: Exposing White Power and Privilege*. New York: Peter Lang Publishing, 2004.

Delp, Linda, ed. *Teaching for Change*. Los Angeles: UCLA Labour Centre, 2002. Available online from www.labour.ucla.edu.

Ellwood, Wayne. *The No-Nonsense Guide to Globalization*. Toronto: Between the Lines, 2001.

Elmear O'Neill. "From Global Economies to Local Cuts: Globalization and Structural Change in Our Own Backyard." In L. Ricciutelli, June Larkin, Elmear O'Neill et al., eds., *Confronting the Cuts: A Sourcebook for Women in Ontario*. Toronto: Inanna Publications, 1998.

Faculty of Environmental Studies and Centre for the Support of Teaching. *Voices of Diversity & Equity: Transforming University Curriculum*. A DVD and User's Guide for Workshops and Classrooms. Toronto: York University, February 2005.

Ferguson, Kathy. *The Feminist Case against Bureaucracy*. Philadelphia, PA: Temple University Press, 1985.

Folson, Rose Baaba, ed. *Calculated Kindness: Global Restructuring, Immigraiton and Settlement in Canada*. Halifax: Fernwood, 2004.

Frankenberg, Ruth. *White Women, Race Matters: The Social Construction of Whiteness*. Minneapolis: University of Minnesota Press, 1993.

Gabel, Medard, and Henry Bruner. *Global Inc.: An Atlas of the Multinational Corporation*. New York: The New Press, 2003.

Galabuzi, Grace-Edward. *Canada's Creeping Economic Apartheid: The Economic Segregation and Social Marginalisation of Racialised Groups*. Toronto: Centre for Social Justice, 2001.

Goldstein, Tara, and David Selby, eds. *Weaving Connections: Educating for Peace, Social and Environmental Justice*. Toronto: Sumach Press, 2000.

Graveline, Fyre Jean. *Circle Works: Transforming Eurocentric Consciousness*. Halifax: Fernwood, 1998.

Griffiths, Linda, and Maria Campbell. *The Book of Jessica: A Theatrical Transformation*. Toronto: Coach House Press, 1989.

Hage, Ghasan. *White Nation: Fantasies of White Supremacy in a Multicultural Society*. Sydney, Australia: Pluto Press, 2000.

Hagey, Rebecca, et al. *Implementing Accountability for Equity and Ending Racial Backlash in Nursing*. ?: Canadian Race Relations Foundation, 2005.

Hatch, Mary Jo. *Organization Theory: Modern, Symbolic and Postmodern Perspectives*. New York: Oxford University Press, 1997.

Henry, F., C. Tator, W. Mattis, and T. Rees. *The Colour of Democracy: Racism in Canadian Society*. Toronto: Harcourt Brace, 2000.

hooks, bell. *Teaching to Transgress: Education as the Practice of Freedom*. New York: Routledge, 1994.

—. *Killing Rage: Ending Racism*. New York: Henry Holt, 1995.

—. *Teaching Community: A Pedagogy of Hope.* New York: Routledge, 2003.

Hughes, Lotte. *The No-Nonsense Guide to Indigenous Peoples.* Toronto: Between the Lines, 2003.

Hull, Gloria T., Patricia Bell Scott, and Barbara Smith. *All the Women Are White, All the Blacks Are Men, but Some of Are Brave: Black Women's Studies.* New York: Feminist Press, 1982.

Jackson, Andrew. "Is Work Working for Workers of Colour?" Research Paper No. 18. Ottawa: Canadian Labour Congress, n.d. Available online from www.canadianlabour.ca.

James, Carl E., and Adrienne Shadd, eds. *Talking about Difference: Encounters in Race, Ethnicity and Language.* Toronto: Between the Lines, 2001.

Jordan, June. *Moving Towards Home: Political Essays.* London: Virago Press, 1989.

—. *Kissing God Goodbye: Poems 1991–1997.* New York: Doubleday, 1997.

Kivel, Paul. *Uprooting Racism: How White People Can Work for Racial Justice.* Gabriola Island, BC: New Society Publishers, 1995.

Kunz, J.L., A Milan, and S. Schetagne. *Unequal Access: A Canadian Profile of Racial Differences in Education, Employment and Income.* A Report for the Canadian Race Relations Foundation, by the Canadian Council on Social Development. Toronto: Canadian Race Relations Foundation, 2000.

Lewis, Stephen. *Stephen Lewis Report on Race Relations in Ontario.* Toronto: Government of Ontario, 1992.

Loeb, Paul Rogat, ed. *The Impossible Will Take a Little While: A Citizen's Guide to Hope in a Time of Fear.* New York: Basic Books, 2004.

Lorde, Audre. *Sister Outsider: Essays and Speeches.* New York: The Crossing Press, 1984.

Lukas, Salome, and Judy Vashti Persad. *"No Hijab is Permitted Here": A Study of the Experiences of Muslim Women Wearing Hijab Applying for Work in the Manufacturing, Sales and Service Sectors.* Toronto: Women Working with Immigrant Women, 2002.

—. *Through the Eyes of Workers of Colour: Linking Struggles for Social Justice.* Toronto: Women Working with Immigrant Women, and Toronto and York Region Labour Council, 2004.

MacDonald, Gayle, Rachel L. Osborne, and Charles C. Smith, eds. *Feminism, Law, Inclusion: Intersectionality in Action.* Toronto: Sumach Press, 2005.

Martin, D'Arcy. *Thinking Union: Activism and Education in Canada's Labour Movement.* Toronto: Between the Lines, 1995.

McCaskell, Tim. *Race to Equity: History of Equity Work at the Toronto Board of Education.* Toronto: Between the Lines, 2005.

McKinney, Karyn D. *Being White: Stories of Race and Racism.* New York: Routledge, 2005.

Memmi, Albert. *Racism.* Minneapolis: University of Minnesota Press, 2000.

Mills, Albert J., and Tony Simmons. *Reading Organization Theory: A Critical Appraoch to the Study of Organizational Behaviour and Structure.* Toronto: Garamond Press, 1999.

Morrison, Toni. *Playing in the Dark: Whiteness and the Literary Imagination.* Cambridge, MA: Harvard University Press, 1992.

Nadeau, Denise. *Counting Our Victories: Popular Education and Organizing.* Vancouver: Peal the Deal Productions, 1996.

Nelson, Camille A., and Charmaine A. Nelson. *Racism, Eh? A Critical Inter-Disciplinary Anthology of Race and Racism in Canada.* Toronto: Captus Press, 2004.

Ngo, Hieu Van. *English as a Second Language Education: Context, Current Responses, and Recommendations for New Directions.* Calgary: Coalition for Equal Access to Education, 2001.

—. *Toward Innovative Vision for Quality, Equitable ESL Education.* Calgary: Coalition for Equal Access to Education, 2003.

Ontario Human Rights Commission. *Paying the Price: The Human Cost of Racial Profiling: Inquiry Report.* Toronto: OHCR, 2003. Available online from www.ohrc.on.ca.

—. *Policy and Guidelines on Racism and Racial Discrimination.* Toronto: OHRC, 2005. Available online from www.ohcr.on.ca.

Rasmussen, Birgit Brander, Eric Klinenberg, Irene J. Nexica, and Matt Wray, eds. *The Making and Unmaking of Whiteness.* Durham, NC: Duke University Press, 2001.

Said, Edward W. *Culture and Imperialism.* New York: Vintage Books, 1994.

Satzewich, Victor, ed. *Racism and Social Inequality in Canada: Concepts, Controversies and Strategies of Resistance.* Toronto: Thompson Educational Publishing, 1998.

Seabrook, Jeremy. *The No-Nonsense Guide to World Poverty.* Toronto: Between the Lines, 2003.

Segrest, Mab. *Memoir of a Race Traitor.* Boston: South End Press, 1994.

Stalker, Peter. *The No-Nonsense Guide to International Migration.* Toronto: Between the Lines, 2001.

Sue, Derald Wing. *Overcoming Our Racism: The Journey to Liberation.* San Francisco: Jossey-Bass, William Wiley, 2003.

Task Force on the Participation of Visible Minorities in the Federal Public Service. *Embracing Change in the Federal Public Service.* Ottawa: The Task Force, 2000.

Thomas, Barbara. *Multiculturalism at Work: A Guide to Organizational Change.* Toronto: YWCA of Metropolitan Toronto, 1985.

Thomas, Barbara, and Charles Novogrodsky. *Combatting Racism in the Workplace: A Course for Workers.* Toronto: Cross Cultural Communication Centre, 1983.

Toronto and York Region Labour Council. *Breaking Barriers, Linking Struggles.* 24 min. 2004. Videocasette.

van der Gagg, Nikki. *The No-Nonsense Guide to Women's Rights.* Toronto: Between the Lines, 2004.

Williams, Jessica. *50 Facts that Should Change the World.* Cambridge, UK: Icon Books, 2004.

Yalnyzian, Armine. *The Growing Gap.* Toronto: Centre for Social Justice, 1998.

Yip, Pearl. "A Case Study Analysis of the ESL Issue." MA thesis, University of Calgary, 1997.

Organizations and Web Sites

Aboriginal Peoples Television Network /
www.aptn.ca
Visit the Web site to join its mailing list for weekly updates. APTN has a national call-in program called *Contact*, which is a "circle for grassroots Aboriginal people to share their views and stories about the forces that shape their lives."

African Canadian Online / www.yorku.ca/aconline
Based at York University, its Web site has information on culture, arts, history, and politics.

Asian Canadian Labour Alliance /
www.buzzardpes. com/acla
This coalition of Asian Canadian unionists hosts a Web site with news and information about issues affecting diverse Asian Canadian communities.

Canadian Centre for Policy Alternatives /
www. policyalternatives.ca
Develops and disseminates progressive social research on a variety of issues, including their annual Alternative Federal Budget.

Canadian Council for Refugees /
www. web.net/ ~ccr/fronteng.htm
This site has information about a variety of issues and about actions and lobbying for fair legislation.

Canadian Heritage / www.pch.gc.ca
This Web site has an A-Z index, links to legislation, publications, and other organizations. The *Racism Stop It* page highlights activities for March 21, the International Day for the Elimination of Racism.

Canadian Labour Congress / www.clc-ctc.ca
CLC's site contains information about its work on equity. Click on the "Rights" section for materials on women, anti-racism, Aboriginal workers, workers with disabilities, solidarity and pride.

Canadian Race Relations Foundation / www.crr.ca
CRRF's site offers organizing news and analysis on a variety of issues in communities across Canada and elsewhere such as their coverage on racial profiling. They do important research on racism and racial equity and their publications are available through their site.

Catalyst Centre / www.catalystcentre.ca
A Toronto-based popular education group with an excellent online bookstore.

Centre for Social Justice / www.socialjustice.org
A research organization with good material on economic and racial inequality.

Coalition for the Advancement of Aboriginal Studies /
www.edu.yorku.ca:8080/caas
This coalition's goal is to create changes in classroom teaching and learning so that all students are exposed to Aboriginal perspective and content.

Coalition of Black Trade Unionists /
www.cbtu.org & www.cbtu.ca
This coalition started in the United States and has chapters in most states, as well as Canada. It provides news about organizing that "addresses domestic and global issues impacting working people." The Ontario chapter's site offers Canadian news about organizing.

Selected Bibliography

Colourlines Race Culture Action / www.colorlines.com
A U.S. magazine featuring writing on race, culture, and organizing.

Colours of Resistance / colours.mahost.org
This grassroots network is consciously trying to develop anti-racist, multiracial politics in the movement against globalization; committed to integrating an anti-oppression framework and analysis into all its work. The site has great articles and organizing tools. Join its list serve to receive information about organizing in a variety of places.

Diversity Appreciation, Training, and Management / www.mapnp.org
This site is linked to a list of resources with more information as you dip into them, assembled by Carter McNamara.

Diversity Watch / www.diversitywatch.ryerson.ca
Managed by Ryerson University's School of Journalism, this site offer background information on different communities, a media watch section, and links to other resources.

National Anti-Racism Council / www.narc.freeservices.com
On this site you'll find information about conferences, materials, and news of interest to racial equity activists.

National Film Board of Canada / www.nfb.ca
The NFB site offers many films by Canadian filmmakers helpful in exploring racial justice and identity in Canada.

National Network for Immigrant and Refugee Rights / www.nnirr.org
This network in the U.S. promotes anti-racism organizing and produces excellent materials.

New Internationalist / www.new int.org
New Internationalist monthly magazine focuses on world inequalities and organizing for justice in communities around the globe.

People's Movement for Human Rights Education / www.pdhre.org
Based in New York, this organization's site shares methodology and learning materials as well as information on global human rights issues.

Rabble / www. rabble.ca
Rabble offers alternative sources on the news and global organizing.

Starhawk's Home Page / www.starhawk.org
Find Starhawk's latest essays and books about global organizing and earth-based spirituality.

Stop Racial Profiling / www.stopracialprofiling.ca
This is a Canadian Web site that is one in a campaign to halt racial profiling in Canada. "It brings together community groups, law makers, lawyers, activists, targets of racial profiling and all affected communities."

Straight Goods / www.straightgoods.ca
Like Rabble, this is a Canadian independent on-line source of news and analysis.

Toronto and York Region Labour Council / www.labourcouncil.ca
This site will give you information about the council's equity agenda and organizing.

Turtle Island Native Network / www.turtleisland.org
The site has educational material as well as many other interesting resources.

Vive, Inc / www.vivelacasa.org/links.htm
Offers a variety of links to sites on immigration, refugee, and human rights.

Women's Wall Project / www.wallworkshop.com
"The wall" is a methodology for doing gender analysis of the global economy, starting with women's experiences. It has been used by women's organizations, unions, community groups, and professional and religious organizations in countries around the globe. The site offers an introduction to the methodology, experiences of people who have facilitated the wall, and access to guides and other tools.

Women, War, Disaspora, and Learning / www.utoronto.ca/wwdl
This site circulates resources that are helpful to activists and academics in the area of women's studies, Middle East studies as well as social services and immigration policy studies. The materials emerge from two research projects at OISE/UT led by Professor Shahrzad Mojab and Dr. Rachel Gorman that focus on Kurdish women.

ZNet / www.zmag.org
Find news and analysis that links you to others committed to social change. While it is based in the U.S., many international authors like Arundathi Roy are regular contributors.

MARQUIS

Québec, Canada